THE ATKINSON FAMILY

IMPRINT IN HIGHER EDUCATION

The Atkinson Family Foundation has endowed this imprint to

illuminate the role of higher education in contemporary society.

The publisher and the University of California Press Foundation
gratefully acknowledge the generous support of the
Atkinson Family Foundation Imprint in Higher Education.

Inclusive Socratic Teaching

Inclusive Socratic Teaching

Why Law Schools Need It and
How to Achieve It

Jamie R. Abrams

UNIVERSITY OF CALIFORNIA PRESS

University of California Press
Oakland, California

© 2024 by Jamie R. Abrams

Library of Congress Cataloging-in-Publication Data

Names: Abrams, Jamie R., author.
Title: Inclusive Socratic teaching : why law schools need
    it and how to achieve it / Jamie R. Abrams.
Description: First. | Oakland : University of California
    Press, 2024. | Includes bibliographical references and
    index.
Identifiers: LCCN 2023047043 (print) | LCCN
    2023047044 (ebook) | ISBN 9780520390713 (cloth) |
    ISBN 9780520390720 (paperback) | ISBN
    9780520390737 (ebook)
Subjects: LCSH: Law—Study and teaching—United
    States. | Law—Study and teaching—United States—
    Philosophy. | Law schools—United States.
Classification: LCC KF272 .A43 2024 (print) | LCC
    KF272 (ebook) | DDC 340.071/173—dc23/
    eng/20231012
LC record available at https://lccn.loc.gov/2023047043
LC ebook record available at https://lccn.loc
    .gov/2023047044

33 32 31 30 29 28 27 26 25 24
10 9 8 7 6 5 4 3 2 1

To Morgan and Gavin

*May you always explore the world around you
with the boundless curiosity of Socrates.*

Contents

Preface

This book seeks to catapult forward the enduring, yet stagnating, dialogue within legal education about the role of Socratic teaching by shifting the discussion to concrete strategies and action items. Candidly, this is not an easy conversation to have with oneself, within our institutions, or across our profession. I have quipped many times while writing this book that my two primary areas of legal scholarship are reproductive rights and the pedagogy of legal education, and I am sincerely not sure which one puts me in a more polarizing and vulnerable place! Talking about reforms to legal education should not be polarizing, but it can be. It requires a very delicate approach that is inviting and empowering for all. It requires navigating our most basic human vulnerabilities.

In approaching this conversation, delicate as it may be, it is helpful to squarely center our students and our expectations of them to provide us with vital perspectives. Every year we bring into our institutions hundreds of new students. We ask them to move out of their comfort zones, challenge their assumptions, bring a growth mindset, and do the hard work necessary to thrive in the classrooms that we design and deliver. We know that it is hard for them to accept feedback and adapt to it. We lament that more students do not go over their exams or graded work to learn from it or come to office hours to address weaknesses in content mastery. We know that it is hard for our students to do what we are asking of them, in part, because it exposes their greatest vulnerabilities. As academics, in contrast, we often stay squarely within our (often narrow) comfort zones.

In fact, we consider staying within that comfort zone as the very essence of being an expert and a scholar. We speak, write, and teach only on topics with which we have robust knowledge. We offer wholehearted disclaimers of "this is not my area" for all other areas of law.

When it comes to *how* we teach, as compared to *what* we teach, however, education is not just about showcasing our expertise or staying in our respective lanes. Like our students processing our feedback of them, so many of us read our own course evaluations with the same fears, vulnerabilities, and reluctance that we urge our students to overcome in their exam reviews and memo rewrites. We regularly share our scholarship with our peers for discourse, feedback, and critique. We generally accept that feedback with grace and gratitude. Yet we often reflect on our teaching in isolation and sometimes even with great disdain for the critiques we do receive. We spend months rewriting our scholarship to address critiques and incorporate new developments. Rarely do we apply the same rigors to reworking our teaching or staying current on developments in *how* to teach. Far too often we collapse being knowledgeable and being a good teacher into the same thing.

Yet education is about what students learn, not how much we know. On this topic one of my coworkers told me an amusingly memorable tale of someone who swore that they could teach their cat to play the guitar in a week. When the week was over, the cat could not play the guitar (surprise!), to which the teacher replied, "I said I could *teach* the cat to play the guitar, not that the cat would *learn* how to play the guitar." This tale reminds us that education—at its core—is about centering the learner and not the teacher. Thus, while this advice falls squarely in the "easier said than done" category, I invite you to approach this book with your own growth mindset, squarely centering the needs of students collectively.

We have done this before in the most surprising of times. Paradoxically, I take great hope and optimism from how legal education transformed to meet the challenges presented by the COVID-19 global pandemic. We *had* to transform rapidly and systemically because the continuity of our students' education demanded it. There was no time for committee deliberations, faculty debate, or institutional bureaucracy. We rolled up our sleeves, attended trainings, talked with peers, learned from one another, and delivered legal education in a way that met that unique moment. We were focused on our students. We were notably *less* vulnerable because we were *all* in it together. The shifts we had to make to address COVID-19 disruptions were not critiques of *my* teaching or *your* teaching, nor were they about racking and stacking our students through assessment. The emergency pivots we made to address COVID-19 were about our collective need to help our students learn. Thus, in the one recent instance when law-teaching reforms (albeit temporary and transitional ones) were perceived as *necessary*, we rallied as a profession, and we got the job done.

I approach this book similarly as a universal call to action. I write from my own lived experiences, with their full authenticity and vulnerability. I come to this book having worn many different hats in legal education. I am now a professor of law at the American University Washington College of Law, where I also direct the Legal Rhetoric Program, which delivers the Legal Research and Writing curriculum to four hundred first-year students. I have taught courses in torts, legal research and writing, family law, appellate advocacy, legislation, and gender and the law. I have taught in "skills" classrooms, "doctrinal" classrooms, online classrooms, hybrid classrooms, flipped classrooms, and traditional Socratic classrooms. I have held positions as an associate dean, a tenured professor, a visiting faculty member, a term faculty member, and an adjunct faculty member.

Through these roles I have a fifteen-year history of teaching law across public and private schools, international and domestic schools, and so-called blue-state and red-state schools. I have experienced teaching across the country and across its steepest hierarchies. From this robust range of experiences, I see transformative potential to build bridges across our classroom categories (e.g., skills, experiential, doctrinal) and our institutional caste systems and into our communities.

I bring to this book my own full and authentic set of teaching experiences. Some of those teaching experiences have been deeply fulfilling and occasionally even celebrated. I have received awards, such as the Blackboard Catalyst Award for Teaching and Learning, the University of Louisville's Presidential Exemplary Multicultural Law Teaching Award, Teacher of the Year at the University of Louisville Brandeis School of Law, and American University Washington College of Law's Innovations in Law Teaching Award. Like many of you, though, none of those awards are as memorable or as defining to my professional identity as the times when I know that I have failed in the classroom. I am far more haunted by the students that have not made it through law school or licensure, the instances where I have bungled a Socratic exchange, and the students who have broken down in my office because they are not getting it or feeling defeated in my classroom than I am proud of any line item on my curriculum vitae. The moments when I realize that I can—and must—do better fuel me to keep at it, try new things, and evolve *with* our students.

Authoring a book on the subject has positioned me in a deeply vulnerable place: self-reflecting and holding myself accountable for the choices that I make in the classroom. I am not a scholar trained in educational best practices. Notably, very few law professors or law administrators are. I was, however, a first-generation law student who entered my own Socratic classrooms full of crushing self-doubt, fear, and anxiety. As a first-year law student in 1999, I had the great fortune of being the first group of students at the American University Washington College of Law to participate in an integrated first-year curriculum. Through my own early experiences with the Socratic method, my 1L professors—many of whom are my professional colleagues today—transformed me from a rural farm girl to a lawyer with a robust skill set, prepared to counsel clients and analyze the law's effects on real communities. To get there I needed committed and savvy professors, for sure. I also benefited from a whole lot of privilege and support that I did not fully appreciate at the time. Rising to the top of law school is in some part about intellect and hard work, but it also requires an extraordinary amount of privilege to avoid being disrupted by housing or food insecurity, physical or mental health disruptions, family hardships, and so much more.

I end this Preface right where I started by acknowledging the great vulnerability that it takes to have meaningful conversations about our teaching practices. When I set out to write a book on the topic of reframing the Socratic method, I thought that authoring a book would make me feel like *more* of an expert, empowered by documenting and sharing my perspectives. I was so surprised to find that the experience of writing these chapters had the entirely opposite effect. I find myself sending this manuscript to print from a place of greater humility than when I started. That humility comes from a couple of places. It comes from the heavy weight of knowing that our students demand so much from us. It comes from a candid realization that I *cannot* meet all those needs. Nor can you. The only way that we can meet the needs of our students is to come together as a teaching community and navigate directionally together. I have the deepest love of legal education. There is not a day that I have walked into the institutions where I have worked without reflecting on what a privilege it is to hold this job. Legal education changed my life before it *became* my life. I have deep gratitude, but I also have a boundless energy to improve legal education so that all of our students can thrive and succeed.

Acknowledgments

I am so grateful to all the readers, reviewers, confidantes, champions, allies, mentors, and role models who helped me see this project through to publication. Aníbal Rosario Lebrón was an unparalleled reader, editor, sounding board, and source of inspiration at so many stages of the project that I am forever grateful. This book is stronger thanks to his deep insights and contributions. Legal education has a bright future with generous, thoughtful, and uplifting scholars and teachers like Aníbal leading us forward.

Maura Roessner, Sam Warren, Susan Silver, and Stephanie Summerhays were such a gracious and uplifting editorial team at UC Press. I am deeply grateful to Maura for seeing potential in my ideas and championing me across the finish line. This publication is stronger because of Maura's masterful "hatchet" and "scalpel," wielded thoughtfully to strengthen the manuscript. Thanks to all the editors and the production team for their excellence.

This manuscript is also stronger because of the feedback I have received at various stages at scholarly conferences and workshops. I am grateful to all the participants in the SMU Dedman School of Law's Don Smart Legal Education Endowment Lecture in 2023 and to Jessica Dixon Weaver for hosting this workshop. I also extend my warmest thanks to the Integrating Doctrine and Diversity Series for including me in their thoughtful webinar on Inclusive Socratic Teaching in September 2023. This event was sponsored by the Roger Williams School of Law, CUNY

School of Law, Berkeley Law, and JURIST and generously hosted by Nicole Dyszlewski. I am also deeply grateful to the Capital Area Family Law Workshop in 2022, organized by Aníbal Rosario Lebrón and Greg Strauss; the 2021 Women in Legal Education Section's pedagogy panel at the Association of American Law School's Annual Meeting; the William and Mary Law School Pedagogy Series; and the COVID Care Crisis I and II convenings in 2021 and 2022, organized by Meera Deo, Shruti Rana, and Cyra Choudhury. I am particularly grateful to Dean Onwuachi-Willig and Dean Sean Scott for their vital insights while serving as commentators on an earlier draft. Thanks also go to so many colleagues for their impactful feedback, including Susan Duncan, Julia Florey, Maya Manian, Andy Popper, Dara Purvis, and Jessica Dixon Weaver.

I also offer my heartfelt thanks to all the research assistants who supported this project at its various stages. These dedicated research assistants were students at the American University Washington College of Law, my current institution; and the University of Louisville Brandeis School of Law, my former institution. Thanks to this amazing cohort of students: Colby Birkes, Allison Bohach, Sydney Brookshire, Taylor Castleman, Samantha Fang, William Garcia, Rachel Gumbel, Brooklyn Hagan, Meredith Harbison, Nia Jolly, Jasmyne Jones, Tyler Melton, Nicole Narvaez, Jacob Rayburn, Paige Reardon, Ruth Schultz, Kenny Schwalbert, Miriam Sopin-Valle, Breanna Stiefvater, Emma Vonder-Haar, and Jazmyn Wood. With their thoughtful insights, rigorous research, and careful editing, these students each left the project stronger than they found it. I also thank the American University Washington College of Law for a summer 2022 research grant, which provided an invaluable springboard for this manuscript.

Finally, I thank my amazing husband, Jason. His loving support and encouragement fueled me from manuscript to publication while navigating a cancer diagnosis, the caregiving disruptions of the COVID-19 pandemic, and a cross-country move and job change.

Legal Education's Curricular Conformity

Socratic classrooms continue to dominate legal education's curricular core. Their dominance necessitates their central role in building inclusive, equitable, and effective law schools. Inclusive institutions cannot be built around the perimeter of traditional Socratic classrooms no matter how many sophisticated niche seminars, cohorts of interested law teachers, or well-orchestrated lunchtime programs are offered. Inclusive Socratic classrooms are vital to systemically, swiftly, and sustainably building inclusive institutions that better prepare students for practice. The forthcoming redesign of the entry-level bar exam, wellness and health challenges, and diversity and inclusion struggles further reinforce this call to action. Inclusive Socratic classrooms are an essential foundational baseline reform from which our institutions can then further innovate and transform.

This Introduction's unifying thread is one of uniformity and conformity. Modern legal education and its structure, economics, demographics, curriculum, and grading practices are quite standardized and stagnant.[1] Working within these constraints and structures, this book offers a roadmap to catalyze Socratic classrooms—the curricular core of legal education—to improve the culture, equity, and inclusion of legal education in scalable and immediate ways. Inclusive teaching is equitable, giving all students an opportunity to achieve their potential. It is welcoming, leaving all students feeling a sense of belonging.[2] Inclusive teaching can be learned, cultivated, and measured, even in a Socratic classroom.

It is the responsibility of the law teacher to build an inclusive learning environment. This book charts the path for law teachers, law schools, and accreditors seeking to cultivate inclusive Socratic classrooms.

CURRICULAR CONFORMITY

Most of modern legal education's core courses are delivered using some variation of the Socratic method, an inquisitive teaching method whereby law teachers lead students through extracting rules from appellate cases using a fluid question-and-answer dialogue to develop reasoning and argumentation skills.[3] This Socratic method of teaching law, first introduced by Dean Christopher Langdell of Harvard University in 1870, grounded law school teaching in a scientific approach and gave legal education increased prestige.[4] This model of legal education was adopted swiftly and uniformly, leaving law schools with little differentiation or distinction.

With legal education's heightened esteem came exclusion and hierarchy, which persists today in both glaring and subtle ways.[5] The Socratic method, in its traditional performance, embeds a hierarchy of teacher and student, and the hierarchy is the point. Feminist scholar Catharine MacKinnon explained how students in Socratic classrooms can be "motivated by fear" and "infantilized," and they are "schooled in hierarchy, taught deference to power, and rewarded for mastering codes for belonging and fitting in."[6] MacKinnon's twenty-year-old critique still rings powerfully true today.

From Professor Charles Kingsfield in *The Paper Chase* to Elle Woods in *Legally Blonde,* our society is deeply intrigued by the curriculum and format of legal education. Formal books and programs abound to prepare students for success in law school, as do widely circulated memes and humor. These materials and depictions are universally applicable because the law school curriculum is structured so similarly nationwide across schools that are private and public, small and large, well resourced and underresourced, and across the perceived hierarchies of prestige ranking various law schools, with only minor gradients of distinction and innovation.

This uniformity is a bit surprising when we reflect on the realization that—in his time—"Langdell's approach and proposals were innovative and responsive to challenges in legal education and the legal landscape," yet "the legal academy has not *continued* to follow Langdell's lead by innovating and responding to new information and new challenges—

or at least . . . the innovations have not been as effective or comprehensive as the passage of so much time would seem to warrant." Rachel Gurvich and colleagues powerfully conclude that what "current law students experience is an artifact of another generation and therefore does not account for today's student body or decades of research about pedagogy and the science of learning."[7]

Yet the economics and trajectories of legal education do largely envision (at least implicitly) the continuation of law school's existing curricular structure. The law school curriculum is three years for most full-time students and four years for evening and part-time students. Approximately 10 percent of students enroll in part-time programs.[8] Over these three or four years, students complete a largely consistent core curriculum. Common law subjects prominently featured on the bar exam dominate this core curriculum, with niche seminars and clinics supplementing the core. For these core classes, students generally read from expensive casebooks compiling appellate opinions and take heavily weighted summative exams. Students also complete a required first-year legal research and writing course and an upper-level writing requirement. They engage in experiential learning that simulates the practice of law in a class or two. Recent accreditation reforms ensure that students get *some* training in cultural competency and professional-identity formation before graduation.

In sum, the vast, sweeping majority of students sit in a large, lecture-hall course with a traditional appellate casebook in a Socratic-style environment more than any other method of instruction. For most law schools, there is little incentive—either economically or reputationally—to innovate the curriculum. Rather, schools largely stay in lockstep together. Thus, Socratic classrooms dominate our institutions. Socratic teaching methods can vary considerably within our institutions from class to class and teacher to teacher. For some the Socratic method remains a traditional means of rigorous critical inquisition to develop analytic skills. Many styles of Socratic teaching ask questions persistently to reveal what students know and motivate students to prepare for class through the anxiety of being called on to answer these questions. For others Socratic teaching is one tool layered on with other teaching techniques such as group work, skills simulations, practice problems, and lectures. Despite its acknowledged decline in exclusive use, the Socratic method persists almost universally in varying styles and intensities across student learning in all institutions.[9]

Notably, most performances of the Socratic method are quite inauthentic to true Socratic dialogue.[10] Even in its most favorable usage, law teachers generally conduct the classroom in a "sage on the stage" approach, with professors centered intellectually and structurally. Langdell's version of the Socratic method positions teachers as the experts and conductors of the Socratic exchange, leaving students disempowered and unable to seek their own wisdom and clarity in understanding the law.[11] The professors in Langdell's traditional model were selected predominantly for their keen intellect, while their teaching skills or practice experience were rarely essential.[12]

The Socratic method, as deployed in many classrooms, can thus distort power dynamics such that *how* the content is taught reinforces the critiques of *what* is taught. For this reason legal education pedagogy scholars sometimes refer to this teaching technique as the "Langdell method" as compared to the "Socratic method." Beth Hirschfelder Wilensky describes the Langdell method as encompassing the pedagogical components of the "case method," the "Socratic method," and "cold calling," which collectively describe law teachers deploying appellate casebooks and questioning techniques that leave students in suspense regarding their participation.[13] Here I am using Socratic teaching to describe broadly the large, lecture-hall classroom with a professor poised at the podium, using an appellate casebook to question students about the material, with a high-stakes summative exam looming at the end of the course.

Traditional styles of Socratic teaching reinforce the positioning of law as an authoritative system and structure *over* students. It teaches the law, but it allows little room to challenge the law's origins or justness.[14] The method of reasoning strictly using edited appellate cases as the framework for learning is a "rigid deductive local structure."[15] We train students to "think like a lawyer," but we do so in a vacuum devoid of culture or context and in a model framed around authority over and control of the discourse.[16] This formalism limits students to engage only with the precedential rule and the selected facts in the case and risks obscuring social and nonlegal context.[17] This narrow focus can keep students from engaging in systemic or comprehensive inquires of law.[18] Absent social, political, and economic context, students lose sight of the larger trajectory of the law, the critiques of its effects on various communities, and broader visions of how else the law could function.[19] Whether out of necessity, efficacy, sustained reverence, or agnostic indifference, Socratic teaching remains foundational to legal education.[20] Law schools continue to design their budgets, curricula, and student experiences around some degree of case-based, Socratic law teaching in large lecture-style classrooms with heavily weighted summative exams.[21] It particularly persists in first-year and bar exam classes.[22]

In recent years the American Bar Association sought to transform legal education to be more outcome driven. Law teachers now include learning outcomes in their syllabi. They might also provide a midterm with a model answer or a light grading sheet to help students assess how they are progressing toward achieving competencies in meeting the published learning outcomes. Students generally receive only light feedback on the summative exam, however. They often do not even receive their own answer or the exam question back to allow for meaningful self-critique because faculty often preserve the possibility of reusing the exam.

This combination of Socratic teaching and summative exams often yields an inordinate amount of student anxiety and fear, but often in ways quite far removed from mastering the material or learning to lawyer. Students receive little clarity regarding how they are supposed to progress in Socratic classrooms from semester to semester and year to year. Rarely do students get feedback regarding how their Socratic engagement tethers to the course exam, bar exam, or law practice. Law schools collectively hope that students graduate at the end of three or four years, having met the school's stated learning outcomes, prepared for the bar exam, and secured a job for which they have the skills to succeed.

The Socratic method does bring one notably reliable and enduring attribute—it is cost-effective and scalable.[23] Its efficiencies also align with the larger demands on law faculty. Teaching in this method ensures that faculty can produce impactful scholarship and serve in their institutions and communities. Faculty workloads have long been cemented around this Socratic classroom model. Our casebooks are built around this model. Our budgets are built around this model. Accordingly, even *discussing* reforms to the delivery of legal education is often stunted heavily by the competing demands already facing faculty and the abundance of existing teaching materials supporting these classrooms.

Legal education has thus generally added innovation, such as clinical programs, experiential learning, and skills development, around the curricular core while simultaneously retaining the hallmarks of traditional legal education.[24] Those teaching in Socratic classrooms generally hold the highest pay and status in legal education. Students then enhance that curricular core with thoughtfully designed clinics, simulation courses, and experiential learning courses. Clinics rigorously center the client in the classroom and position faculty and students to collaboratively solve the client's problems. The client comes from the local community.

Students might also receive academic credit for placement in a practice setting to obtain real-world experience. When scheduling permits, niche seminars focused on race, sexuality, economics, gender, and more allow select students to explore critical perspectives with the self-selecting cohort of students that enroll. From the student perspective, though, these core Socratic courses might be perceived as disconnected from these other components of legal education without a purposeful pedagogical pipeline from Socratic classrooms into more client-centered and community-centered learning experiences.

After graduation law students generally lose an additional semester's worth of employment and pay an outside vendor thousands of dollars to prepare for the bar exam. The process of preparing for the bar exam is sometimes described disdainfully as too pedestrian for a typical law school classroom. It is often, instead, jettisoned into academic success curricular offerings that are optional and disconnected from both the core law school curriculum and the vendor-administered bar courses that students purchase at a hefty price. The optional nature of bar success programming requires students to invest time that they rarely have. It leaves some of the students who would benefit the most from this programming unable to attend for bandwidth reasons (e.g., caregiving responsibilities, employment obligations, or extended commutes).

Historically, the bar exam has not assessed whether students have acquired practice skills. Rather, the legal profession has long taken on the work of training law students to be lawyers in their firms, chambers, offices, and entities. Many practitioners have expressed persistent frustration with law schools for not adequately equipping students with the skills that they need to succeed in practice, like client counseling, problem-solving, task management, and communication skills. Changes to the bar exam are imminent to address this disconnect.

Despite this curricular consistency over the past century, the costs to complete a JD degree have risen dramatically, and the stratification of costs is steep. The average cost of law school tuition has increased by $35,000 over the past thirty-five years.[25] Law school debt differs based on several factors, such as geography, LSAT scores, grade-point averages, and state funding provided to the school. Nonetheless, 74 percent of law students graduate in debt, with an average borrowing amount of $118,400. This debt substantially affects students in school choice, satisfaction, and job options.

Debt further stratifies by race and gender. Black students owe 97 percent more and Latinx students 49 percent more than their White counterparts after graduation. White students on average owe 17 percent less than the national average.[26] Women also leave law school with more debt than men.[27] Rates of loan repayments also differ greatly by race, ethnicity, and gender, as women and students of color make less on average after graduation, thus extending the time it takes to repay loans.[28] These debt disparities, in turn, can raise access to justice issues, compelling students into higher-paid government and private-sector jobs and compromising the ability of students to work in public service.

Legal education's curricular conformity also comes at a heavy psychological cost to many. Teri McMurtry-Chubb reveals the stagnant trend of conformity and the systemic harms that it perpetuates across legal education in this powerful statement: "We press, purposely and deliberately, under the guises of 'course coverage' and 'bar passage' . . . [but in doing so we] perpetuate microaggressions, microinequities, microassaults, microinsults, microinvalidations, and stereotype threat—all of which act as barriers to minoritized law students experiencing equitable and inclusive classroom and curricular environments. When viewed in this light, our curricular and pedagogical goal is conformity, not diversity, equity, or inclusion." While schools have made considerable strides in increasing the aggregate number of women and students of color studying, teaching, and working in law and law schools, as described in the next section, notably the pedagogy has not adapted universally to support more diverse communities or to adapt to evolving professional trends.[29]

STAGNATING DEMOGRAPHICS, SILOED ACCOUNTABILITY, AND STEEP HIERARCHIES

Law schools have stagnated on diversity and stratified in hierarchies. The numbers are problematic on their own and even more so if considered as a reflection of entrenched institutional values. The Supreme Court's recent decision in *Students for Fair Admissions v. University of North Carolina* and *SFFA v. Harvard College* present additional challenges to retaining and improving law school diversity.[30] In 2022 there were 196 accredited law schools nationwide, with a total of 39,294 first-year students enrolled and 26,440 faculty (of which 9,360 were full-time and 17,080 were part-time).[31] The budgetary model relies largely on scalability, filling large classrooms to deliver content efficiently in ways that are replicable year to year.

Legal education is heavily ranked, stacked, and steeped in hierarchies. Law schools dedicate tremendous time, energy, and expense to position themselves favorably in the *U.S. News and World Report* rankings, even while law schools almost universally hold searing critiques and frustrations with the dominance of these rankings. These pressures particularly came to bear in the 2022–23 academic year, when many law schools refused to participate in the rankings, and the *U.S. News* dramatically altered its rankings methodologies.[32] The external job market is also steeply hierarchical, with students competing mightily for elite jobs. Faculty recruiting committees, likewise, compete in their hiring processes to recruit elite pedigrees of new faculty colleagues.

Law schools also have entrenched institutional hierarchies that affect pay, status, and governance that are deeply relevant to designing effective and equitable institutional reforms.[33] L. Danielle Tully powerfully writes that "legal education is shrouded in stories of gatekeeping and exclusion," with decades of "vagaries and vicissitudes." The hierarchies are not merely about labels; they are "containers" that "limit faculty's ability to collaborate, innovate and integrate best practices for legal education across the curriculum."[34] The compensation, status, and workload differences among staff, faculty, and various categories of law teaching are often inverted relative to the degree of student support and skills instruction compelled by the role. The most student-intensive and skills-intensive classes are often taught by legal research and writing, clinical, and experiential law faculty.[35]

Likewise, the institutional employees who interact most with students are often staff. The Dean of Students Office generally supports student wellness, campus programming, and student groups. The Academic Affairs Office generally manages the course schedule, teaching loads, accommodations, and exam administration. Perhaps a Director of Diversity monitors campus climate, hosts programs, and provides training. Professional development offices support students and alumni in job searches. The staff who fill these various roles are often supporting students in time-intensive, one-on-one relationships, mentoring students needing academic support, counseling students in job searches, and supporting students as individuals and in student organizations.

Our institutions collectively put the weight of admissions, academic success, and career placement in staff positions. Most diversity and inclusion efforts have also been housed in staff roles. This structure inhibits moving the cultural needle because it leaves unaddressed calls for reform straight through legal education's curricular core. These hierarchies house some of the important functional tasks of law school success in positions with lower pay and prestige and higher turnover than tenure-track faculty. It heavily immunizes tenure-track faculty within the curricular core from accountability for outcomes such as bar passage, inclusion, job placement, student satisfaction, and student wellness.

Race

To build inclusive Socratic classrooms, we must also understand the racial demographics of our law schools and then examine the structural hierarchies shaping our institutions. Law schools, "by almost any definition, are still white spaces."[36] Most students study in majority-White institutions under majority-White faculties. Reflecting a steady upward trajectory when examined in the aggregate, 34 percent of enrolled law students are students of color.[37] The aggregate numbers still vitally lag behind the US population at large though. For example, Latinx students comprise 12.7 percent of all law students and 18.3 percent of the US population. Asian students comprise 6.36 percent of all law students and 5.9 percent of the US population. Black students comprise 7.94 percent of all law students and 13.4 percent of the overall US population.[38] While the overall enrollment of students of color has trended upward, enrollment for Black students has trended downward for four consecutive years.[39] Aggregate law school enrollment numbers also obscure stark institutional and geographic differences. States such as Texas, Arizona, California, Florida, and Hawaii have 45 percent students of color enrolled in their law schools. Other states, in contrast, remain dramatically lower, in the 10–20 percent range.[40] Students of color are also disproportionately enrolled in lower-ranked schools.[41]

The enrollment of women of color in law school generally exceeds that of men of color, with Black women's enrollment doubling that of Black men.[42] Yet women of color generally disproportionately contemplate withdrawing from law school (31 percent) compared to men of color (26 percent), White women (24 percent), and White men (22 percent), suggesting inclusion and belonging concerns. Attrition rates for all students of color are also disproportionate, deepening the disparities that begin with admissions.[43] While White students were 62 percent of law school enrollment in 2016, they accounted for 49 percent of attrition in the first year. In contrast, first-year law students of color began with 30 percent of total enrollment but accounted for 44 percent of law school attrition.[44]

Perhaps driving these attrition issues, students of color report considerable culture and campus-climate concerns, as explored further in

Chapters 2 and 3.[45] For example, despite their statistical advantage, women of color report more negative experiences in law school than their male peers when measured by their overall satisfaction, reinforcing the importance of an intersectional analysis of law school cultures.[46] Only 21 percent of Native American and Black law students agreed that they were a "part of the community." A full 25 percent of Black students and 18 percent of Latinx students reported that they did not feel comfortable being themselves in their law school, relative to 9 percent of White students.[47] These statistics hold true in the legal profession as well, revealing that the "White space" of law school feeds into the "White space" of lawyering too.

Yet a sense of belonging is vital to academic success, motivation, student engagement, and achievement. A sense of belonging is about how well students perceive that they fit in and cohere with their classmates, faculty, and institution. Generally, law students' sense of belonging differs by race and gender, with women of color having the lowest sense of belonging. This sense of belonging is heavily affected by perceived bias and stereotype concerns. For example, White women worry at a rate of 7 percent higher than White men do that their professors "underestimate their intelligence," and women of color worry 13 percent more than White men do about this. These findings are critical. These data suggest that inclusion will not derive from a lunch program or savvy seminar offering. Rather, inclusion requires all institutional stakeholders striving to ensure the success of all students.[48]

Yet most existing diversity, equity, and inclusion efforts sit squarely, if not exclusively, in the admissions, financial aid, recruiting, student organization, seminar, and mentoring spaces of law school. These siloed centers of accountability place heightened vigilance at the entry points to law school but do little to explore the exit points and the day-to-day lived experiences of students during their course of study. Thus we keep recruiting students, staff, and faculty of color into law schools even when we are not fully supporting them. Carliss Chatman and Najarian Peters lead us to think meaningfully about the inadequacies of our approaches, concluding that many recruiting techniques are "shams" and "deep-shallow fakes" that can "draw Black and Brown students into the hostile waters." Thus Chatman and Peters conclude that, when we are talking about diversity, equity, and inclusion, we need to differentiate between performative gestures and effective practices. This includes positioning the dialogue squarely in legal education's curricular core.[49]

Disproportionalities in recruiting and retaining diverse students, in turn, feed into professional disparities. Law school diversity gains have not held in the legal profession. The Black population at large is 13.4 percent of the overall population, while representing only 7.94 percent of law students, 4.76 percent of associates in US law firms, and 1.97 percent of partners.[50] Only 5 percent of all lawyers are Black, 2 percent are Asian, and 5 percent Hispanic or Latinx, leaving these communities woefully underrepresented compared to the overall population.[51]

The diversity of law faculty "lags behind" the student community.[52] In 2020, 21 percent of law faculty identified as "minority," up from 14 percent in 2000 and 10 percent in 1990. Again these aggregate numbers obscure a more nuanced picture. These numbers are considerably lagging behind the student population and the population at large. Many schools are still staggeringly lacking in diverse faculty. The Committee for Faculty Equity and Inclusion in the Clinical Legal Education Association concluded that racial and ethnic inclusion in law faculty clinical hiring has been limited and stagnant.[53] While the aggregate percentage of faculty of color in clinical teaching has grown from 9 percent to 20 percent from 1981 to 2017, Black clinical faculty have not exceeded the peak of 7 percent in 1999. While the numbers of Latinx clinical faculty has grown to 5 percent from 2008 to 2017, it is still a fraction of the overall Latinx population. The percentage of Asian clinical faculty rose from 2 percent to 6 percent from 2008 to 2017. Indigenous faculty have never attained 1 percent of representation, while comprising 1.7 percent of the US population.[54]

Gender inequality persists in law faculties too. Women of color in law teaching remain dramatically underrepresented and even more so in the tenure and tenure-track ranks. Women of color were just 7 percent of law faculty in 2009 when these data were last released. A closer look at aggregate numbers also reveals hierarchies and segmentation. Women faculty of color occupy lower-status and lesser-paid jobs, thus often doing more work for less job security and pay.[55] Experiential faculty are often women and faculty of color with less secure jobs, status, and pay.[56] On the legal research and writing side, the gains in diversity have not been as strong. The 2020 Association of Legal Writing Directors and Legal Writing Institute Survey identifies 13 percent of legal research and writing faculty as non-White, multiracial, or other, only a 1 percent increase since 2010.[57]

This is, again, about the difference between performative gestures and effective practices. Regarding faculty recruitment efforts, for example, Chatman and Peters conclude that "around and around the tables of faculty meetings, heads nod in agreement to the delivery of a homily of regret, confounded but nonetheless resigned to the poised self-reverence that gives the straight-faced and well-meaning faculty the spine to say unspeakable things about how much they tried. They tried." Chatman and Peters conclude that existing efforts are "half-hearted and incremental" theater, "mostly for show." They urge us toward more transformative, sincere, and effective approaches.[58]

Consistent with trends in student and faculty demographics, there is a pronounced lack of diverse representation in the ranks of deans across law schools, though diversity is increasing. According to a study compiled by the National Opinion Research Center at the University of Chicago, women headed 41 percent of law schools in 2020, compared to 18 percent in 2005. In 2020, 31 percent of all law schools had deans who identified as people of color or Hispanic, compared to 13 percent in 2005. According to the study, 18 percent of the law school deans in 2020 identified as Black or African American, up from 8 percent in 2005, and 6 percent identified as Hispanic or Latinx. The number of law school deans who identify as American Indian, Alaska Native, Asian, Native Hawaiian, or other Pacific Islander was also increasing, in small amounts.[59] Notably, 90 percent of deans surveyed asserted that they were the first of their gender and or race to serve as dean of their current law school from inside academia.[60] Harnessed fully, the increasing diversity of leadership within law schools can create the conditions necessary to ignite, catalyze, and institutionalize the changes needed to establish more inclusive Socratic classrooms.

Gender

There is work to do on gender too. While law school is no longer exclusively male, masculinities continue to explain much of legal education's hierarchies and structures.[61] Gender is deeply entrenched in the hierarchies and siloes of legal education, leading to a "stubborn persistence of a gender gap."[62] Legal education reflects strong gains for women in the aggregate but steep hierarchy and segmentation when reviewed more carefully. Legal education hit a milestone in 2016, when women's enrollment exceeded men's, an achievement that has held through the latest published data.[63] In 2020–21, 54 percent of enrolled JD students were women.[64] Only 36 percent of attorneys are women, though, revealing a pipeline myth that gender equality will organically improve over time.[65]

Legal education is also losing women from undergraduate studies into law school. Women secure 57 percent of undergraduate degrees, thus comprising the majority of the law school–applicant pool, yet men are admitted into law school at a higher percentage of the applicant pool. Women also attend lower-ranked law schools than their male peers, limiting job outcomes based on placement data. Women comprise 55.2 percent of all students in the bottom quarter of *U.S. News*–ranked law schools and 50.5 percent of the student body at the top twenty law schools. Seven of the schools ranked in the bottom quartile have more than 60 percent women students.[66]

Researchers explain that women express more hesitation around the costs and debts incurred in law school than their male peers. Women are also more likely to opt out of law school because they perceive its academic rigors as a deterrent, at a differential of 29 percent to 20 percent when comparing women to men, a vital area for further research. Work-life balance can also be a bigger deterrent for women. Women cite a higher interest in jobs that are helpful to others and that achieve social change compared to men, who are more likely to seek prestige and status. The heavy emphasis of the LSAT in law school admissions (which favors men) relative to undergraduates' grades (which favor women) also yield disparities in admissions outcomes. The LSAT emphasis further incentivizes the distribution of scholarships, financial aid, and price discounts to alleviate the burdens of law school for male students disproportionately.[67]

While legal education accreditors discussed the possibility of dropping the LSAT for admissions consideration, in February 2023 the American Bar Association's policy-making body rejected a proposed change to its accreditation standards that would allow law schools to go "test optional" beginning in 2025. The bid to end the long-standing requirement failed for a second time in six years. The controversial proposal has divided the legal academy and the association itself, with law student diversity emerging as the primary point of contention. Opponents have cautioned that eliminating the LSAT requirement would make admissions offices more dependent on subjective measures such as the prestige of an applicant's college, which they say could disadvantage minority applicants.[68]

The number of women faculty has grown mightily over the decades. In 1977 there were 391 women law professors nationwide, comprising 8.6 percent of all tenure and tenure-track faculty.[69] By the mid-80s this percentage had doubled to 15.9 percent.[70] By 2000 it was at 32.5 percent, and in 2011 it was 40 percent.[71] The 2020 *ABA Annual Reports* reveal that 47 percent of all full-time law faculty are women, reflecting strong trajectories in the aggregate.[72] Women of color remain dramatically underrepresented and even more so in the tenure and tenure-track ranks. Women faculty occupy lower-status and lesser-paid jobs, while more male faculty hold full professorships at more prestigious schools.[73] If we look at just "vertical segregation," approximately 64 percent of traditional tenured faculty are men.[74] Two-thirds (67 percent) of all clinicians and field-placement professors are women. That number rises to 73 percent if only new clinical faculty are considered.[75] Clinical faculty, as well as legal research and writing faculty, are often not in tenure-track roles.[76] If the aggregate numbers remove clinical faculty and legal research and writing faculty, then women make up only 38 percent of law faculty.[77] These statistics notoriously also omit library faculty. Law librarians are 68–70 percent women.[78]

These data reveal "status inequities" that cluster women faculty members.[79] These roles, in turn, hold less status, security, governance, and pay.[80] Nontenure-track legal research and writing faculty, for example, are paid an average of $32,000 less than their tenure-track peers.[81] Yet legal research and writing faculty are doing vital work for accreditation, formative feedback, and professional-identity formation. Legal research and writing, upper-level writing, and experiential learning are curricular requirements for an accredited law school. Yet the accreditation standards perpetuate these hierarchies, even in the face of mobilized opposition and documented disparities.[82]

Issues still fester in the faculty hiring process, biased student course evaluations, peer faculty hostility, vague and secretive tenure processes, and disproportionate service and emotional labor.[83] At nearly every step of the academic career trajectory, persistent barriers still impede women's success. Women faculty are often saddled with disproportionate institutional service and support tasks, described as the school's "housework."[84] They are also often managing the "Second Shift," performing disproportionate caregiving and household management at home.[85] COVID-19 intensified many of these inequities, particularly for untenured faculty, junior faculty, caregivers, faculty of color, and women faculty.[86] A demoralizing and harmful "presumption of incompetence" painfully governs the careers of women and all faculty of color too, reminding these communities that they have yet to attain a sense of meaningful belonging in spaces they have occupied for more than half a century.[87] Many women and faculty of color describe suffering from imposter syndrome and a lack of belonging.[88]

In addition to growth in law student and faculty representation, women have risen in the leadership ranks. In 2018, 41 percent of Association of American Law Schools–member schools had women deans, 6.7 percent of whom were women of color.[89] As of 2023, the percentage of deans who are women of color has grown to 18.69 percent.[90] Yet careful observers watch these numbers warily for their long-term predictive power. Skeptics observe that the rise in women deans has notably coincided with nationwide law school budget cuts, admissions declines, job placement challenges, and COVID-19 leadership challenges, presenting these leaders with deep institutional challenges from day one.[91] Black women have played a particularly influential role, leading law schools in transformative ways through the COVID-19 pandemic and through resounding calls for racial justice.[92] As with students, aggregate numbers reveal entrenched hierarchies and segmentation. Women, for example, are playing distinctly supportive roles as assistant and associate deans. While 62 percent of law school deans are men, 51 percent of the associate deans who support the day-to-day operations of law schools (e.g., preparing course schedules, supporting students, advising about careers) are women, and 68 percent of assistant deans are women.[93]

Even with more diverse student bodies, faculties, and leaders in legal education, the core power systems, substance, and method of delivering legal education remain remarkably unchanged. If anything, law schools only steepened their stratification and silos relating to who is accountable for diversity, equity, and inclusion outcomes in law schools. Vitally, colleagues in legal research and writing, clinical teaching, experiential courses, and law libraries reveal the exact path forward for the reform of traditional Socratic classrooms. These colleagues have long taught in student-centered, skills-centered, client-centered, and community-centered ways. They have long worked as a community to build best practices around inclusive and equitable classrooms. They have long worked to refine and develop assessment practices. Thus changing how we teach in the curricular core must align with structural reforms to value faculty who already prepare our students for practice.

This book is organized in two parts. Part I (Chapters 1–4) sketches out critiques of legal education and the legal profession. Part II (Chapters 5–8) maps a path forward to reform. Chapter 1 describes the concrete harms produced by the traditional Socratic classroom, concluding that the persistence of the Socratic method is both surprising and worrisome. It is woefully out of step with pedagogical trends outside of legal education. Chapter 2 reveals that the endurance of the Socratic classroom ignores a half century of well-documented quantitative and qualitative challenges. Chapter 2 sketches central themes that have emerged from critical legal theory scholarship to contextualize and inform modern curricular reforms. It examines the scholarly contributions of feminism, critical legal studies, critical race theory, LatCrit, and queer theory in identifying the marginalizing effects of legal education. These scholarly strands contest the rigid professor-student hierarchy of instruction, challenge the disconnect between the skills and values rewarded and revered in law school relative to those needed in practice, and reveal how the law reinforces hierarches of gender, class, race, and sexual identity.

The largely enduring Socratic classroom model might suggest that the status quo persists because most students are thriving in this model, which then constrains reforms. But the data and student experiences presented in Chapter 3 starkly reveal how most students are struggling in the existing model. Students enter law school as well adjusted and optimistic as the population at large. Very early into their first year, they become isolated, anxious, stressed, and depressed. By graduation many students struggle with depression, suicidality, and substance abuse. Many of our students are overwhelmed by legal education, its methods, its culture, and its pressures. Chapter 4 then examines the continuation of dysfunction—and even despair—that permeates the legal profession. Collectively, Chapters 1 through 4 reveal that innovations are necessary, urgent, and compelling. They also reveal that innovations need to be grounded in the curricular core of legal education. They remind us that scholars have raised these points for half a century.

Part II reveals that, while legal education sits in a state of relative stagnation and conformity, change is happening in accreditation, other academic programs, learning theory, bar exam methodology, and the professional job market. Chapter 5 addresses the questions of "Why now?" and "What is different today?" to explain why reforms are achievable after decades of critiques. Legal education is at a tipping point. A tipping point occurs when the "beliefs and energies of a critical mass of people are engaged," allowing new ideas to take root and fundamental change to occur.[94]

Legal education has experienced disruptive forces. COVID-19 seismically disrupted the delivery of legal education, as faculty made the seemingly overnight shift that the public health crisis demanded. COVID-19's curricular disruptions aligned with a tectonic racial justice reckoning, as professors and law schools reconsidered content coverage and the cultures that our institutions and classrooms foster. These shifts remind us that change *can* occur rapidly and systemically. Today's reforms and transformations should look to the legacy of scholarly critiques for guidance. More inclusive law schools are not just isolated ad hoc innovations to aspire to achieve as a branding tool. Meaningful reforms need to sit in the day-to-day core of our students' curricular experiences—the Socratic classroom.

Chapter 6 argues that it is time to "raise the floor" on legal education, by eliminating "problematic performances" of the Socratic method across all courses and institutions. This is a call to end the presumptive reverence and implicit immunity given to Socratic teaching to make space for greater innovation, experimentation, dialogue, study, and critique. These reforms sit harmoniously as an undergirding, foundational support for far more ambitious and transformative calls to reform modern legal education—proposals to "raise the ceiling" on "legal education's possibilities and purpose," such as Dean Danielle Conway's work to build antiracist law schools, Bennett Capers's call to "*radically* reimagine" law schools from the bottom up, and Etienne C. Toussaint's argument that examining how legal and political systems "further racism, economic oppression, or social injustice must be viewed as endemic to the purpose of legal education."[95] As these transformative discussions take root and flourish, we need an urgency to raise the floor of legal education's curricular core. More innovative and ambitious goals are undermined and thwarted by problematic Socratic performances festering in the center of the curriculum.

Chapter 7 proposes a set of shared institutional values rendering Socratic teaching more student, skills, client, and community centered. Shared values would give the Socratic method modern purpose and professional relevance. They respond to long-standing critiques of the harmful effects and deficiencies of Socratic teaching. Socratic classrooms can engage students with enhanced purpose and context on behalf of clients and within professional communities. Paradoxically, this book thus draws on the existing curricular conformity, using it as a catalyst for sweeping change. Chapter 8 carries these reforms through to revamp our assessment practices to value and measure equitable and inclusive learning environments. This book seeks to modernize, align, authenticate, and adapt the existing Socratic classroom in ways that are achievable, systemic, and transformative.

Part I

CHAPTER 1

Socratic Classrooms Dominate Legal Education's Curricular Core

The Introduction describes modern legal education's structure, economics, demographics, curriculum, and grading practices. This chapter focuses on the central dominance of the traditional Socratic classroom as the curricular core of modern legal education and the pointed critiques of it. While innovative seminars, experiential courses, and clinical lawyering offer enriching pedagogical opportunities to modern law students, the traditional Socratic classroom remains the dominant curricular experience for students. The Socratic classroom positions the professor as the power center of the classroom, while serially engaging each student. It relies on an appellate casebook to introduce students to legal rules. It is typically held in a packed lecture hall filled with students nervously waiting to participate.

While the curricular core relies heavily on the Socratic method to deliver content, these classrooms are about more than *just* deploying the Socratic method. They are built to varying degrees on broader systemic institutional hierarchies that dominate legal education. That is why our focus on inclusive institutions needs to *begin* with Socratic classrooms, not navigate around them. This chapter describes the concrete harms relating to equitable and inclusive student learning that can be sourced to the traditional Socratic classroom's structure and method. It first presents an account of this curricular core from the student perspective, then from the law teacher perspective, and finally from the staff perspective.

STUDENT EXPERIENCES IN LEGAL EDUCATION'S
CURRICULAR CORE

Socratic Classrooms

Traditional law school first-year and bar exam classes have remained largely unchanged in their teaching materials, economic structure, assessment methods, and teaching techniques for more than a century. These clusters of classes center one usually tenured or tenure-track professor reverently with fifty to one hundred students spread throughout the room. Each of these students spend $150 to $400 purchasing the assigned materials, primarily a book compiling appellate cases from various geographies and historic periods.

It is unlikely the syllabus outlines how professors will conduct their classroom, whether they will use the Socratic method, or how students should engage with this teaching technique or prepare for it. Maybe students received some mentoring on successful Socratic participation through upper-level peers or at orientation. Some students may have learned how to brief a case at orientation or in a summer bootcamp program. Some might learn how to brief a case in their legal research and writing course. Few students likely learned what to do with that case brief when they bring it to the Socratic classroom. Instead, they will watch and observe.

What they will soon learn is likely that the professor uses Socratic dialogue to work through the cases in the casebook for most of the semester, perhaps with some breaks for lectures, student questions, or group work. If there is any chance that students will be on call in a particular class, they will likely stay up late or wake up early, obsessively reading the material granularly to prepare for any question the professor might ask. The preparation to be on call rarely includes students generating their *own* questions or considering the deeper connections of the material to their lives or communities.

In addition to the edited appellate opinions, the casebooks further make *secondary* references to diverse communities, lawyering skills, historical context, or modern legal trajectories in notes and callout boxes, which students likely read entirely unsure of what the professor intends the students to do with this content. Particularly in first-year classes, the students likely nonetheless read these notes meticulously, although unsure of whether they matter to the class or its assessments. Law teachers might also assign or recommend a skills supplement to apply the content through exercises that do not exist in the primary text.

Participation in a Socratic classroom is often an anxiety-ridden and atomistic exercise for students to get through one class session and one case at a time. Participating students answer questions from the professor about the who, what, when, where, and why of the case, followed by some higher-order questions interrogating the breadth and scope of the rule set out in the case. Getting through a Socratic class session is about learning the material for all, but for some it might also be consumed by trying to avoid embarrassment or any signs of weakness generated by the risk of intimidating or belittling Socratic exchanges.[1] If students are worried about being on call for the next case, they might spend the entire class discussion time of case A freshening up on case B instead of listening.

For students not actively participating, these Socratic classroom exchanges are often "digestive" experiences, where students are passive learners absorbing and "banking" new information.[2] When students are active participants, often the loudest and most dominant voices are valued as the most competent.[3] Indeed, silence in Socratic classrooms can be interpreted as a lack of preparation, inadequacy, and weakness.[4] Yet there are also social pressures to navigate too, leaving some students worried of being perceived as the "gunner" and thus reluctant to participate, even though prepared. The professor might occasionally recap the substance of the material, but generally there is no other learning arc to the semester other than progressing through the sequential book chapters. There are likely well-crafted learning outcomes listed in the course syllabus, but they are rarely, if ever, discussed explicitly in class. The professor generally works through the assigned material in this manner until the exam nears.

Assessment Techniques

Historically, most Socratic classrooms were based almost entirely on a singular summative exam. American Bar Association reforms have since prioritized the use of formative assessment more robustly. Most Socratic classroom faculty have implemented that charge, however, by offering a practice exam or midterm as a sneak preview of the final exam, just replicating the same uncertainty and anxiety the final exam previously held. Professors might respond to some substantive exam review questions from students or even go over a practice exam closer to the final exam. It is unlikely faculty have a grading rubric for the exam available to the students in advance.

Outside of class, though, the students begin cramming excessively, often at the expense of their physical, emotional, and mental health, isolating themselves from friends and family, as the exam approaches. The exam grades are nearly always still heavily weighted, even if a midterm is also given. If there is another course grade component, it is often a murky "bump" for participation. This component likely has little transparency or candor for students regarding what it takes to receive a bump or whether one was awarded, a murkiness ripe for implicit bias to permeate assessment practices. The exam grades are generally posted privately for students to see a few weeks after the course ends. Weeks or months pass before the students see their faculty again, if at all. A handful of students trickle into the professor's office the following semester to go over the exam and raise questions or concerns, some compelled to do so by academic counseling requirements. Most students, however, accept their grades and march forward to "rinse and repeat" the following semester, without modification, reflection, or growth.

Some students will withdraw, disproportionately students of color.[5] This only exacerbates the existing disparities in enrollment of students of color. White students are already overrepresented in law school, comprising 64.8 percent of the law school population compared to just 57.9 percent of the US population.[6] Little is done to study why these students departed or whether the law school or law teachers could learn from these departures or even hold accountability for the departures. Yet these attrition numbers are revealing about the isolating, competitive, and all-consuming climate of law school and its effects. They compel us to ask tougher questions about the equities of our teaching and assessment practices, including digging into what factors or events compromise some students' sense of belonging.[7]

FACULTY EXPERIENCES IN LEGAL EDUCATION'S CURRICULAR CORE

Socratic Classrooms

Just as Socratic classrooms can be anxiety-provoking for students, Socratic teaching is demanding and has high stakes for the faculty that teach in this approach too. Acknowledging the full breadth of faculty constraints and institutional expectations that shape Socratic teaching is critical to thinking through effective reforms that are sustainable and realistic for law teachers, students, and institutions alike. There are intense preparation demands for Socratic law teachers, particularly in the first couple of semesters teaching a course. Newer law teachers, just like their students, likely also cram and exhaust themselves preparing to lead this classroom dialogue. Law teachers need to plan the dialogue arc of each class, sketch out their questions, anticipate student questions, and master the material in the casebook meticulously. There is really no course of study or prior professional role that can prepare professors to thrive in this model.

When deploying Socratic teaching methods, law teachers must listen with laser-sharp precision to the student responses to craft responsive follow-ups. Simultaneously, law teachers must monitor the understanding of *other* students while remembering what content has been covered and staying focused on where to go next. Law teachers might also simultaneously be managing classroom participation, taking notes regarding who is participating and who will be next. This is far more complicated to navigate than straight lectures would be. Indeed, a Socratic teaching style demands unparalleled attention to the clock, materials, microexchanges, and the macroclassroom climate. It is fatiguing and high pressure. One wrong word, misphrased question, or snarky response can torpedo the law teacher. Some of those Socratic classroom pressures are authentic to maintaining one's status as a subject-matter expert, but not all. The burdens are not experienced equally.

The Socratic classroom responsibilities, like all classrooms, are buttressed by other law-teaching functions. Law teachers balance office hours appointments, student email inquiries, proactive student outreach, mentoring, job support, and emotional support in their professional roles. For some law teachers, particularly women and faculty of color, these mentoring and support demands are heightened, as are the likelihood of student critiques.[8] For faculty of color and women faculty, students do not always grant the same presumption of competence that they give to White male professors who align with some students' entrenched stereotypes and expectations of a law professor.[9] Faculty of color and women faculty instead often have to fight against a presumption of incompetence to be viewed as subject-matter experts by their students, in the same way that their White, male colleagues are viewed by default. Indeed, the "shadow of Professor Kingsfield continues to dog women and other outsiders on law faculties because expectations play such an important role in the social construction of reality."[10]

Assessment Techniques

Through all of this, law teachers are expected to secure strong course evaluations from their students. These course evaluations are essential to check the box in the professional trajectory toward tenure or contract renewal. The questions are likely about the professor's availability, classroom management, and subject-matter knowledge. Other than checking that effective-teacher box, there is virtually no incentive to do more in the classroom. If the law teacher is up for promotion, other colleagues might come in the class and observe the teaching and write an evaluation. These peer-teaching reviews can be part of the curricular conformity too. While being reviewed, teachers might paradoxically be *less* likely to show innovation or distinction. They might be more inclined to show that they conform to the Socratic approach as implemented in their institution.

Far too often, after a semester of Socratic classes with a summative final exam, law teachers submit their end of semester grades and stop there. Most professors stop there because they must turn to other pressing demands. Thus, most professors annually update their materials for current events and developments but not for deep self-reflection or adaption to feedback. Law teachers are not necessarily expected to self-critique or analyze whether either the exam results or the course evaluations reveal anything about their teaching, their assessment techniques, or their classrooms. The tools and training do not exist to do this with ease or with savvy; thus there is no incentive to do this type of intensive reflection autonomously. Annual performance reviews and tenure reviews rarely ask for any meaningful reflection on teaching beyond evaluation scores and courses taught. In fact, the period immediately following exams is often the most intensive time for scholarly research and writing, networking, and conferencing.

Competing Service and Scholarship Demands

The Socratic classroom holds an important economic and pragmatic role in balancing the overall professional demands on law teachers, who have many other professional expectations, many of which often hold even greater weight in the promotion and tenure process. Faculty demands broadly relate to teaching, service, and scholarship. At many schools the hierarchies of scholarship, service, and teaching position scholarship as the most important professional obligation of tenure-track faculty. Traditional law faculty have pressure to publish, demonstrate a scholarly impact, and lead their institutions and communities. In stark contrast, an extra article, book, conference, keynote address, or legislative testimony yields concrete professional rewards that are economic (e.g., stipends, honorariums, grants); noneconomic (e.g., prestige); and quantifiable (e.g., articles downloaded, scholarly rankings). It is thus these scholarly benchmarks that are more likely to move the needle in job advancement through awards, marketing coverage, recruitment, course releases, and leaves. These scholarly tasks thus tend to sit higher on the faculty task hierarchy, and they are also more likely to advance law teachers professionally (e.g., lateral recruitment, named chair distinctions).

In fact, there can be reverse incentives relating to teaching in legal education. Designing simulations, hosting review workshops, offering formative assessment, meeting with students in small groups, taking students into the community, and other teaching enhancements that improve student experiences can spiral tremendously in time-consuming obligations for law teachers. Meaningful formative assessment jolts many students into realizing that their performance is not what they thought it was, thus adding office hours, consults, and referrals to the time of providing the formative assessment in the first place. Simulations, field trips, and experiential opportunities yield more letters of recommendations and reference requests because the students know that law teachers have seen them in action and can speak to their qualifications concretely. Like winning the prize of pie after a pie-eating contest, law teachers who really engage and energize students in the traditional doctrinal classroom are thus often rewarded with *more* large lecture-hall classes, fewer seminars, and more course-coverage pleas following institutional scheduling disruptions. Rarely do these teaching innovations yield heightened faculty status, lateral offers, or other marks of distinction. Yet students still need concrete job training from somewhere. Consequently, it is more likely that the most robust feedback and innovative teaching sits in *other* law school classrooms, not Socratic classrooms, such as legal research and writing, clinics, seminars, and experiential learning. These classes, of course, are much more likely to be taught by colleagues who are *not* on the tenure track and thus have less prestige, job security, institutional power, and compensation.[11]

Scrutinizing the traditional model of Socratic legal education reveals that it is indeed time-intensive, with high stakes for law teachers and students alike. The model plays a pragmatic and efficient role in legal education, however, while allowing law teachers to meet intense scholarly expectations. Although newer law teachers might initially exit these classrooms feeling tremendous pressure, fatigue, and scrutiny, over time the process becomes quite replicable and sustainable. Yet students continue to leave most traditional Socratic classrooms with few concrete job skills, minimal formative feedback, and high anxiety and stress to boot.

STAFF EXPERIENCES IN LEGAL EDUCATION'S CURRICULAR CORE

Beyond just the teacher and student, many other stakeholders shape legal education. Particularly for Socratic classrooms, academic success personnel often play vital roles preparing students for the demands of performing in Socratic classrooms. Academic success professionals might offer programming on rule-based legal reasoning, case briefing, outlining, exam performance, time management, and more. They might also deliver critical individual-support through mentoring and one-on-one advising and counseling roles for students struggling with academic performance. These roles can sometimes be deployed in partnership with the Socratic law faculty, but more often these events and support systems are separately managed and delivered out of sight of the faculty. There are surely many efficiencies and professionalization benefits of this approach. Student affairs offices can also be mobilized to help a student through disruptions, such as moving, illness, deaths in the family, and more. Disability and accommodation offices can be called on to help students and law teachers navigate testing condition parameters.

There are several implications of this bifurcation between student support and the Socratic classroom though. This infrastructure puts the burden on students to gain these study and performance skills by identifying the value of the programming in the first instance and then setting aside the time and bandwidth to attend ad hoc events. It also houses vital student-support functions with staff who are often undercompensated and overworked, thus often yielding a high turnover.[12] What is notable from this structural picture, however, is that there is a general sense that students *need* support in Socratic classrooms. We have built entire trainings and staff departments around helping students through class preparation, note-taking, and exam performance. This reveals how we continue to accept that we fix students through preparation, mentoring, and support instead of fixing the teaching model.

THE LIMITS AND HIERARCHIES OF THIS CURRICULAR MODEL

The dominant centering of Socratic classrooms at the apex of the law school hierarchy has several problematic implications for inclusive, equitable, and effective teaching. This section surveys the general critiques that have emerged of Socratic teaching. Chapter 2 deepens this foundation considerably by surveying how critical theorists have analyzed Socratic classrooms and spotlighting the reforms they have proposed and catalyzed over fifty years. These critiques of Socratic teaching are thus not fads or trends. Rather, strong voices have challenged the dominance of the traditional Socratic classroom throughout the past half of a century of modern legal education. Yet institutional momentum remains strongly skewed toward retaining Socratic classrooms. Accordingly, as Kathryne Young colorfully contextualized, student experiences will not be altered by waiting it out while some "cranky old professors . . . refuse to 'change with the times'; rather it is a fidelity to a system's long-standing structures even when those structures do not serve all students." Young powerfully directs us to interrogate Socratic pedagogy head on: "Instead of asking why we are choosing to rely so heavily on a pedagogy that creates disparate effects, we ask what is wrong with the students it disadvantages. The mistake lies in seeing the pedagogy, not the students, as the nonmoving piece in the equation. . . . But the more transformative approach is a structural one: entertaining the possibility that if a pedagogical tool consistently produces negative results for certain people, perhaps the problem is with the tool, not the people."[13] We need to center these Socratic critiques in our larger legal education-reform dialogues. Socratic reforms can yield enduring, sustainable, and scalable improvements in legal education when deployed with intentionality, collaboration, and purposefulness. Let's consider the core arguments critiquing Socratic classrooms.

Magnifying Some Voices and Marginalizing Others

The Socratic classroom has long been critiqued for magnifying some student voices while silencing others. The teacher dominates at the podium, and students orient toward that central power figure, only minimally interacting with one another. This classroom setup socializes students around when to speak and to whom.[14] Feminists and intersectional feminist scholars have documented quantitative disparities in women's Socratic class participation for decades.[15] They have captured how male students dominate, while women remain silent in ways that compromise academic and professional success.[16]

The implications are real and harmful. The iconic 1994 publication of "Becoming Gentlemen: Women's Experiences at One Ivy League Law School" particularly highlights how similarly qualified male and female candidates diverge as they move from their first year to their third.[17]

Coauthored by Lani Guinier, who would go on to become the first woman of color granted tenure at Harvard Law School, the study reveals that women students receive relatively lower grades, class ranks, and honors than their male peers.[18] While prior studies had documented women's reduced classroom participation, "Becoming Gentlemen" exposed women's institutional and cultural alienation resulting from the Socratic method, even though this pedagogy dominated (then and now) across nearly all 1L instruction and much of the upper-level curriculum.[19] Women characterized their first year as a "radical, painful, or repressive experience" with psychological and employment consequences. The Socratic classroom symbolizes legal education's values and hierarchies more broadly, and there are "few winners and many losers." The Socratic method takes the differences among students and makes it into their disadvantage in legal education.[20] Other scholars continue to build on these findings, both replicating them and concluding that time will not resolve these disparities, only pedagogy reform and institutional changes will.[21]

These observed disparities—skewing toward the dominance of male and White students in Socratic participation—have persisted through COVID-emergency remote teaching, as have the calls for institutional responses. Several student respondents to a 2020, in-depth, qualitative study attributed the disparities in Socratic participation to socialization, whereby women were more likely to participate only when they knew their answers were relevant or correct. The students also surmised that women were more concerned about critical judgment when participating than their male peers. In contrast, one male respondent, for example, reported how he viewed the class as an opportunity "to get what's in my head out to see if I'm right or wrong," revealing a stark comfort (entitlement even) in the classroom space and an "imperviousness to negative peer judgment."[22] Many students are not thriving in the traditional Socratic classroom, including women students and students of color. These critiques cannot just isolate the Socratic exchanges, however. Cemented into the Socratic teaching model is a more systemic degree of hierarchy and formalism that too can be disengaging and distortive.

Formalism

Formalism limits how lawyers think about their work and the tools they have to solve client problems. Formalism is a method of reasoning grounded in "obsession with precedent." It limits the use of "history, literature, religion, morality, and other humanistic bodies of knowledge on legal problems," yielding "intrinsically less interesting, less rich" law practice. This is about both the substance of law and the structure of law practice. The formalism of law is further reinforced by the billable hour requirements, specialization, and competition found in many law practice settings. This contrasts with earlier conceptions of law as a helping profession with a strong emphasis on service.[23]

Formal reasoning structures further constrain and shape the Socratic instructional model. Students study existing rules from appellate cases. They learn how to issue spot when those rules apply and how to reason through to compelled outcomes based on the facts. This IRAC method (issue, rule, application, conclusion) of legal reasoning sets the boundaries for classroom dialogue. IRAC "has the power to construct reality." It embraces a "straight-line structure [that] limits what meanings can be construed," cementing rules in existing power structures and hierarchies.[24]

But existing rules are not neutral, of course. Rather, they construct "a foundational system that is deeply interlaced with inequality that preserves concentrated power in a select group of predetermined elites." This hierarchy can reinforce inequalities of class, race, and gender through powerful categorizations that need to be contested. Because existing law "benefits those groups who are already in power, law reifies majoritarian norms and tends to ignore and silence minority voices."[25] This formal method of instructions thus teaches the law, but it allows little room to challenge its origins or justness, unless the law teacher pursues that line of inquiry.[26] For students to question a rule or case, they are expected to cite another case or another rule, making legal education "intrinsically justify the existing legal order and the social authority of the state."[27] This limits students' understanding of "what matters" as well as "their vision of what law can do, and what the law should do," leaving them blindfolded instead of exposed.[28] And this methodological critique has persisted for decades.[29] The Socratic teaching method using appellate cases and formal reasoning thus teaches students to replicate existing hierarchies and uses traditional legal analysis to preserve it.[30]

These layers of hierarchy come at a cost to law teachers and students alike. We give core classes that deploy these formal teaching techniques privilege and hierarchy in the curriculum, and we often pay these professors more and bestow them with higher status.[31] Further, the student-reward structures of law school and job searching exacerbate the weight of these core Socratic classes for students.[32] Students are socialized early on to seek these top 1L grades to increase their likelihood of securing a prestigious job.[33] In this way the hierarchy and competitiveness of "case-law method and student culture reinforce one another."[34]

Socializing Perspectivelessness

The structure and methods of Socratic classrooms also perpetuate and socialize a problematic "perspectivelessness," which marginalizes students of color, women students, and LGBTQ+ students. Socratic teaching pretends to adopt a position stripped of culture, politics, and identity. Yet it instead standardizes norms built around dominant cultures and communities without acknowledging the privilege and oppression this approach creates and sustains. This classroom model thus entrenches hierarchies while paradoxically wrapping them securely around a pedagogy of neutrality. Bennett Capers describes how Black students and faculty in this dynamic are "typically absent, not expected, or marginalized when present," while White students and faculty can then regard these law school spaces as "unremarkable, or as normal, taken-for-granted reflections of civil society."[35]

This can in turn limit the success, professional development, and perceived possibilities for students of color. Teri McMurtry-Chubb powerfully explains how "navigating law school and joining the legal profession meant presenting less of ourselves and embracing who we were told we must become." She explains that "the path presented was narrow, and what lay outside of it was context, explanation, and the lived experiences of the parties in our casebooks who stand eternally at the ready to guide class after class of law students to 'the law.'"[36]

The harms of perspectivelessness are searing for students of color. Patricia Williams emotively frames it as "spirit murder," as students of color abandon their identities and adopt a perspective infused with a White, middle-class worldview. Students of color are left to provide marginalized "testimony" to challenge the dominant norms and are then perceived as presenting "biased, self-interested, or subjective opinions" when they voice their experiences, creating "twin problems of objectification and subjectification."[37] Mari Matsuda describes this vacillating between a student's lived consciousness and "the white consciousness required for survival in elite educational institutions" as "multiple consciousness."[38] Dean Spade explains that "law school is a place where white masculine norms and behavior are exacerbated . . . and ostracism of people who fall outside the norm is par for the course."[39] It is harmful to students of color when instructors adopt this perspectivelessness approach because it devalues the backgrounds, experiences, and identities of many students.[40] This cultivates an alienating and marginalizing experience for students of color.

LGBTQ+ students and faculty have also critiqued law school's perspectivelessness approach.[41] Classroom discussions and content can be marginalizing and isolating for LGBTQ+ students. Experiential accounts document classroom encounters that are sometimes hostile to the perspectives and contributions of LGTBQ+ students.[42] These accounts align with overall climate surveys, in which LGBTQ+ students report that they do not always feel like they belong.[43] Likewise, the expectation that law teachers teach in a "detached, objective manner" can be "not only disingenuous, but dangerous."[44]

The fiction of neutrality distorts the dialogue. LGBTQ+ students and teachers sometimes have to "leave their personal skins on hooks outside the door of the law school to be collected (if remembered at all) on the way out." Incorporating LGBTQ+ issues into the curriculum can go a long way to creating a welcoming climate for students. Avoiding these topics in the curriculum "only encourages the invisibility of these issues in legal education and allows bias and discriminatory assumptions to go unchecked."[45] The magnification versus marginalization of certain voices, the limits of formalistic classroom discourses, and the socializing of perspectivelessness are three sweeping critiques of the dominance of Socratic classrooms that occupy the curricular core of legal education.

. . .

This section presents the centrality of Socratic teaching from the student, law teacher, and staff perspective. It reveals the murky, anxiety-ridden, and competitive framework governing the Socratic classroom for students. It then contextualizes the pragmatic and professional drivers that make Socratic classrooms so foundational to legal education infrastructure for faculty. It notes the support structures in place to help students. Underlying each of these perspectives is the vivid reality of legal education's hierarchies—hierarchies that position scholarship and tenure-track roles over other law-teaching roles, hierarchies that position the grades in first-year Socratic classrooms over skills and experiential courses, and the hierarchies of which voices, methodological approaches, and perspectives are centered in the dominant curricular core of Socratic classrooms. Next Chapter 2 reviews the sustained challenges and critiques that communities of critical theorists have documented and developed for decades. These scholarly perspectives chart our path forward.

CHAPTER 2

Sustained Calls for Curricular Reforms

Socratic teaching remains the curricular core of legal education, even as its leaders, students, and teachers have become far more diverse. Law schools continue to privilege a traditional model of Socratic teaching with appellate casebooks in large lecture-style classes. While this technique has softened and diversified over the decades, on balance it remains competitive, impersonal, adversarial, and marginalizing in many classrooms. Chapter 1 summarizes the concrete harms to students and law teachers that can be sourced to the traditional Socratic classroom.

Yet critical voices across many institutions, communities, and decades have long championed steady and resounding calls for reforms to make legal education more inclusive and more effective for more than half a century. This chapter sketches the central themes that have emerged from feminism, critical legal studies, critical race theory, Lat-Crit, and queer theory to inform modern legal education reforms. These critical theories (and others) have unpacked various oppressions in society, centered missing voices in law and society, and revealed how legal doctrine embeds and privileges dominant insider perspectives. These scholarly critiques have made vital contributions to both the substance of law and the theories underlying the law and its limits. They have also aligned in synergistic and sustained ways in their critiques of and proposed reforms to the dominant Socratic-teaching pedagogy. This chapter highlights the lessons these theories collectively bring to modern curricular reform.

FEMINIST CRITIQUES

Feminism offers vital insights into how legal education functions today and its ongoing critiques. Feminism has influenced legal education over more than a century of critical engagement.[1] Feminist critiques have challenged the substance of legal rules, the methods of law teaching, and the culture of legal education in ways that inform modern pedagogy. Following decades of advocacy, feminism has generated new fields, courses, laws, leaders, and spaces.

Early liberal feminist activism focused on removing formal barriers to legal education and bar admission. While educating *women* lawyers was considered radical at the time, formal legal education was itself an innovation. Most lawyers at the time trained through apprenticeships, but these too were unavailable to women or restricted to fields like family law.[2] In 1896 Ellen Spencer Mussey and Emma Gillett made history by establishing the Washington College of Law in Washington, DC, to educate women lawyers.[3] They incorporated some unique structural protections to support women students, such as night classes and low tuition; they even allowed a student to attend under a pseudonym to protect her identity.[4] But aside from the radical move of seeking legitimacy as a women-run law school for women students, its pedagogy was entirely conventional.[5] And even as a law school for women, the radicalness of Mussey and Gillett's fledgling feminist institution was severely undercut by the exclusion of African American students for fifty more years.[6] Entry to law school was only one of many barriers facing women in the profession. When women could not vote or serve on juries, it was common for local bar associations to exclude women as well. These external barriers led Mussey and Gillett to establish the Women's Bar Association of the District of Columbia in 1917, an important foreshadowing of the external partnerships between law schools and the local bar associations necessary to secure change.[7]

While the liberal feminist agenda succeeded in getting women in the door, at the podium, and in the dean's suite of law schools, integrating women into the curriculum proved more complex. Ironically, after centuries of women's exclusion based on presumed differences from men, once admitted, women were assumed to be the same, and the culture remained unchanged. Women endured sexism, tokenism, and sexual harassment.[8] Women's initial law school presence compelled them "to simply join the academic procession, not to question its direction."[9] The next challenge feminists faced was thus transforming the delivery of legal education itself, following in the footsteps of feminist pedagogical reforms emerging from other disciplines. Across disciplines feminist pedagogy sought to include multiple perspectives, value all voices, contextualize experiences, and reorient away from the notion of one absolute, objective truth in fields of study. Feminist pedagogy also directed learning toward the goal of achieving transformative changes in society through action.[10] These feminist visions for an improved pedagogy notably stood to improve the experiences of all learners and communities.

Feminist pedagogical influences did partially take root in legal education. Feminists challenged core doctrinal premises, problematic legal rules, and ineffective teaching methods through their teaching, scholarship, and advocacy. This mobilization also brought law teachers out of law schools and into the community in scholarly discourse and activism. In the late 1960s, for example, a group of scholars organized a Women and the Law Conference to discuss topics such as family law, criminal law, discrimination law, reproductive rights, and constitutional law.[11] Law-reform efforts targeted substantive areas like sexual harassment, rape, domestic violence, employment, family law, and reproductive rights. These public feminist reforms inevitably transformed learning inside the classroom.[12] Pioneering scholars began to publish casebooks on women and the law, sex-based discrimination, and feminist jurisprudence.[13] These materials, borne out of scholarly faculty communities, created opportunities for specialized study and community building.

As feminist spaces and academic materials emerged to deepen discourse within select pockets and courses, questions of the best approaches to scale and transfer feminist methods emerged. Scholars considered whether specialized courses and programs would have the paradoxical effect of marginalizing women's issues in ways that reinforced the myth of law's neutrality throughout the rest of the law school curriculum.[14] While urging feminist courses to continue, Catharine MacKinnon and other contemporaries called for the "mainstreaming" of gender issues across legal education.[15] Feminism was not something to be deployed in fragments in select spots of courses or books. Rather, it required a wholesale effort to rethink the legal education curriculum holistically.

Feminists accordingly pushed to transform legal education's threshold assumptions, approaches, and methodologies. They contested the "add woman and stir" model, declining to limit feminism to a "narrow, one-dimensional, one-note, geographically limited, thin set of problems, questions, and people."[16] Feminist theorists particularly challenged the very premise of a gender-neutral person positioned at the law's center.

This perceived neutrality rendered gender invisible in law while exalting a system designed around privileged male norms.

Feminists particularly exposed the unidirectional process of professors transmitting knowledge through objective discussion.[17] They challenged the method of teaching with appellate cases because it obscured factual context and lawyering strategy. They contested the Socratic method's dominant role in legal education. Indeed, feminist law teachers excoriated the Socratic method for failing in both teaching and learning. It sits at a "level of abstraction" that is "both too theoretical and not theoretical enough" in that it fails to examine the foundations of legal rules and fails to teach students how to use these rules.[18]

In seeking to transform how legal education was delivered, feminists sought to inject women's perspectives and experiences into law study. This marked a transformative pedagogical move away from trying to assimilate women *into* law schools toward aligning the culture of legal education *with* women's learning styles. Difference strands of feminist theory particularly explore how values traditionally associated with women are marginalized in legal education and need to be pedagogically centered.[19] Difference feminism celebrates a relational ethic of care that values collaboration, community, context, and cooperation as critical values in law beyond abstraction and competition.[20] Valuing relational skills might, in turn, improve the quality, depth, and breadth of lawyering. Shifting cultural approaches offered a promise to transform the legal profession by rethinking long-standing obstacles to women's success, such as billable hour requirements and the absence of family leave.[21] Feminists notably advocate that *all* law classes could be more participatory, inclusive, and nonhierarchal. Finally, the buildings themselves require adaptations, such as inclusive bathrooms for students and lactation spaces for students who are nursing.

But not all feminists sign on to a cultural feminist agenda for legal education or otherwise. Others within feminism argue that there is no singular approach or learning style that is inclusive of all women. Indeed, to suggest otherwise is to ignore rich variations across ages, cultures, classes, disability statuses, races, and more.[22] Embracing a "women's perspective," the critiques proffer, risks engaging in a type of essentialism that erases differences, privileges dominant voices, and reinforces exclusionary hierarchies, repeating the exact same deficiencies that feminists sought to overcome in legal education.[23] Still, feminists do broadly agree on the need to expand the repertoire of skills and values traditionally centered in legal education. Feminists align in moving beyond a model designed by and for men, even as they differ in what model best responds to the critiques. Robust debates continue across various stands of feminism.

CRITICAL LEGAL STUDIES

Critical legal studies (CLS) offers an additional critical lens into the law and legal education, focusing more squarely on class hierarchies. CLS emerged in the late 1970s and the early 1980s and left its mark on legal education. Evolving from early legal realism schools of thought, the CLS vision is to build a more cohesive intellectual community of existing politically left-leaning scholars who see the law as more indeterminant and politically intertwined.[24] CLS particularly focuses on how the law is used to produce class hierarchies, thus calling into question liberal rights, the impartiality of law, and the public-private divide. CLS seeks to destabilize this unjust order. It explores how wealthy ruling classes can use the law to advance existing privilege and class stratification. While CLS comprises a diverse group of thinkers with differing views, it aligns in wanting to transform the law to foster "a more decent, equal, solidary society—less intensively ordered by hierarchies of class, status, 'merit,' race, and gender—more decentralized, democratic, and participatory."[25]

CLS is distinctly critical of legal education pedagogy and its relationship to reproducing the hierarchies that shape the law. Duncan Kennedy's iconic 1983 work, *Legal Education and the Reproduction of Hierarchy*, describes the law school classroom as "hierarchical with a vengeance," with a "demand for a pseudo-participation in which you struggle desperately, in front of a large audience, to read a mind determined to elude you." Kennedy critiques the lack of classroom connection to the actual practice of law. He distinctly connects and intertwines the hierarchies of legal education and the legal profession itself. He describes how the rankings, titles, and prestige hierarchies of the profession precisely parallel the infrastructure of law schools, and how the professor-student relationship replicates the supervisory relationship in practice.[26]

Kennedy's work has a "revelatory power" in its poignant descriptions of the hierarchies shaping legal education.[27] It is, however, perhaps less concrete in its call to action for legal education reform.[28] CLS "is attempting a project as ambitious as Langdell's—to reinterpret law and legal education."[29] CLS's impact on legal education, however, is surely more than just intellectual. It leads many law teachers to help students critique the law and its systems to acquire a broader set of tools as advocates and counselors. CLS leads to richer instruction, challenging students to deconstruct what the courts are doing in deploying conventional argumentation moves and the "backstage devices" that attorneys can deploy to shift the outcomes, for example, identifying when courts deploy rigid rules versus discretionary ones.[30]

With that more critical lens, students can frame advocacy strategies and respond to counterarguments more robustly. Robert W. Gordon summarizes that "the basic method here is just to bring out the submerged premises, empirical assumptions, narrative artifices; to elaborate them; to encourage students to elaborate them; to show there is a limited number of basic moves, endlessly repeated across doctrinal fields; to demonstrate that they are all in conflict with one another; and to examine how they can all be drawn upon in the analysis of every case." These strategies, in turn, leave students with more "suppleness and flexibility than can be derived from teaching the law as an authoritative set of solutions."[31] CLS has been criticized for advancing left-leaning political views. Its advocates, however, emphasize that all students are empowered to read texts more critically, with a broader critique of institutions and systems.

CLS faces criticism from both outside and inside its ranks. Many CLS scholars are also women and scholars of color who want to further unpack how gender and race are situated within the law. These communities critique CLS's "inability to incorporate the authentic experience of minority communities," particularly in its focus on theory over action.[32] Over time, feminism, critical race theory, LatCrit, queer theory, and other critical discourses have all challenged the role of law propping up existing hierarchies and subordinating power structures. These strands have deepened and expanded the CLS foundations by interrogating the construction of racial hierarchies.

CRITICAL RACE THEORY

The field of critical race theory (CRT) emerged from a community of scholars working at the intersections of antidiscrimination work and CLS, who came together to discuss their integration struggles and race work at their respective institutions.[33] CLS had offered a scholarly space to contest the law's neutrality.[34] Within that space a "gender turn" pivoted toward the emergence of FemCrits, followed by a "race turn" of identified RaceCrits, articulating the core themes that became CRT. Kimberlé Crenshaw succinctly defines the scholarly shift as a "left intervention into race discourse and a race intervention into left discourse."[35]

CRT, like other critical theories, is not one unified theory but a diverse range of voices and perspectives.

Broadly defined, CRT is "a body of legal scholarship . . . the majority of whose members are both existentially people of color and ideologically committed to the struggle against racism, particularly as institutionalized in and by law."[36] Like other critical communities, it is equal parts substance, analytic methodologies, and community. The roots of CRT took hold in the mid-1970s, as many of the gains of the civil rights movement had sputtered, and founding scholars came to see that new tactics and theories were necessary for the next era.[37] These scholars saw the law as central to understanding racial subordination, "not merely *regulating* race and the relations between the various races, but . . . actively *constituting* race and the relations between various races."[38] CRT thus emerged in the 1980s from a "unique confluence of temporal, institutional, and political factors."[39] It spawned from CLS and other movements, such as ethnic studies and women's studies.[40]

CRT notably emerged along with vital efforts to diversify legal education. In 1980 renowned scholar and CRT pioneer, Derrick Bell, left Harvard to become the University of Oregon's law dean, leaving curricular gaps at Harvard. Students organized and agitated in response to Harvard's failure to hire a new professor and to adequately cover courses after Bell's departure.[41] Harvard responded to the criticism by raising merit arguments, citing the absence of a qualified pool of candidates from which to recruit. This response only increased and mobilized student agitation. These events revealed how little legal education's core considered issues of race and how "sluggish" legal education was to rethink its curriculum after transformative civil rights shifts. Critics countered Harvard's "merit" argument, arguing that Harvard was relying on structures that reproduced racially disparate outcomes without contesting how those systems had built a virtually all-White institution. These structures normalized racial subordination and stratification and failed to reward innovative legal theories. Harvard's responses revealed how antidiscrimination approaches that yielded a "colorblind" approach left the institutionalized structures of racism unchallenged. Ultimately, this mobilization and advocacy after Bell's departure led to a course offering that was heavily enrolled and featured a slate of scholars, which revealed the breadth of scholarship and knowledge that was being "embargoed at Harvard's gates."[42]

CRT has since spent decades centrally positioning the inquiry around how race and racism define and structure the law.[43] CRT challenges the standard institutional and educational models framed around "objectivity, meritocracy, color-blindness, race neutrality, and equal opportunity." It exposes how these myths obscure the power, privilege, and hierarchies that sustain these models. CRT pedagogies instead seek to infuse the classroom with the lived experiences of students of color to analyze race and racism in the past and the present.[44]

Much of the past work of CRT and critical race feminism particularly included efforts to improve hiring practices and reform the institutional culture of law schools.[45] These initiatives are still vital today. Seminal published works such as *Presumed Incompetent* continue to reveal the intersecting roles of race, class, and gender and the ongoing reform agenda of legal education.[46] CRT more recently has faced highly politicized critiques, backlash, and distortions in politics and the media.[47] These political attacks collectively only reveal the depth and breadth of the work of the CRT agenda and its ongoing importance to legal education. CRT further birthed many additional critical communities, not all of which are profiled in this chapter, such as Asian Pacific American critical race theory (APA crit), tribal crit, and class crit.[48] The next section introduces the contributions of LatCrit to ongoing pedagogy reforms, a discourse also spawned from the CRT movement.

LATCRIT

The LatCrit movement offers further insights into curricular reforms in both its methods and approaches. LatCrit is "a genre of critical outsider jurisprudence" that emerged from CRT, interrogating CRT's Black/White paradigm to further unpack how racial hierarchies and subordination impact Latinx communities.[49] The movement addresses the "marginality and invisibility of Latinos/as/x in law, theory, policy and society."[50] Notably, when LatCrit emerged, only an astonishing 94 out of 5,064 law professors identified as Latinx.[51]

LatCrit formally emerged from a 1995 colloquium to develop a "critical, activist, and interdisciplinary discourse on law and policy toward Latinos/as/x." The movement seeks to develop "coalitional theory and practice as well as the accessibility of this knowledge to agents of social and legal transformative change." It centers on the experiences of Latinx identities while rejecting Latinx exceptionalism, seeking to sustain intersectional discourses and cultivate a "diverse, participatory community."[52]

LatCrit recognizes the vast diversity of Latinx people as a vehicle through which to examine and improve the law because of the community's complexities and diversities. LatCrit theory deploys shifting lenses to study the law from various perspectives, such as class, religion, culture, language, sexuality, imperialism, ethnicity, and colonialism. While its goal is to center the Latinx condition, its methodologies rely on broadly inclusive and multilateral discourses incorporating Latinx experiences and others. LatCrit theory is thus informed by diverse "outside" viewpoints as well as diverse "internal" viewpoints.[53] From this substantive work have emerged both community and solidarity.

LatCrit is distinctly intentional about identifying its values and its commitments as a movement. It has developed its own values and guiding principles, in ways that are deeply respectful and collaborative with other critical movements. From the outset it has espoused an uncompromising commitment to creating an inclusive community welcoming of all.[54] It blends substance (*what* it seeks to accomplish) seamlessly with method (*how* it operates) and deploys a "rotation of centers" and "bottoms-up" approach. LatCrit fosters critical discussions about Latinx people, but it does so distinctly without privileging any one Latinx identity over another. It executes a "rotation of centers" approach that continually shifts the lens to see various similarities and differences. LatCrit methodologies also critique legal systems from the bottom up to reveal sociolegal hierarchies.

The LatCrit movement is robust in its substantive contributions to knowledge generation, theory development, legal reforms, and community. LatCrit is actively engaged in real-world projects, living out its values through amici projects, accredited NGOs, and various community projects.[55] These purposeful methodologies offer vital insights into how legal education too can achieve inclusive reforms. LatCrit teachers and students have particularly agitated and advocated for legal education reforms for decades. As their CRT and feminist colleagues have done, the Latinx community likewise forms student groups and faculty communities of support, creating spaces for scholarship and teaching on issues affecting the Latinx community. These efforts yield more courses on LatCrit issues and more materials using LatCrit methods.[56]

LatCrit also focuses on the recruiting and hiring of faculty, as well as recruiting and retaining Latinx students, thereby resulting in demographic shifts in law schools and the profession.[57] Through these efforts there has been an increase in the number of Latinx students enrolling in law schools. In 2012, 13,556 Latinx students attended law school out of a total of 139,504 students, comprising 9.72 percent of the overall law student population.[58] In 2022, 16,005 Latinx students attended law schools out of a total of 116,725 students, reflecting 13.71 percent of the law student population. Thus there has been just under a 4 percent increase in Latinx students enrolling in law schools over ten years.[59] Despite this growth in student enrollment, the number of Latinx deans has been low compared to that of Latinx students. As of July 2023, there are 13 Latinx law school deans out of 199 deans (6.5 percent).[60]

LatCrit has also considered innovations in law teaching at nearly every annual law school conference and symposia. It unpacks the role of "identity, power, law, and knowledge" in legal education and exposes the "absences, distortions, and limitations of formal legal training." LatCrit accepts as a premise that "legal rules and actions are both manipulable and manipulated in light of their basic indeterminacy" and that identity can shape how that indeterminacy is resolved. Like CRT, LatCrit seeks to expose the legal fictions that obscure social realities and the lived experiences of all. LatCrit embraces interdisciplinary and counterdisciplinary texts, projects, and programs.[61]

LatCrit has joined its other critical theory allies in squarely focusing on the Socratic method as a target of reform. The LatCrit community keenly understands that the Socratic method's positioning as the dominant method for delivering legal education sits in tension with LatCrit's goals to "engage and embolden, rather than to stifle or silence, outsider students *and* teachers." One study of Latinx student experiences with the first-year curriculum, for example, reveals that cultural differences merit further understanding of the Latinx Socratic student experience. The Socratic method might be perceived as "irreverent" or "disrespectful" within some students' cultural experiences.[62]

LatCrit instead champions a critical pedagogy that centers race and racism in legal education, challenges dominant ideologies, advances social justice principles, applies knowledge experientially, and uses interdisciplinary perspectives. It also seeks deeper connections in the classroom between the past and the present, the personal and the structural, the social and the legal, the particular and the general, and knowledge and practice.[63]

LatCrit methodologies embed more collaborative learning in the traditional law school classroom to avoid entrenching classroom power and subordination. LatCrit approaches intentionally seek to minimize the privilege and hierarchy of the traditional teacher-student relationship. These intentional pedagogies extend to supporting students beyond the walls of the classroom and into the community. LatCrit also unpacks how institutional rewards and incentives in law schools can undermine the work of students and faculty in fully engaging with their community, thus stifling innovation and activism.[64] For example, scholarly writings like legislative testimony, white papers, and other engaged scholarship rarely carry the same panache and weight in internal scholarship reviews.

The LatCrit community offers a powerful template to shape the development of inclusive legal education. It reveals the benefits of a community holding intentional values and shared principles. Socratic law teaching could benefit greatly from many of these approaches. While strong teaching communities exist in other pedagogies, such as legal writing and clinical teaching, Socratic teaching has been largely individual and autonomous. LatCrit methods and practice powerfully teach us how to embed the Socratic classroom more authentically in and around the community, as well as how to use the richness of the community to explore the law from many perspectives. LatCrit reveals the benefits of collaboration through a participatory process in generating shared teaching values and advancing innovation. This multidimensional lens in turn yields a more fulfilling and welcoming environment for all. Queer theory provides further insights and guidance into implementing successful legal education reforms.

QUEER THEORY

Queer theory has also thoughtfully influenced legal education pedagogy. Queer theory interrogates the role of sex, gender, and sexual identities within the law.[65] It examines the social construction of sexuality. It goes further than feminist theory in upending the binary male/female thinking that dominates mainstream feminism. Queer theorists particularly reflect skepticism about the identity-based nature of feminism and gay and lesbian studies as scholarly fields.

Queer theory proffers its own well-developed vision for legal education pedagogy. This momentum came after scholars Kim Brooks and Debra Parkes observed that, other than some experiential accounts of students and teachers and Ruthann Robson's 1998 iconic publication, *Sappho Goes to Law School: Fragments in Lesbian Legal Theory*, queer theory had not yet articulated a distinct queer legal pedagogy. Indeed, before 1985 there were no published materials to teach a class focused on LGBTQ+ issues. Yet student and faculty accounts had already robustly revealed the harms of traditional pedagogy not directly addressing LGBTQ+ issues. For example, one student highlighted how traditional courses problematically covered gay and lesbian persons only in

criminal cases. Another student observed how little familiarity and terminology his classmates had with issues of sexual orientation and how
isolating that felt as a student.[66]

Queer theory pedagogy thus applies its pedagogy principles to all
learners in all classrooms, while acknowledging that this initiative was
necessarily focused on the curriculum, "side-stepp[ing] the larger imag-
inative project of reinventing law school" more systemically. The
rationale for this approach is squarely rooted in lawyering, recognizing
that all students would work with clients of various identities. The
foundation of queer theory's approach thus became a commitment to
legal education as vital training for citizenship and civic participation of
lawyers. Brooks and Parkes introduce the following eight principles of
queer law pedagogy. These principles reveal important insights into
modern curricular reform.

BROOKS AND PARKES'S PRINCIPLES OF
QUEER LAW PEDAGOGY

- Centering queer experiences in all of their diversity
- Denaturalizing heterosexuality
- Cultivating community and coalition
- Seeking connections between disciplines
- Advancing professional transformation
- Embracing activism as method
- Uncovering perspectives
- Responding to changing contexts, periods, and climates

These principles reform both *what* is taught and *how* it is taught,
embracing the full "multiple consciousness[es]" of LGBTQ+ students as
a community. These reforms again sit in the curriculum for all students
to benefit, not leaving these topics or methods marginalized or sidelined
in seminars or student groups. The "what was taught" critique centers
queer experiences and "denaturalize[es] heterosexuality."[67]

There are also pragmatic lessons for legal education to learn from
queer theory about fostering inclusion. For example, many Socratic law
teachers might use gendered naming conventions that can cause anxiety,
and even harm, to students who do not classify themselves or others into
a gendered binary. Likewise, the assigned name in one's university
records may not align with the student's preferred name. Simple practices to use the proper gender identity and name, even if it differs from
the course enrollment software, can help create an inclusive classroom
in which all students have a *"presence."* This intentionality in classroom

management is important for both inclusion and substance: "Legal education is impoverished when it is based only upon the experiences of dominant groups and . . . it will be improved by the infusion of queer experiences."[68] These practices, too, have come under grave political attack.

Queer theory pedagogy also reminds us to build communities and coalitions. Students should not be passively submissive to a professor at the front of the class. Rather, students should be working in communities on projects. It emphasizes cultivating a learning environment that positions all students to be successful and build connections. Queer theory pedagogy also builds interdisciplinary connections, recognizing that other disciplines enrich legal work.[69]

These pedagogy principles are also squarely focused on "advancing progressive transformation" through social justice work. Brooks and Parkes candidly admit that this is likely the most contentious of their eight principles, but they note that "it would be a start" to "simply raise consciousness about how power operates in the classroom and to begin to link the social justice aims of law to our academic material." The focus on pedagogy "embrac[ing] activism as [a] method" would go a long way toward ending the passivity of legal education. Queer theory, like so many of its critical theory allies, seeks to uncover and unpack perspectives and stop pretending that the law is neutral and perspectiveless. Instead, it seeks to provide students with real-world experiences to translate theory into practice. Skills like oral advocacy, lobbying, and policy work, for example, can benefit students in their practice readiness. Finally, queer theory seeks to keep legal education dynamic in responding to "changing contexts, periods, and climates."[70] Queer theory offers vital contributions to legal education pedagogy.

. . .

This chapter reveals that, for more than half of a century, consistent strands of critical theory have challenged the curricular core of legal education—the traditional Socratic classroom. Iconic critical scholarly discourses have long proffered key pedagogy reforms to the Socratic classroom. This chapter is not a comprehensive survey of all strands of critical discourse. Adding other strands of scholarship, such as class crit, disability justice, and APA crit to this analysis, would surely reveal vital additional contributions beyond those presented here.[71] While each theoretical strand presented in this chapter has unique goals, methodologies, and critiques, they each align notably in identifying the

Socratic method as problematic to both learning and inclusion. Thus, critiques of the Socratic method's dominance in law school classrooms have spanned decades, with a remarkably sustained focus. These arguments compel timely and systemic action to make legal education more inclusive, equitable, and effective. Collectively, the strands of critical discourse presented in this chapter present a strong call to action to strengthen traditional legal education by centering the recommendations of critical pedagogies and implementing core themes more systemically.[72] We have the roadmap of where and how to begin this work, thanks to decades of work by scholars.

Chapter 3 surveys the broader health, wellness, and satisfaction levels of law students. It concludes that the existing delivery of legal education is not leaving *any* cohort of students thriving or satisfied with their law school experience. Situating specific Socratic critiques within the context of the larger wellness concerns of modern law students reveals that reform and innovation in the curricular core stand to help everyone. The status quo is not working for anyone such that it justifies ignoring fifty years of sustained critique. Rather, innovating through the curricular core of legal education can benefit all students without disrupting the economics or staffing structures of legal education.

Chapter 4 describes how stark dissatisfaction—and even despair—permeate the legal profession too. These chapters support the need for timely teaching innovations centered in the curricular core of legal education. Reforms to the traditional Socratic classrooms used in 1L and bar exam courses will have effects that scale culturally and institutionally more than incremental reforms around the Socratic classroom. Reforms of Socratic classrooms have the potential to strengthen legal education *and* improve the profession with haste and breadth.

CHAPTER 3

Students Reveal That We Should Not Fear Curricular Change

Outlining the concrete harms of Socratic teaching and the legacy of critiques begs the question of why are we *not* reforming Socratic teaching, given the breadth and depth of these accounts. Indeed, the lack of curricular reform might suggest that perhaps traditional legal education is working so well for some students that there is strong momentum to keep the status quo. This chapter debunks this notion by zooming out to offer a more generalized picture of the wellness and satisfaction of modern law students. This widened picture deeply informs the calculus of whether to transform and innovate . . . because **spoiler alert** we have little to lose. Surveys of modern law students reveal issues of detachment, dissatisfaction, depression, and dependencies.[1] Collectively, these concerns should yield a "wellness reckoning in law schools," as wellness issues have reached "crisis level."[2] This wellness reckoning is not just a warm and fuzzy aspirational goal. Rather, making legal education more sustainable and satisfying for all is a critical priority for legal education and the legal profession.

Understanding law students' basic human needs directs us toward an *imperative* of inclusive law teaching. Existing approaches have failed in two critical ways. Modern curricular reforms are occurring largely *around* the architectural core of legal education—the Socratic classroom. Additional institutional support structures have also been built around the Socratic classroom, such as academic success programming, which further immunizes the Socratic classroom from accountability for change. This chapter moves us away from thinking about inclusion as an undefined, murky, or lofty goal, as explored further in Chapter 5. It shifts us from understanding inclusion as *differentiation* and toward positioning it as a classroom baseline. We need an urgent call to action, and—for better or worse—the Socratic classroom is an efficient and pragmatic site for scalable reform to move the needle toward institutional progress.

A WELLNESS RECKONING

Both legal education and the legal profession have identified wellness issues yielding systemic cause for alarm. This chapter presents the student picture, and Chapter 4 presents the state of the legal profession. Notably, our students start law school "no more or no less happy or healthy than demographically similar peers who are not in law school." Yet something happens *in law school* such that our students leave "less intrinsically motivated, less hopeful, and less happy" than they arrived.[3] They experience high levels of psychological distress that manifest in many ways.[4]

The raw statistics are flooring: "One in ten [law students] physically self-harms, one in six has clinically diagnosable depression, one in three has clinical anxiety and one in four has developed alcohol dependence."[5] Students also experience other generalized manifestations of increased psychological distress, such as "somatization, obsessive-compulsive symptoms, interpersonal sensitivity, depression, anxiety, hostility, phobic anxiety, paranoid ideation, [and] psychoticism." These manifestations of distress distinctly emerge within the first six months of law school.[6] Over the first year of law school, students in one study "experienced large reductions in positive affect, life satisfaction, and overall [subjective well-being], and large increases in negative affect, depression, and physical symptoms."[7] The stress levels only continue to rise from the first year through graduation.[8]

As you read those abstract statistics, take the time to humanize these data points across your own student community. Concretely picture a student who struggles with each of these manifestations of distress. If you cannot identify one, perhaps discuss this with colleagues and self-reflect on why these issues are not revealing themselves to you through the faces and struggles of real students. Student affairs offices and academic success offices might offer insights for your own institution. I can identify a *representative* example of students who have struggled with each manifestation, such as depression, anxiety, suicidality, dependency, and so on, but I cannot identify enough students to get to the one-in-ten, one-in-six, one-in-three, and one-in-four pervasiveness of some of the statistics. That reality itself is insightful to me because it reveals that many of my students are suffering in isolation, no matter how supportive and available we might perceive ourselves to be.

These manifestations of distress are all important to reflect on as teachers. As explored more in Chapter 7, inclusive teaching begins by knowing our students so that we can create classrooms in which they can be successful. Student-wellness issues are not new, and they are not unique to legal education or US law schools.[9] They are, however, vital to address to create effective learning environments. Our students' basic physiological and psychological needs do not lighten or dissipate when they embark on their law studies. Lawrence Krieger outlines the "universal physiological needs" of law students, identifying "self-esteem, relatedness to others, authenticity, competence and security." The core questions are what physiological needs legal education is undermining and why.[10]

We know that lawyers and law students experience high levels of depression and emotional distress. Our students "lose self-confidence and self-esteem after beginning law school, and become insecure and isolated." These setbacks, according to Krieger, derive from the "legal 'success' paradigm," grounded heavily in "grades, external recognition, and money or position." This paradigm promotes "inherently competitive goals, values, and motives [that] promote tension and insecurity." These goals "minimize satisfaction and well-being in the lives of many law students and lawyers."[11]

From on-campus recruitment programs to competitive law review and moot court selection processes, law school compels students to constantly compare themselves with their classmates. This keeps students from instead cultivating their own unique professional identity that harnesses the distinctive strengths and contributions that they will bring to the practice of law. This "success paradigm" creates a "cycle of inherently unfulfilling activity," and that cycle "supplants the intrinsic drive for growth, actualization, intimacy, and community, thereby exacerbating the negative effects on well-being." Students are no longer looking for the right career path or extracurricular opportunities *for them.* Instead, the hierarchies that are plainly visible and uniform across legal education drive student behaviors. The result of these areas of emphasis and deemphasis in legal education are the conditions that allow anxiety and depression to flourish, leaving students (and later attorneys) with little "internal satisfaction."[12] Students instead chase the institutionally and professionally prescribed markers of success, which often distinctly overemphasize success in Socratic first-year courses.

Janet Thompson Jackson introduces a "Wellness Matrix" to think about the interconnectedness of wellness needs. She describes that physical needs include movement, health and medical care, and nutrition and sleep. Relational needs include community, personal and professional relationships, consensual intimacy, and service and justice work. Emotional and spiritual needs include mindfulness and meditation, faith and spirituality, emotional expression, and creativity. Mental needs include learning, career and professional development, and entertainment. Finally, material needs include finances and credit, housing, and physical security.[13]

The annual Law School Survey of Student Engagement (LSSSE) powerfully reveals the hardships many of our students are facing in meeting these needs and the escalation of these hardships since COVID. LSSSE's 2021 survey reveals heightened levels of "loneliness, depression, and anxiety." A staggering 85 percent of law students stated that they had experienced depression that compromised their daily functioning in the past year, with women reporting considerably higher percentages. The survey also reveals student challenges in meeting their basic needs. Nearly a third of our students (29 percent) had "increased concerns about eviction and housing loss," 63 percent were more worried than the prior year about paying bills, and over 40 percent of students reported being food insecure.[14]

For food insecurity and worry about paying bills, these numbers were higher for women and students of color. Latinx (57 percent), Black (55 percent), and Asian American (52 percent) students reported food insecurity at astonishing rates. These studies reported equally high concerns about financial security, with 71 percent of Latinx students, 68 percent of Black students, 67 percent of multiracial students, and 64 percent of Asian American students reporting financial insecurity, compared to 60 percent of White students. Financial concerns spread into concerns about paying for law school too, again with the highest percentages of concerned students being students of color.[15]

The effects of these hardships during the global COVID-19 pandemic also took a toll on students' physical health, according to the LSSSE data, with 75 percent of students reporting a decline in physical health and women reporting a nearly 10 percent higher decline than men. The pandemic also left 69 percent of students reporting some increase in loneliness and 45 percent significantly so. Again, women and students of color reported higher levels of loneliness.[16] Law schools have a vital role to play in graduating students with the coping mechanisms and skills needed to thrive in the realities of practice. Research reveals increasing rates of law students' alcohol consumption relative to prior decades, as well as higher usage than graduate students in general.[17] The picture of drug and alcohol use among law students suggests these substances play unhealthy roles by helping students cope with the pressures and demands of law school.

Research on student alcohol and drug use also reveals a critical intersection with law practice in that students are afraid to seek help because of licensure barriers. The Hazelden Betty Ford Foundation reported that 72 percent of law school respondents who "reported three or more serious substance use behaviors in the previous two weeks (including behaviors such as two or more binge drinking episodes, use of street drugs, and use of prescription drugs without a prescription) believed they had a better chance of being admitted to the bar if they hid their problems rather than sought help."[18] Nearly 12 percent of law student respondents revealed using drugs without a prescription in the past year, including stimulants and sedatives.[19] Critically, these respondents reported *academic* reasons for usage:

- To concentrate better while studying (67 percent)
- To increase alertness to study longer (64 percent)
- To enhance academic performance (49 percent)
- To increase alertness to work longer (46 percent)
- To concentrate better while working (45 percent)[20]

These studies only begin to scratch the surface of understanding the depths of student well-being concerns, but they give us vital directional guidance. They notably direct us to look carefully at the cultures we foster in legal education and the incentive structures we propagate for students. No on-campus counseling, therapy dogs visiting campus, or wellness workshops will adequately address the need to help law students feel valued, connected, and authentic. Reforms need to sit squarely in the curricular core of student experiences because—for better or worse—that still occupies the critical mass of the overall law student experience.

Of course, curricular reform is only one piece of the larger wellness puzzle. Meeting student needs demands existing (and enhanced) programs and resources (e.g., mental health counseling services). Critically, however, adding resources and programs that burden student schedules or costs is not a sustainable solution. We need to improve the spaces where students *already* spend the bulk of their time and energy.

Meeting the basic needs of students is not just a feel-good exercise. It is about building the legal profession and effectively preparing the next generation of lawyers. The negative effects of legal education carry into the legal profession, as explored further in Chapter 4. However, the problems of the legal profession distinctly *begin* in law school and, more pointedly, they begin in the first year. Students leave law school changed, often "more depressed, less service-oriented, and more inclined towards undesirable, superficial goals and values."[21] Pinpointing negative health outcomes emerging early in the first year is notable because nearly all 1L courses, other than research and writing, are styled around an appellate casebook, Socratic dialogue, and a heavily weighted summative exam. This realization directs us to look squarely at reforms within the Socratic classroom as a scalable and systemic source for building sustainable and inclusive law schools.

The goal of this chapter is not to prove that these health and wellness concerns are caused by the defining characteristics of Socratic classrooms. Rather, it is to center the Socratic classroom as a vital site for change, given its centrality to the law school experience. Improving student wellness is not about reducing stress for the sake of reducing stress but about improving students' overall life satisfaction. A survey of law students' life satisfaction concluded that students were the most satisfied when they faced "an appropriate level of challenge," when students perceived themselves as successful in law school, and when they experienced the "social support of family, faculty, and peers."[22]

Two significant ways to improve the life satisfaction of law students are to engage them in meaningful work and embed them in strong communities. Generally, when people believe their work is meaningful, they report higher life satisfaction, as do people who feel that they are part of a community.[23] Yet so many students experience the Socratic classroom as distinctly abstract, competitive, and marginalizing—frankly, the opposite of community. So many such classrooms are motivated by the fear and nerves of being on call as compared to meaningful endeavors training for client-centered lawyering as part of a noble profession. Thus, our challenge is to build law schools that cultivate environments where students are a part of a common exercise in which students have the power to influence their education and they learn that lawyers can shape the law. We need our students to care deeply about the work and see themselves and their communities in it.[24]

Students want to feel a sense of belonging and a strong sense of connection.[25] Incidentally, these are the buildings blocks of *both* student happiness *and* more inclusive classrooms.[26] Outside of orientation activities, mandatory trainings, and student groups, law schools generally do very little to build social connections purposefully.[27] Indeed, many of the social connections that do occur among students tend to involve alcohol, which compromises and exacerbates the wellness concerns presented in this chapter. Some schools' emphasis on honor-code compliance might even instill a culture of fear and worry surrounding collaboration on academic work.[28] Yet relationships are central to wellness, lawyering, and learning. Community and connection need to be embedded in law classrooms in ways that are efficient, engaging, and purposeful, as explored in Chapter 7.

In stark contrast, current models of legal education instead often yield "emotional detachment," which can negatively impact student well-being.[29] Kathryne Young interviewed fifty-three law students across thirty-six law schools in 2020. Her research revealed that students had trouble reconciling their personal identity with their future professional one, explaining that it required some detachment from themselves to do so.[30] This reveals the interconnections between abstract perspectiveless-ness described in Chapter 1 and the general malaise of modern law students captured here.

Standard summative exam techniques can also compromise students' belonging and connection. Most often exams are quite formal, in which students strictly apply the rules that they have studied to the hypotheticals that their professors present. Those hypotheticals generally lack social, political, and economic context to shape a connection from attorney to client or law to community. They often situate students in roles lawyering on behalf of *all* clients and without any research or materials, which distorts ethical rules and practicing norms. They are often tests of competency versus creativity, substance versus strategy, and generic versus customized client counseling. This leaves little room for students to *be* a lawyer connected to the service of clients and the profession.

It is not that law school does not foster meaningful connections. Many law students are actually quite surprised by the strength of the community that they build in law school with professors and classmates early on. Students reveal that their "hope for genuine social solidarity is undermined by the fact that—arguably for reasons having more to do with tradition and convenience than pedagogical rigor—students compete with each other in every doctrinal class and often in their legal research and writing class as well." Law students are quick to internalize that "success is relative, not absolute." This creates a tension between striving to build community and professional identity while rigorously stacking students against one another. Students sense that this is often competition for competition's sake because it does not fully mirror the legal profession. These grading practices cost students their "self-efficacy," meaning that they perceive that they cannot control the outcome.[31] Self-efficacy is an important skill for lawyers, and it serves as a strong protector against those experiencing mental illness.

The lack of transparency regarding performance also undermines students' sense of self control. One study out of Melbourne Law School, seeking open-ended suggestions to improve law student well-being, yielded the most frequent response category of pinpointing assessment techniques as the area for improvement. Students sought more continual assessment, more choice in assessment, and less stress surrounding the exams. They wanted to know more about what was expected of them and see more models of high-performing work product.[32] These requests align with other research, such as Levit and Linder's research on law student happiness, suggesting that a sense of control is critical to one's happiness. Students pinpointed the value of teachers engaging with them and taking a personal interest in them as students as central to their happiness. Students wanted their teachers to understand what their experiences studying law were like.[33] Students wanted a stronger environment where they could work together to succeed instead of in competition. Ultimately, students wanted a more collaborative and inclusive environment.[34] Thus, notably students are not seeking reforms that require budget approval, committee resolutions, or even deep imagination. They are simply seeking connection, purpose, belonging, and control.

CENTERING RESPONSES IN THE CURRICULAR CORE

Notable reform efforts are surely underway. For example, in 2006 the Association of American Law Schools created a new section on Balance and Well-Being in Legal Education, which has worked to build community, scholarship, and pedagogy around wellness practices. The section hosts seminars and creates a place for teachers and administrators to share ideas and learn the best methods to ensure quality education for their students, while also being mindful of the mental health needs of the student body. Most reforms to date, however, have been reactive to existing needs, such as strengthening response systems to students in crisis through on-site counseling or referrals to counseling and lawyer-assistance programs. Some student services offices have also begun to embed general wellness programs into their offerings.[35] Current best practices are focused on detecting students in distress, preparing stakeholders to intervene, providing resources, organizing wellness events, countering stigma, and having "well-being" content in the curriculum.[36]

These existing approaches are still incremental. These intervention models do not get at the day-to-day experiences of law students interacting with the curricular core and all of its known and revered hierarchies. These programs are "decidedly remedial" in that they are not integrated into the daily structure of law school and instead siloed to orientation, lunch events, and elective activities. These approaches can offer very useful supplements, but they cannot achieve their valiant goals independently because they "lack the structural power and institutional legitimacy needed to transform law schools into places where students do not suffer from alarmingly high rates of anxiety, depression, self-harm, alcoholism, and the other health problems that plague so many practicing lawyers."[37] They also do not align with student behaviors, as only 13 percent of students reported that they would be likely to seek help for a drug or alcohol issue from student affairs leaders on campus and only 15 percent for a mental health issue. Students are hampered by worries regarding bar admission and confidentiality.[38]

Thus, existing approaches tend to silo accountability and reform efforts in the student service and wellness roles. They do not address the underlying conditions that lead to these negative outcomes of isolation, detachment, and marginalization. In fact, current approaches simply do not alter *the curriculum* or learning environment at all. Legal education needs to synergistically integrate wellness reforms *as* curricular reforms. Curricular reforms can—and must—build healthier classrooms and institutions. Successful approaches need to collaborate with the legal profession and related stakeholders too, as explored further in Chapter 4.[39]

The Legal Profession Faces Symbiotic Struggles

Unsurprisingly, both legal education and the legal profession face similar reckonings. The hierarchies, marginalization, and anxieties constructed in legal education do not just magically disappear when students enter law practice. Rather, the stressed-out, disengaged, disenchanted law student of today enters the legal profession to become the overworked, anxiety-ridden attorney of tomorrow. The same cultural challenges of competition, skewed rewards, and rigid hierarchies plague the profession.[1] There is a bit of a chicken-and-the-egg circularity here. Law schools justify many of their practices as necessary to prepare students for the real demands of the profession. Changing legal education thus requires symbiotic alignment with the profession.

As with legal education reform, we have little to fear in reimagining the structural and cultural landscape of lawyering. Lawyers are also generally dissatisfied with their work. One American Bar Association study in 2007 concluded that only 55 percent of attorneys were satisfied with their profession (lower than workers generally), and only 44 percent would recommend the career to others.[2] This chapter previews these parallel satisfaction and sustainability concerns to inform and bolster curricular-reform momentum.

DIVERSITY, EQUITY, AND INCLUSION
CHALLENGES IN THE PROFESSION

Like legal education, the legal profession is languishing in its efforts to cultivate a diverse, equitable, and inclusive profession. In 2022, 81 percent of attorneys were White, and 62 percent of attorneys identified as male and 38 percent as female. There has been a 6.6 percent increase in the total number of lawyers in the United States between 2012 and 2022, growing about 1.4 percent each year.[3] However, women attorneys, attorneys of color, and LGBTQ+ attorneys remain disproportionately underrepresented in the legal profession when compared to the general population. Drilling deeper into these general statistics of disproportionality reveals further insights. This section explores the profession through the lenses of gender, race, sexual identity, and intersectionality.

Gender in the Profession

While women are dramatically better represented in the profession than in prior decades, the gains are both stratified and stagnating. They are also complicated by retention and advancement obstacles. Until 1970 women represented only 3 percent of all attorneys, but the percentage has risen gradually in the following decades. Women composed 8 percent of all attorneys in 1980, 20 percent in 1990, 27 percent in 2000, and 37 percent in 2021.[4] These general numbers obscure hierarchies in pay, status, and field segmentation. Women attorneys are paid less than their male counterparts across all fields.[5] There is a 2–5 percent gender pay gap between women and men.[6] When looking at median weekly earnings for attorneys in 2021, women received $1,912, while men received $2,495.[7] Women associates were paid 95 percent that of their male counterparts, women nonequity partners were paid 95 percent that of their male counterparts, and women equity partners were paid 78 percent that of their male counterparts.[8] Generally, women partners' compensation rose at a higher rate than male partners; however, women partners were still paid less than men. In a 2022 survey of 1,755 partners at Global 100– and NLJ 350–size firms, women were paid $905,000 annually, and men were paid $1,212,000 annually.[9] Additionally, only 2 percent of firms reported that their highest-paid attorney was a woman, dropping 6 percentage points from a prior 2005 survey.[10]

The idea that men attorneys are paid more than women attorneys because they have more billable hours than women is a myth. Gender and racial biases explain the pay gap.[11] When origination, billable hours, partner tenure, and size of the firm are controlled, men equity partners still receive higher compensation than women equity partners.[12] These findings suggest that compensation is not based solely on merit and achievements.

One reason for the gender pay gap is that fewer women than men raise formal complaints about their compensation to the firm. This silent resignation to compensation inequities stems from the fear of negative ramifications and worries about the need for future leave time and the flexibility to address family schedules.[13] Women are already treated differently after marriage and childbirth in law practice. A new mother recalled that she was given "less access to good cases, and therefore ha[d] less access to promotion." Other new mothers are passed over for promotions, given "mommy track" low-quality assignments, demoted or paid less, and unfairly disadvantaged for working part-time or with a flexible schedule.[14]

Another reason for pay disparities is that women are underrepresented in higher-paying positions in law firms. Some of the reasons for this are that men receive significantly more internal firm referrals for new work from senior male colleagues, have a higher percentage of the origination from internal referrals, and are overall quicker to get origination credit even when they did not do the majority of the work.[15] Women are excluded from these internal networks and referrals that ultimately help senior associates become partners. Consequently, in 2022 women represented 32.7 percent of nonequity partners and only 22.6 percent of equity partners.[16]

Women disproportionately occupy lower levels of law-firm hierarchies. In 2022 women represented 38.68 percent of overall attorneys.[17] In law firms women represented 26.65 percent of partners, 49.42 percent of associates, 38 percent of counsel, and 54.85 percent of nontraditional-track or staff attorneys. There is some growth in these numbers. In the past decade, there has been a 5.6 percent increase in partners who are women, with a 5.5 percent increase in women equity partners and a 4.5 percent increase in women nonequity partners. The number of women associates has increased 4.48 percent, and the number of women of counsel has increased 3.37 percent. There has accordingly been a 0.89 percent decrease in nontraditional-track and staff women attorneys.[18]

Women attorneys also reported in a 2019 study considerably less recognition and opportunity than their male counterparts. Only 50 percent of women attorneys were satisfied with the recognition they received at work, compared to 71 percent of men. Only 45 percent of women were satisfied with the opportunity for advancement in their career, compared to 62 percent of men. Reduced job satisfaction may also be due to the stereotypes and microaggressions women attorneys can face. A staggering 63 percent of women attorneys reported that they were perceived as less professionally committed, and 75 percent reported that they had experienced demeaning remarks or behavior (e.g., jokes, interruptions).[19] Women also reported in a 2018 study gendered pressure to perform in ways perceived as "feminine" and backlash for performing in ways perceived as masculine, leading to more "office housework" and fewer billable hours. Women reported that they are more likely to be mistaken for nonlawyers and receive fewer desirable assignments.[20]

Women lawyers can also face harassment and incivility of varying degrees. The #MeToo movement revealed numerous accusations of inappropriate behavior perpetrated by judges and attorneys.[21] Chief Justice John Roberts Jr.'s 2018 *Year-End Report on the Federal Judiciary* notes a "special risk for abuse" within the law clerk–judge relationship and flags problems within the federal judiciary of "inappropriate workplace conduct." Roberts proposes code of conduct revisions, prohibiting "abusive or harassing behavior" and requiring "civil and respectful dealings with co-workers and subordinates."[22] New terms have emerged over the years to describe other problematic behaviors, such as microaggressions, mansplaining, hepeating, sidelining, and tokenism.[23] Many of these terms reflect new phrases for long-standing barriers distinctly framed around communication tones, patterns of deference, and perceptions of dominance in professional communications.[24]

Women lawyers have also been leaving the legal profession in droves. These issues persisted long before the COVID-19 global pandemic, but the pandemic greatly exacerbated them.[25] Research estimates that more than eight thousand women attorneys departed from their employment in 2021 during the COVID-19 pandemic, many leaving the profession entirely. One in four women lawyers has considered leaving the profession—one in three if only women with children are considered. The legal profession's so-called she-cession seems to come from insufficient opportunities for promotion, billable hour pressures, lack of scheduling control, health and wellness concerns, discrimination, lack of mentorship, pay disparities, and isolation. Childcare concerns were also a big concern for working mothers who felt unsupported while balancing increased family and work obligations during the pandemic.[26] These challenges surrounding gender in the profession are deeply interconnected to the kinds of Socratic classroom cultures we cultivate and revere.

Race in the Profession

The law profession is also staggeringly lacking in racial diversity and stagnating in the gains that it has made. In 2022, 81 percent of all lawyers were White, only a modest improvement in racial diversity from 88.4 percent in 2012. This is a stark disparity to the overall US population. People of color constituted 41.9 percent of the US population, while only 19 percent of attorneys were attorneys of color. Specifically, Asian attorneys constituted 5.5 percent of the profession, close to their percentage of the US population (5.9 percent). Latinx attorneys were 5.8 percent of the profession, despite comprising 18.5 percent of the US population. Mixed-race attorneys were 2.7 percent of the profession, close to their percentage of the US population (2.8 percent). Black attorneys were 4.5 percent of the profession, despite comprising 13.4 percent of the US population. Native American attorneys were 0.5 percent of the profession and 1.3 percent of the US population overall.[27]

Law firms have invested considerable resources in diversity leadership, mentorship programs, pipeline programs, and other measures. Most firms have a committee, council, or task force charged with coordinating diversity efforts. For instance, Wilmer Cutler Pickering Hale and Dorr has a diversity committee of six partners representing the firm's six offices, with each partner responsible for heading a separate committee on diversity in each office. Large law firms also generally have a dedicated budget for diversity, through which they sponsor trainings, speakers' programs, retreats, formalized mentorships, and sponsorship initiatives. Notably, McGuireWoods is the first firm to introduce the reverse mentoring program, where diverse associates mentor department chairs.[28]

These efforts and investments, however, generally scale only into large law firms. Small law firms are much less likely to have this infrastructure for pragmatic reasons, although no less likely to suffer from the same biases and hiring disparities. Nor have these initiatives significantly increased the representation of attorneys of color. The National Association of Law Placement reported that "law firms have made steady, incremental progress in increasing the presence of women and people of color in the partner ranks, [but] that progress has been excruciatingly slow and nowhere near matches the increases seen in the summer associate and associate ranks. . . . In just over thirty years, the representation of people of color at the partner level has increased by less than 10 percentage points and women by less than sixteen points. At this rate, we still won't be anywhere near parity in another thirty years."[29]

The data underlying the National Association of Law Placement's conclusion indeed suggests only sluggish gains. The percentage of attorneys of color grew incrementally between 2012 and 2022: there was a 2.21 percent increase in Asian attorneys, 1.01 percent increase in Black attorneys, 1.81 percent increase in Latinx attorneys, 1.28 percent increase in mixed-race attorneys, and a 0.01 percent decrease in both Native American and Native Hawaiian attorneys. More specifically, there was a 2.09 percent increase in Asian partners, a 0.59 percent increase in Black partners, 1.06 percent increase in Latinx partners, 0.93 percent increase in mixed-race partners, a 0.02 percent decrease in Native American partners, and neither an increase nor decrease in Native Hawaiian partners. There was a 2.11 percent increase in Asian associates, a 1.58 percent increase in Black associates, a 2.65 percent increase in Latinx associates, a 1.71 percent increase in mixed-race associates, a 0.03 percent decrease in Native American associates, and a 0.02 percent decrease in Native Hawaiian associates.[30]

Attorneys of color also experience biases within the profession. An experimental study found that when partners were given the same memo written by a third-year associate, partners critiqued the memo as needing "lots of work" and "average at best" when they were told it was written by a Black associate. When the partners were told the same exact memo was written by a White associate, partners praised the memo, saying the memo had potential and was "generally good." This study illuminates the ways in which biases harm the careers of attorneys of color. Another study concluded that men of color had to prove their commitment and competence 25.43 percent more than White men, and women of color had to prove their commitment and competence 34.77 percent more than White men. This study further concluded that men of color were held to higher standards 22.99 percent more than White men, and women of color were held to higher standards 32.75 percent more than White men. Attorneys of color also had their ideas valued less: men's ideas were valued 2.65 percent less than those of White men and women's ideas were valued 13.05 percent less than that of White men.[31] Attorneys of color also widely reported that they have been mistaken for administrative or janitorial staff.

Attorneys of color are also paid less than their White counterparts. Women of color reported in 2022 that their pay was 31 percent lower than that of White men.[32] On average partners of color were paid 10 percent lower than that of White partners. When looking at those in partnership ranks, on average, Native Hawaiian partners were paid the least at $350,000, followed by Black partners ($752,000), Latinx partners ($930,000), mixed-race partners ($1,158,000), American Indian partners ($1,225,000), and Asian Pacific partners ($1,227,000). Attorneys of color were not afforded equal access to networking opportunities, business-development opportunities, and advancement opportunities as their White counterparts.[33] Women of color were also denied desirable assignments, resulting in less experience when they were third- or fourth-year associates and ultimately lowering their prospects for career advancement.

Considerable segmentation persists by sector too. One longitudinal study followed lawyers from the class of 2000 in 2004, 2009, and 2014, revealing that White attorneys were most likely to be found in law firms (40.2 percent), while Black attorneys (28.4 percent) and Latinx attorneys (24.9 percent) were more likely to work for the government. Asian lawyers were most likely to be in-house counsel (20.7 percent), while Native American attorneys were most likely to be employed in the tribal sector (22 percent). In the judiciary attorneys of color comprised around 20 percent of state judges.[34] These sector disparities, in turn, yield divergent salary trajectories. In 2020 the median salary for a first-year associate at a private firm was $155,000, which is double a first-year public service attorney's pay. Lower salaries undermine the ability to pay back debt, which affects housing, stability, and wellness. These disparities leave attorneys of color more likely to postpone marriage and home buying.[35]

Finally, the legal profession is also confronting its own legacy of racism.[36] "Lawyering While Black: Examining the Practice of Law through the Prism of the Black Experience" explains how attorneys of color are coping with the legacy and persistence of racial trauma on top of the grueling demands of the profession, which affects the workplace, day-to-day lawyering, and social dynamics.[37] Exploring the status of the profession through the lens of race reveals the need for symbiotic changes that begin in law school and carry through to practice settings.

Sexual Orientation and Identity in the Profession

LGBTQ+ lawyers also face obstacles in the legal profession. Here the data is a bit murkier. The number of identified LGBTQ+ attorneys employed at law firms has been trending upward since data collection began in 2002.[38] Still, LBGTQ+ attorneys represented only 2.99 percent of US attorneys surveyed across 910 law firms in 2019. LGBTQ+ attorneys represented 2.10 percent of all partners, 4.10 percent of all associates, and 6.89 percent of summer associates. LGBTQ+ representation is growing quicker in summer associate ranks, possibly suggesting pipeline growth in the coming years.[39] However, statistics reflect only the attorneys who have self-identified to their employers, while surely others are not self-identifying in their place of employment due to fear of discrimination in the workplace or for other reasons.[40] Further, reliable data does not exist systemically across all law sectors.[41]

LGBTQ+ attorneys may also face discrimination. As of 2023, fifteen states had no statewide prohibition on workplace discrimination on the basis of sexual orientation and gender identity, but federal law prohibits employment discrimination based on sexual orientation or gender identity.[42] Yet LGBTQ+ attorneys still face stereotyping and discrimination in the workplace, such as bullying, harassment, abuse or vandalism, bias, and isolation.[43] Nearly half of LGBTQ+ employees (46 percent) have experienced unfair treatment in the workplace. Many employees engage in "covering" behaviors, such as changing their physical appearance; changing when, where, or how frequently they use the bathroom; and avoiding talking about their families or social lives at work. Employees have reported that they experienced unfair treatment due to religious motivation. For example, attorneys have reported that coworkers have quoted from the Bible and told them to pray they were not LGBTQ+ and that they would "go to hell" or were an "abomination." Overall, transgender employees experience more discrimination in the workplace than their cisgender counterparts.[44]

The Layers of Intersectionality

There are also deep intersectional considerations here too. For example, *both* racial bias and gender bias can permeate law hiring, assignments, evaluations, and compensation. A report by the American Bar Association's Commission on Women in the Profession and the Minority Corporate Counsel Association concluded that women and people of color have to regularly "Prove-It-Again" and that they face tighter regulation of behavior and conduct. Biases particularly arise in collaborative settings in which women's, particularly women of color's, ideas are valued less, their contributions are credited to others, and they are mistaken for administrative personnel.[45] Women of color report having to repeat themselves for their contributions to be heard and prove themselves to be perceived as competent, while others are presumed as such. Black women particularly face an added layer of stereotyping in communication styles: "I am allowed to be passionate, even to demonstrate some level of anger, but it better not be personal. It better not be about me. If I become angry about anything personal, then that is perceived as being an angry black woman."[46] These biases need to be interrupted systemically, comprehensively, and early in the careers of attorneys—beginning in law school.

The legal profession has worked for decades to address issues of bias, with countless commissions, studies, and conferences.[47] In 2016, acknowledging this enduring issue, the ABA added a professional responsibility rule prohibiting attorney conduct that "the lawyer knows or reasonably should know is harassment or discrimination on the basis of race, sex, religion, national origin, ethnicity, disability, age, sexual orientation, gender identity, marital status or socioeconomic status in conduct related to the practice of law."[48] Rule 8.4(g) arose from a joint letter drafted by the ABA's Commission on Women in the Profession, the Commission on Racial and Ethnic Diversity in the Profession, the Commission on Disability Rights, and the Commission on Sexual Orientation and Gender Identity, pleading for an antidiscrimination and antiharassment provision. The joint letter argued that prior approaches to harassment, discrimination and bias—a prohibition only when it was "prejudicial to the administration of justice"—ignored the bias and prejudices manifesting in countless other professional settings, along with their pervasive effects.[49] This rule revision reflects a recognition that such bias persists, which is an important normative commitment to equality and a possible enforcement tool. In "Don't Call me Sweetheart!," Kristy D'Angelo-Corker argues that the ABA reforms to amend rule 8.4(g) are just the first steps in addressing these issues.[50] The challenges facing the legal profession align in vital ways with those in legal education. These realizations direct us to craft synergistic and mutually reinforcing reforms.

ATTORNEY WELLNESS

The legal profession is also wrestling with deep and complex issues relating to attorney wellness. The depression, dejection, and disillusionment that plague law students also compromise practicing attorneys. Understanding these professional struggles is critical to designing effective solutions beginning in law school. I first started writing this section by segmenting out categories such as depression, suicidality, and anxiety, but I quickly realized that there are no clear boundaries when it comes to attorney wellness. For example, one national study of lawyers revealed a 28 percent prevalence rate of depression, a 19 percent rate of anxiety, a 24 percent to 36 percent rate of problematic alcohol use, an 11 percent rate of substance abuse, and a 15 percent rate of burnout.[51] These prevalence rates are interconnected.

Lawyers have the fourth highest rate of suicidality by occupation, after dentists, pharmacists, and doctors. A staggering 11.5 percent of practicing attorneys in a 2016 study of thirteen thousand attorneys throughout nineteen states reported experiencing suicidal thoughts.[52] Male attorneys are committing suicide at higher rates than women.[53] In contrast, female attorneys are more likely to leave their job and the profession. Notably, these health concerns of practicing attorneys begin in law school and continue in the profession.[54] Many aspects of lawyering lead to the prevalence of suicidality and mental health concerns. The high billable hours requirements, the adversarial nature of the profession, secondary or vicarious trauma, and the stigma that surrounds mental health all contribute to these rates.[55] Secondary or vicarious trauma, compassion fatigue, and PTSD particularly affect lawyers practicing criminal law, family law, immigration and refugee law, and personal injury law.[56]

A vicious cycle underlies these data. Lawyers are unhappy and chronically stressed in their work. Chronic stress can trigger depression. Attorneys are 3.6 times more likely to suffer from depression than nonattorneys, rendering attorneys as belonging to one of the most depressed professions. Data reveal that 26 percent of the attorneys who seek professional counseling support do so for depression and anxiety. Attorneys report that they experience increased rates of depression manifesting in many ways, such as decreased pleasure in everyday activities, difficulty sleeping, low energy levels, poor eating habits, and suicidal ideation.[57]

The connection between depression, stress, anxiety, suicidality, and alcohol and drug use is also important to study. There is surely a complex interconnection between *how* lawyers cope with the stress, anxiety, and depression and the role of drugs and alcohol exacerbating those underlying struggles. Attorneys struggle with drugs and alcohol at rates that exceed professional peers. The Hazelden Betty Ford Foundation reported that 36.4 percent of attorneys' self-reported conduct qualified as problematic drinking, compared to 15.4 percent of surgeons.[58] For women attorneys, respondents yielding "problematic drinking" classifications were notably above the general population, at a full 20 percent

(39.5 percent v. 19 percent), while male attorneys were about the same as the general population (33.7 percent v. 32 percent).[59]

A culture of drinking is indeed embedded in the profession. Increased alcohol consumption can yield higher social capital through heightened status and earnings in the legal profession—to the staggering degree of 10–14 percent higher pay for drinkers than nondrinkers.[60] There are real professional risks in alcohol and substance abuse too. One study of California disciplinary proceedings concluded that 25–35 percent of disciplinary charges involved substance abuse.[61]

Most attorneys who have alcohol or substance-abuse problems are reluctant to report incompetent or impaired work for fear of disbarment. However, by not reporting, attorneys ultimately harm their clients. Several attorneys reported that they required others to help them cover their "decreasingly effective performance of responsibilities." Attorneys worked less, failed to file court papers, neglected correspondences and phone messages, forgot to attend scheduled court appearances and appointments, missed deadlines, and "borrowed" money from client trust funds to support their alcohol or substance use.[62]

The "solutions" so far have been largely symbolic and incremental. Law firms are starting to engage in discussion. Some firms have implemented modest strategies to improve attorney well-being. For instance, Goodwin Proctor's partners are planning to reduce the number of meetings, add structure to meetings, and leverage more workload-management resources available to the firm. Foley and Lardner offers burnout prevention and team programming for the management committee, department chairs, and office-managing partners. These programs address issues impacting team trust, such as talking to partners who may not be living up to the firm's culture and core values. Sheppard, Mullin, Richter and Hampton offers team-based strategies to senior leaders as well as a program allowing associates and special counsel to use up to forty hours of billable credit time each year to rest and recharge. ArentFox Schiff shares results from an associate survey to the firm partners regarding associates' sources of stress and different signs of burnout. ArentFox Schiff also has a three-year leadership-development program to teach and prioritize leadership at the firm, while incorporating well-being principles and conversations. Last, Sidley Austin offers programs to senior associates and counsel regarding psychological safety and motivation.[63] Again, these wellness efforts scale effectively to large international firms like those identified here. Smaller firms and other practice settings are much less likely to have these formal resources or initiatives. There is, however, no evidence that these other practice settings yield improved wellness outcomes.

Each state has a Lawyer Assistance Program, providing confidential services and support to judges, lawyers, and law students struggling with substance-use disorders and mental health issues.[64] There are also private entities providing help. In California, for example, there is a network known as The Other Bar, composed of recovering attorneys, judges, and law students dedicated to assisting others within the profession who are suffering from alcohol- and substance-abuse problems.[65]

A coalition including the ABA's Commission on Lawyer Assistance Program, the National Conference of Bar Examiners, and the National Conference of Chief Justices convened a National Task Force on Lawyer Well-Being and published *The Path to Lawyer Well-Being: Practical Recommendations for Positive Change*. The report concluded that the profession is at a crossroads: "To maintain public confidence in the profession, to meet the need for innovation in how we deliver legal services, to increase access to justice, and to reduce the level of toxicity that has allowed mental health and substance use disorders to fester among our colleagues, we have to act now." Some concrete Task Force recommendations included working to reduce toxicity in the profession, reducing stigma surrounding seeking help, weaving attorney competence together with attorney wellness, offering more educational programs, transforming the culture, reimagining what it means to be a lawyer, and reducing the centrality of alcohol at professional functions.[66]

The ABA also recently launched its "well-being pledge campaign." This campaign calls on employers to "(a) recognize that substance use and mental health problems represent a significant challenge for the legal profession and acknowledge that more can and should be done to improve the health and well-being of lawyers; and, (b) pledge to support the campaign and work to adopt and prioritize its seven-point framework for building a better future." Going forward, the ABA campaign will measure and track steps to advance these shared objectives. Threshold action items include robust educational programming, reductions in the expectations surrounding alcohol usage at firm events, partnering with support networks, and confidential support programs.[67] As of July 2023, 223 law firms, companies, and schools have adopted this well-being pledge. The ABA hosted a panel for an update on the campaign in 2021, noting a positive, if only anecdotal, increase in the overall happiness of the employees at firms that signed onto the pledge.[68]

One vital example of the need for solutions that bridge legal education to the legal profession is the role of bar licensure. In 2014 the Survey of Law Student Well-Being examined law student alcohol and drug use and found that 42 percent of respondents reported needing help in the past year with mental health problems, but less than half of those respondents actually received counseling.[69] Having invested years in schooling and tens of thousands of dollars to become an attorney, students are deterred from receiving help due to the threat of not being admitted to the bar.[70] At present thirty states and the District of Columbia include at least one question in the "Character and Fitness" portion of the bar application, referencing an applicant's mental health status. The questions typically fall into three categories:

1. Diagnosis or existence of a mental health condition that could affect an applicant's ability to practice law

2. Treatment, in-patient or out-patient, of the aforementioned condition

3. Whether the applicant has ever been party to conservatorship or court-appointed guardianship proceedings[71]

There is currently a movement to revise or eliminate these questions. Arizona, Washington, Illinois, Massachusetts, and Mississippi eliminated mental health questions in its licensure application. California bar examiners are prohibited from reviewing mental health records unless they are offered by the applicant. Connecticut and New York have moved to focus on conduct and behavior.[72]

. . .

The legal profession is wrestling with many similar challenges of hierarchy, exclusion, and wellness. The solutions are as interconnected as the problems. An inclusive profession is a healthier one. A healthy profession invites further inclusion. Law schools need to think now about how to symbiotically reform along with the legal profession. Our students need us to be innovative, collaborative, and committed. The profession as a whole will be stronger for it.[73]

Part II

CHAPTER 5

The Imperative of Inclusive Socratic Classrooms

The time to reform is now. Legal education has sat in a state of relative stagnation and conformity for decades. The relative stagnation of legal education since the emergence of Socratic teaching is both notable and surprising for two reasons. First, transformative changes, driven by learning theory and client-centered lawyering, are underway in the legal profession, in the bar exam, and in higher education. Legal education can and should do more to lead instead of lag. Second, decades of scholarly and anecdotal critiques reveal that the Socratic method is not meeting the needs of all students. While episodic and isolated innovations are occurring, they have not altered the institutional or cultural fabric of legal education. The COVID-19 pandemic and racial justice activism have catalyzed our institutions toward reform, reflecting that our institutions have reached a tipping point toward inclusive Socratic teaching.

A TIPPING POINT FOR CURRICULAR REFORM

Legal education has reached a tipping point. The dual forces of a public health pandemic and a racial justice reckoning present a pedagogical tipping point toward inclusive Socratic teaching that compels action. Like viruses, changed behaviors can spread rapidly throughout communities and institutions.[1] A "tipping point" is a unique window, in which the "beliefs and energies of a critical mass of people are engaged," such that conversion to a new idea can "spread like an epidemic, bringing about fundamental change very quickly." A tipping point requires critical mass and focused energy, but not necessarily a majority view.[2] A committed minority position can evoke change and achieve a tipping point that can in turn trigger a "cascade of behavior change that rapidly increases the acceptance of a minority view."[3] Tipping points allow new ideas to spread rapidly and bring "fundamental change very quickly."[4]

Legal education has experienced two seismic disruptive forces that can catalyze systemic curricular change. The COVID-19 global pandemic meaningfully disrupted the delivery of legal education. Law teachers underwent frenzied training to make the seemingly overnight shift that the public health crisis demanded. Many teachers, administrators, alumni, and students wondered particularly how the Socratic method would transfer into an online-delivery format.[5] Yet Socratic law teachers did transform their teaching styles and materials and acquire new skills and abilities to meet the needs of students. Law teachers first had to access an online platform to teach the course. They then quickly realized that the seventy-five-to-ninety-minute live classes did not translate well to an online format. Law teachers started to break up their material into more manageable chunks, followed by opportunities to apply the content interactively. Others learned to "flip the classroom," with short, recorded videos followed by more interactive work online for shorter blocks of time. While these reforms were frenzied and flawed, they were also systemic and universal across law schools. Law teachers had to navigate "on calls" a bit more carefully, as they were no longer able to confirm that every student was able to participate at every moment. Many law teachers also softened the weight of the summative exams. Some of these innovations were distinctly, yet collaterally, in alignment with the calls for pedagogy reforms that had come for decades, such as the softened emphasis on rigorous grading curves and the more diverse array of learning tools deployed in the classroom. These COVID-19 pivots taught us that law teachers *can* change how they deliver content, that they *can* prioritize student needs, and that they *can* move rapidly and systemically.

Some law teachers actually concluded, as a matter of first impression, that online teaching was surprisingly "*more* genuinely Socratic" than the traditional classroom. Particularly compared to a large lecture hall, where the room's spacing and layout are hierarchical and distant, in an online format, students and law teachers are more equally positioned in side-by-side dialogue, with equal space allotted to students and teachers alike—a very symbolic shift.[6] There is no front seat, no digital professor podium, no microphones to amplify certain voices, and everyone's window is equal in size. The exchanges accordingly felt like less of a performance and more of a dialogue. This can diffuse the hierarchies of traditional classrooms in substantive ways.

COVID-19 dramatically upended long-standing teaching norms. Many of these transformations were surely rushed, chaotic, and problematic, but law schools also made strides in technology usage, the integration of formative assessment techniques, flexibility and adaptability to students' needs, and more purposeful content coverage. Law teachers worked more collaboratively across fields and across campus departments to learn new skills and to adapt their courses. They attended trainings, helped one another, accessed campus resources, and shared ideas and syllabi. Colleagues worked collaboratively and rapidly across all institutions.

Notably, Socratic teaching during COVID-19 did not just replicate old teaching techniques in front of a camera. Rather, 69 percent of surveyed faculty with no online-teaching experience changed the types of assignments they gave, and 60 percent of faculty already teaching online also changed assignments or exams formats.[7] Many law teachers dynamically adapted their courses to be more visually appealing, more interactive, and more diverse in teaching methods (e.g., practice problems, group work, discussion groups). Socratic law teachers used their classroom time differently to apply the doctrine to problems and hypotheticals. Law teachers interacted with their students in new ways, checking on their well-being, learning more about their current lived experiences, and soliciting more real-time feedback regarding how the course was working for students.[8]

Perhaps most notably, the pandemic made teaching transformations less personal, minimizing the vulnerability inherent in identifying one's weaknesses and working to improve them. All teachers had to transform through COVID-19 regardless of their skills or styles. Law teachers were not revising courses because of personal shortcomings in ways that accordingly triggered deep vulnerabilities. Instead, they changed because students *needed* their teachers to adapt and be resilient. The early months of the COVID-19 pandemic presented great uncertainty and fear among many students and teachers alike. It was humbling, frankly. That is a critical difference relative to prior discussions of reforming Socratic teaching, which could be perceived as judgmental of peer teaching. The COVID-19 changes were motivated by students and done in a community-centered way. This book seeks a similar wholesale effort toward achieving enduring Socratic-teaching reforms.

The spring and summer of 2020 also brought a powerful racial reckoning to all societal institutions, including legal education. Nationwide demands for change sounded in protests, marches, legislation, and activism.[9] Communities wrestled with the harmful consequences of policing practices, hyperincarceration, and the presence of monuments and naming practices celebrating white supremacy and white supremacists.[10] These conversations called for all institutions and individuals to reflect on their role in dismantling racism in their communities and institutions.[11] Cohorts of deans, law schools, faculty, and staff swiftly organized robust programs on racial justice that were widely attended by many who were newly active in the work.

Law schools were essential sites for reflection and transformation. Legal education advanced various initiatives, albeit episodically. Schools worked to expand program and course offerings addressing systemic racism in various capacities.[12] Schools hosted community programs engaging the public. Educators examined the inclusivity of their classrooms, their teaching methods, and their content coverage. For example, the Society of American Law Teachers organized well-attended programs on antiracist work and teaching methods.[13] Boston University hosted a symposium titled "Racial Bias, Disparities and Oppression in the 1L Curriculum: A Critical Approach to the Canonical First Year Law School Subjects."[14] As a result, law schools' websites now prominently feature their work on antiracist practices and racial justice.[15] Thus, for every training and program geared toward the *delivery* of legal education, many law teachers and institutions also disrupted the *substance* of their teaching in new ways with an emerging or enriched focus on racial justice and antiracism in the subject matter and the delivery.

COVID-19 presented many challenges, but it also presented an "opportunity and responsibility to make our schools more student-centered, effective, and inclusive."[16] These dual disruptions, supported by the deep rigors of the long-standing calls for Socratic reforms, collectively present a vital tipping point for transformative and enduring curricular change in Socratic classrooms. Law teaching *can* change. Time and resources *can* be devoted to improving teaching. We *can* all learn from one another across generations, institutions, and geographies. While the teaching disruptions during the COVID pandemic were surely a frenzied and flawed implementation, they reveal promise and hope for the speed and breadth of systemic, student-centered change. The next section previews what inclusive teaching *is* before later chapters apply these concepts to Socratic classrooms.

WHAT IS INCLUSIVE TEACHING?

Inclusive teaching can be learned, cultivated, and measured. Inclusive teaching is equitable, giving all students an opportunity to achieve their potential. Inclusive teaching is welcoming, leaving all students feeling a sense of belonging.[17] A sense of belonging is a foundational human need. The accounts of women students and students of color interfacing with the Socratic method and feeling marginalized are critical evidence affecting students' sense of belonging. If some communities of students inherently feel like they belong and others feel like outsiders, this undermines inclusion and needs to be addressed.[18]

More inclusive classrooms are also inherently more student-centered classrooms in ways that have the effect of promoting student wellness.[19] Feeling connected to others results in lower levels of stress and anxiety and higher levels of self-esteem and empathy. Peer-to-peer, student-faculty, and student-staff relationships are "the foundation of learning, belonging, and achieving" in education. These relationships and interactions "positively influence the breadth and depth of student learning, retention and graduation rates, and a wide range of other outcomes, including critical thinking, identity development, communication skills, and leadership abilities."[20] Professors hold responsibility and accountability for cultivating a sense of belonging in their classrooms.

An inclusive classroom is about structure, intentionality, and accountability. All professors are cultivating a classroom environment, whether intentionally or unintentionally. Most Socratic law teachers cannot develop a realistic sense of how inclusive or equitable their classrooms are without intentional examination, which is structurally problematic as a threshold matter. Inclusive instructors hold several key characteristics; they "take responsibility for making their teaching and their curriculum inclusive," "continue to learn about both their students and teaching," "care about and for each and every student they teach," and "change their teaching based on evidence about the practices that support and challenge all students to thrive."[21]

To be an inclusive Socratic instructor requires intentionality in class, office hours, and assessments. Socratic classrooms typically hold large student enrollments, which can skew a professor's understanding of *who* is participating and *how* all students are experiencing the classroom dynamics. There will always be enthusiastically eager students to answer the professor's questions. With the pressures to navigate the dialogue, flow, and content of a Socratic classroom falling largely on the law teacher, they are often just anxious to continue the momentum and the flow. Accordingly, Socratic law teachers can leap at questions and volunteering hands in the air. This large classroom setup with the law teacher in control can accordingly perpetuate the mistaken belief that, so long as *some* students are engaging, answering, and participating, *all* students are learning inclusively.

The same is often true for office hours. So long as *some* students are coming through office hours and asking thoughtful questions about the course, law teachers can superficially and perhaps falsely conclude that their courses are accessible to all students. If students needed more support, they would come to office hours and seek it out, right? Law teachers assume that access equals equity. If students needed different support measures, they would just ask, right? Law teachers also assume that silence is belonging. If students found a classroom anything *other* than welcoming, they would raise concerns, right?

Anonymous grading can further compromise a law teacher's best intentions to acquire an accurate and meaningful sense of how inclusive or equitable their classrooms are. At the tail end of the course, law teachers generally deliver a summative exam. That exam reveals that a handful (hopefully, just a handful) of students performed quite poorly. Because most of the other engagements, such as on-calls and office hours visits, were largely ad hoc and unstructured, there is not really a consciousness to how Socratic classroom performance aligns with classroom assessments. Are the students who performed poorly on the exam *also* the ones who were not actively engaged in classroom discussions and who did not seek out extra support? Chapter 8 introduces dialogue about how to better monitor and measure engagement and participation in Socratic classrooms and how to align the classroom structure with the assessment structure.

Socratic classrooms can also be distinctly elusive in setting out expectations for how to engage with the course from class to class. Most syllabi set out the readings, the learning outcomes, and any course policies (e.g., attendance). Rarely do syllabi define the expectations for Socratic engagement or supplemental support. An inclusive classroom, however, has clear expectations readily available to all students, avoiding reliance on the "whisper networks" that often selectively pass on legacy strategies for surviving and thriving in each classroom with each professor's style, values, and norms. Students need to know what is expected in class and on the exam. This includes explaining what students should do with the information they have acquired: How will they be tested, assessed, and measured? For Socratic classes this distinctly involves transparently connecting Socratic classrooms to the exam, lawyering, and student success. Chapters 7 and 8 further address this need for curricular tethering.

Notably, two separate topics are at play when it comes to inclusive and equitable classrooms. One is methodological: *How* is legal education delivered? The other is substantive: *What* content is taught? Typically, law schools have generically lumped "diversity, equity, and inclusion" efforts into one amorphous topic or area of focus, despite their different objectives and focuses. Socratic classrooms have largely responded to institutional emphases on diversity, equity and inclusion by adding more robust content, if at all.[22] That is squarely about *what* is taught, not *how* it is taught. Notably, the robust critiques presented in Chapter 1, though, are about *how* the law is taught as well as *what* is taught.

Embedding more robust and diverse content into a syllabus is important, but it is not the same as building an inclusive classroom or an equitable one. Substantive changes tend to work in a limited fashion as "existing content-enhancing work" by episodically featuring a case or current event, a video clip, a guest speaker, or a supplemental reading. These types of "add-on approaches" risk leaving diverse topics hanging in the air without threading them through to measuring learning outcomes and designing learning activities.[23] These curricular add-ons are often still packaged in the Socratic method. These improvements—at best—improve the diversity of course *coverage*. That in turn *might* also make the course incrementally more inclusive, but it certainly does not move the cultural needle on the sense of belonging or the equitable positioning of all students with the opportunity for success in the classroom overall. These "add-on approaches" leave unaddressed *how* we teach and the learning environment we create and foster overall. It is time for further action on this metric.

GROUNDING INCLUSIVE TEACHING IN THE SOCRATIC CLASSROOM

Cultivating an inclusive learning environment for students is an educational imperative for all law teachers. It is not a marketing tool to innovate. Nor is inclusive teaching an initiative for *tomorrow*. It is an initiative for *today* that we owed our students *yesterday*. Transforming our teaching is admittedly hard, vulnerable, and raw, even more so if it is time intensive. In that sense, though, it is important to remind ourselves that this challenge to overcome and persevere in a new environment with new methods is exactly what we ask of our students every day in our classrooms. We push our students to learn new vocabularies, analytic approaches, and rules. We compel them to perform despite their greatest vulnerabilities and fears. We can do the same, and we can do it collaboratively, collegially, and efficiently. To meet the needs of all students, building an inclusive classroom is a minimum baseline educational expectation. Law schools owe students of all backgrounds, races, religions, genders, learning abilities, ages, and socioeconomic, immigration, and military statuses a learning environment in which they feel like they belong and thrive . . . in every classroom.

Chapters 1 through 4 map out the landscape of current legal education and the profession and voice the deep and robust critiques that scholars have set forth. These earlier chapters reveal enduring concerns regarding the inclusivity of the curricular core of legal education and the general malaise and dejection of many law students. Calls for more inclusive Socratic classrooms have endured for over half of a century and are well supported by theorists and both quantitative and qualitative research. The experiences of law students and lawyers alike further reinforce that we have little to lose by innovating to build more welcoming learning communities for all. These prior chapters reveal that the Socratic classroom is an essential, effective, and scalable place for reform.

Law schools have historically responded to these institutional critiques by building in expertise and accountability for diversity, equity, and inclusion with student services, admissions, and dedicated staff. These professional colleagues are generally segmented, however, from the full teaching faculty. This specialization and segmentation approach generally immunizes the law faculty from accountability for building an equitable and inclusive institution through their classroom learning environments. Further, this specialization and segmentation response alone is misaligned with students' experiences, given the dominance of the curricular core in shaping the culture of law school. This approach ignores the long-standing calls for systemic reform to the architectural core of legal education—the Socratic classroom.

Law schools accordingly need to analyze *how* we teach our students to assess effectiveness, equity, and inclusion. Many law schools have committed to looking inward and reforming their institutions to become antiracist and inclusive institutions. This involves a powerful examination of all aspects of legal education, including—and especially—the Socratic classroom. Other law schools are critically examining job placement and bar-exam results. Reforms must also include a

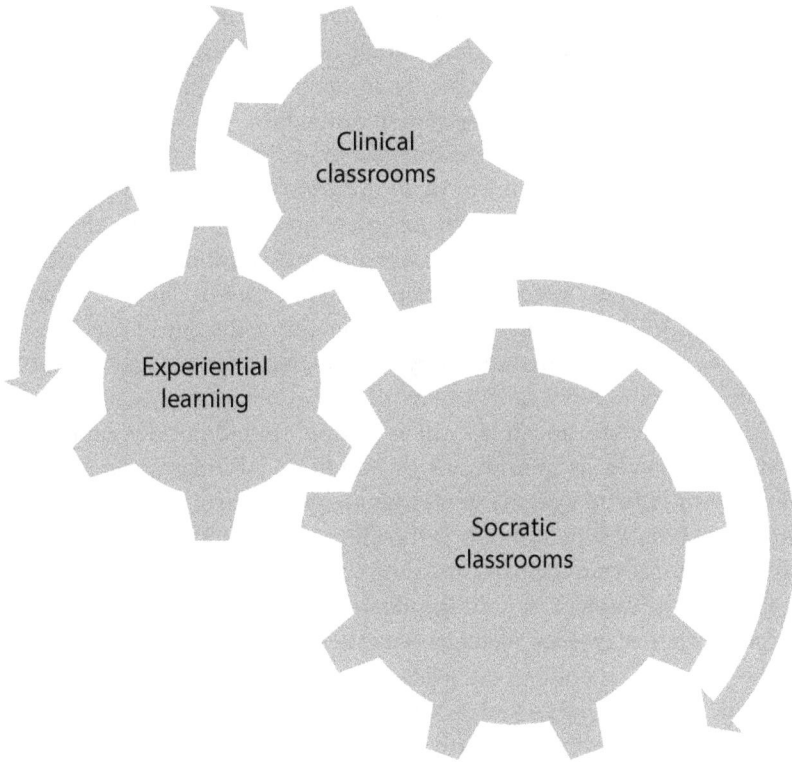

FIGURE 1. The catalyzing role of Socratic classrooms in building inclusive law schools. Illustration by the author.

rigorous examination of Socratic classrooms. Socratic classrooms are not leaving legal education any time soon, so let's harness their efficiencies, repetition, familiarity, and scalability to move the cultural needle more than any seminar or pizza lunch program can.

The dialogue regarding Socratic teaching has historically been quite polarized. The debate seems to be framed around ditching the Socratic method or not. While navigating that binary and entrenched conversation, the result has been to innovate *around it*. As explored further in Chapter 6, that avoidance approach has insulated the curricular core from scrutiny in ways that undermine other hearty and well-intentioned efforts to build inclusive institutions and prepare practice-ready graduates. Thus, this book argues that we need to *catalyze* the Socratic method as the baseline "floor" of building an inclusive law school to support other curricular innovations. Figure 1 helps depict this catalyzing role for

Socratic classrooms. Instead of legal education offering various gears that separately turn to teach skills, substantive rules, or client-centered lawyering, what if the dominant Socratic classroom was thought of as catalyzing all the innovations that have been built around it?

Because of its dominance, persistence, and efficiencies, revamping *how* we deliver the curricular core of legal education is the only way to achieve truly inclusive institutions. Inclusive institutions involve more than just episodic attention to diverse communities and more than just isolated courses and support systems. Inclusion is an institutional endeavor that is inherently defeated if legal education immunizes the curricular core of legal education from accountability for building inclusive and equitable classrooms.

These proposals and this "call to action" paradoxically cannot be framed, however, as innovations or "add-ons." Modernizing Socratic classrooms with educational pedagogy to be inclusive, measurable, and responsive to all student needs is the minimal baseline that we *owe* our students to provide inclusive learning environments. Notably, professors and institutions can (and should!) do dramatically more than just reform the pedagogies framing Socratic classrooms.[24] This chapter issues a call to action on the *who, when,* and *where* of inclusive law schools. The COVID-19 global pandemic revealed to us that this *can* be done, and it can be done swiftly and systemically. We have hit a curricular tipping point that compels moving the inclusion needle more rapidly and systemically using Socratic classrooms as a catalyst. This imperative for inclusive Socratic classrooms aligns with other shifts in legal education.

INCLUSIVE SOCRATIC CLASSROOMS ALIGN WITH OTHER PROFESSIONAL REFORMS

Inclusive Socratic teaching also aligns with trajectory shifts in educational pedagogy in other professional fields and in law. Other professional fields and educational programs have done far more than law in this area. We have models to draw on and examples to follow. Other professional schools, like medical, nursing, social work, and dental schools, have already included a formal educational requirement tied to cultural competency in their accreditation processes.[25] The accrediting body for medical education, for example, has a standard requiring that "faculty and students must demonstrate an understanding of the manner in which people of diverse cultures and belief systems perceive health and illness and respond to various symptoms, diseases, and treatments."[26] This includes accountability for students *and* faculty. In contrast, the ABA language regarding cultural competencies is generically charged to the law school, with no measurement of student outcomes. This reinforces the point that accountability for cultivating cultural competencies in students likely sits with our segmented specialists outside of the classroom.

Social work programs have an even stronger commitment to strengthen cultural competency by "engag[ing] diversity and difference in practice": "Social workers understand how diversity and difference characterize and shape the human experience and are critical to the formation of identity. . . . Social workers understand that, as a consequence of difference, a person's life experiences may include oppression, poverty, marginalization, and alienation as well as privilege, power, and acclaim. Social workers also understand the forms and mechanisms of oppression and discrimination and recognize the extent to which a culture's structures and values, including social, economic, political, and cultural exclusions, may oppress, marginalize, alienate, or create privilege and power."[27]

The changing legal profession also reinforces the momentum for curricular reform. The Institute for the Advancement of the American Legal System surveyed practicing attorneys from various practice settings and seniorities and identified twelve building blocks to develop minimally competent lawyers:

- The ability to act professionally and in accordance with the rules of professional conduct
- An understanding of legal processes and sources of law
- An understanding of threshold concepts in many subjects
- The ability to interpret legal materials
- The ability to interact effectively with clients
- The ability to identify legal issues
- The ability to conduct research
- The ability to communicate as a lawyer
- The ability to see the "big picture" of client matters
- The ability to manage a law-related workload responsibly
- The ability to cope with the stresses of legal practice
- The ability to pursue self-directed learning[28]

These building blocks chart a course forward for legal education, but they also liberate the Socratic method distinctly. The goal of a Socratic classroom need not be focused so narrowly on filling a "brain full of mush" with common law rules and compelling their application on heavily weighted final exams, as Professor Kingsfield memorably declared in *The Paper Chase*. Modern lawyers candidly acknowledge that in practice it would be nearly malpractice to rely on the cache of written rules learned in law school. The Socratic method has its strengths, but it can also be an impediment to reform if legal education innovates *around* it. The legal profession stands poised for change too.

EXISTING ACCREDITATION STANDARDS ARE SILOED AND BIFURCATED

Existing approaches to build inclusive institutions through accreditation are ineffective currently. Inclusive classrooms are an imperative that law school accreditation should support in both structure and substance. All law teachers and institutions hold accountability for inclusive teaching, and accreditation plays a significant norm-setting role. Existing accreditation standards problematically bifurcate law school classrooms entirely from diversity, equity, and inclusion accountability.

Current accreditation approaches primarily rely on monitoring diversity efforts at the law school front door. These standards are implemented largely through mentoring, programming, recruitment, scholarship, and pipeline programs. Success is measured largely by admissions and hiring metrics. These initiatives happen *outside* of the classroom and without large-scale faculty involvement. Mentoring and event programming, for example, would likely be managed through a Dean of Students Office outside of the classroom and unbeknownst to most faculty. Recruitment, scholarships, and pipeline programs would likewise likely be managed by Admissions, Financial Aid, and Development Offices, also outside of the classroom. These segmented implementation strategies silo staff colleagues with accountability for diversity and inclusion metrics. While this is effective in yielding expertise, specialization, and accountability, it collaterally immunizes the curricular core of legal education from diversity and inclusion measurement and accountability.

The following list visualizes this bifurcation in the accreditation standards. Observe structurally how accreditation standards silo diversity, equity, and inclusion under the law school administration side of accreditation standards. The program side of accreditation standards— law school classrooms—is wholly disconnected from diversity and inclusion metrics. Thus, the law school *as an entity* is measured for its compliance with standards, while the classrooms in which student learning is delivered is not explicitly measured. Accreditation has thus done little to build an inclusive or equitable culture in the *learning environments* of legal education.

ACCREDITATION STANDARDS

ORGANIZATION AND ADMINISTRATION	PROGRAM OF LEGAL EDUCATION
Governance	Objectives of legal education
Resources	Learning outcomes
Nondiscrimination	Curriculum
Diversity and inclusion	Academic standards
Accommodations	Academic advising
	Assessment of student learning
	Evaluation of legal education, learning outcomes, and assessment
	Bar passage

However pragmatic this approach—housing diversity and inclusion under law school organization and administration—might be institutionally, it is out of sync with the student experience and misaligned with best educational practices. Accountability to achieve inclusive institutions must include the spaces where students spend the bulk of their time and credit hours—in traditional Socratic classrooms.[29]

Once diversity and inclusion are housed under the organization and administration of law school accreditation standards, most law schools then rely on diversity specialists, student affairs, student organizations, mentoring, and financial aid to support students of color, women students, LGBTQ+ students, nontraditional students, international students, and students with disabilities. These campus constituencies can act as powerful catalysts to faculty and staff hiring, student recruitment, student wellness, course offerings, career support, and more. These approaches are not *enough*, however, to ensure an inclusive climate exists *throughout* institutions. Indeed, many of these approaches circle a full 360 degrees around the perimeter of legal education's Socratic core.

Yet all constituencies in institutions need to be accountable for building an inclusive institution. Inclusive teaching is not an aspirational goal to differentiate or distinguish one classroom or school from another as an add-on or piecemeal effort. Indeed, when inclusive classrooms are one-off innovations, specific law teachers breaking from the status quo can face considerable backlash. Inclusive teaching cannot be the exclusive work of faculty of color, skills faculty, staff, or any cohort of the larger campus community. Rather, inclusive classrooms are a baseline expectation of *effective* teaching in any course in any institution. True inclusion requires the "purposeful investment" of all law teachers to be successful.[30] This is not a problem with students.[31] This is about ensuring *institutions* meet the needs of all students.[32]

The imperative to achieve inclusive institutions involves the intentionality of individual actors, such as law teachers, *and* the development of supportive infrastructure. Valuing institutional inclusion needs to carry through, for example, to tenure and review processes and institutional workload considerations. Reforms, even modest ones, require implementation with accountability and rigor. Effective initiatives need the backing of the deans, monitored implementation, consistency, community building, and even celebration. All-in approaches to inclusion move the community forward *together,* avoiding curricular outliers.[33]

Notably, however, the American Bar Association has doubled down on this bifurcation in its most recent 2022 reforms. The ABA recently added a cultural competency requirement to its accreditation standard. It approved the following reform to Standard 303:

> (c) A law school shall provide education to law students on bias, cross-cultural competency, and racism:
>
> > (1) at the start of the program of legal education, and
> > (2) at least once again before graduation.
>
> For students engaged in law clinics or field placements, the second educational occasion will take place before, concurrently with, or as part of their enrollment in clinical or field placement courses.[34]

While it is a modest step forward, it is not likely to move the needle on inclusive Socratic classrooms.

Legal education is grossly overdue to implement such a substantive metric. Some law schools had already independently added learning outcomes focused on students achieving competency in cross-cultural communication or cultural competency on their own.[35] Schools would notably have been adding this learning outcome, however, to *differentiate,* not to *align* with the core shared values of legal education under the prior ABA standards. Legal education's new accreditation standard deploys a "check-the-box" approach, though, to delivering content on bias, cross-cultural competency, and racism. It does not tether this content to student learning of legal doctrine or legal skills. In fact, it does not seem to hold *classrooms* accountable as the sites for "provid[ing] education" in these areas at all.

The ABA's previous accreditation-reform initiative focused on imposing measurable learning outcomes to achieve student competencies. Yet the ABA's language governing *this* accreditation requirement is out of sync with its own efforts to shift best practices, an astute point made by my colleague Lisa Taylor.[36] Interpretation 303-6 explains that "the importance of cross-cultural competency to professionally responsible representation and the obligation of lawyers to promote a justice system that provides equal access and eliminates bias, discrimination, and racism in the law should be among the values and responsibilities of the legal profession to which students are introduced."[37]

The interpretation notably deploys the passive voice to obscure *who* will be introducing these concepts to students. This seems to say that *legal education* needs bias, cross-cultural, and racism education only to *tell* students that lawyers need to promote such values. It is as if we are just previewing for students that, when they leave this institution, lawyers will care about bias, cross-cultural competency, and racism, but right now we will just teach them that this matters *prospectively*. Most notably, despite the prior wave of ABA accreditation reforms focused on measuring student competencies in meeting learning outcomes, this accreditation standard does not measure anything about what students are able to do upon graduation.[38] It just requires schools to "provide education," ensuring nothing about what our graduates can do or how our students will tether this content to the rest of their legal education.

Interpretation 303-7 suggests that schools can satisfy the requirement through programming in "(1) Orientation sessions for incoming students; (2) Lectures on these topics; (3) Courses incorporating these topics; and (4) Other educational experiences incorporating these topics." The interpretation is clear that this requirement does not require an additional class and no set form of implementation is required.[39] Interpretation 303-7 merely frames the obligation around mandatory infrastructure, not effective student learning, stating that "law schools must demonstrate that all law students are required to participate."[40]

This is a notable deviation from the other new accreditation requirement that schools provide opportunities for students to engage in professional-identity formation. With respect to *that* recent requirement, the ABA sees the importance of learning theory, whereby new skills take time, growth, and reflection to acquire: "Because developing a professional identity requires reflection and growth over time, students should have frequent opportunities for [developing professional identity] during each year of law school and in a variety of courses and co-curricular and professional development activities."[41]

Professional-identity formation is explicitly housed in a "variety of classrooms" and bias, cross-cultural competency, and racism is explicitly exempted from a requirement of classroom implementation. This isolated, bookended, add-on approach to bias, cross-cultural competency, and racism renders it doomed to mandatory "pizza will be served" events. This suggests the content will be presented as *adjacent to* the core curriculum, likely implemented by specialized staff with great expertise but out of sight from most law teachers. This approach glues a modern brick *around* the traditional architecture that still dominates and overpowers the student experience—the Socratic classroom. It introduces values "in the air," but it does not pull the values into how we teach the law. It does not address whether we are *teaching* in ways that remove bias, confront racism, and model cross-cultural competency.

In sum the ABA accreditation standards currently reinforce the same existing approaches that immunize the Socratic classroom from accountability. As explored more in Chapters 6, 7, and 8, it is not enough to require schools to just *measure* learning outcomes in the abstract and take steps to meet them by separately providing some programming on cultural competency. We need to end the presumptive reverence and implicit immunity given to Socratic classrooms. We need to identify shared values driving our Socratic classrooms and align our assessment practices accordingly. We need our programmatic and organizational commitments to diversity and inclusion to shape our curriculum, assessment, learning outcomes, and program objectives.

. . .

This chapter makes the case for individual and institutional accountability for inclusive Socratic classrooms. Many dynamic innovations are happening in legal education. These innovations, however, are generally occurring *around* the curricular core of legal education. Traditional teaching and grading practices are thus framing and shaping the dominant values and norms undergirding legal education. Whether intentional or not, we collectively set the values and norms of legal education. "*We* create the social and institutional structure of law school through the administrative and pedagogical choices we make."[42] It is up to us to pivot, adapt, and reform to build inclusive institutions, which necessarily must include Socratic classrooms. The time is now.

CHAPTER 6

Pivoting Away from Problematic Socratic Performances

The time to reform Socratic classrooms is now, to make them more inclusive, equitable, and effective. That effort begins by ending the presumptive reverence and implicit immunity given to all performances of Socratic teaching to make space for greater innovation, experimentation, dialogue, study, and critique. This chapter first concedes that the Socratic method will continue to play a dominant role in legal education, whether because of economics, inertia, or sincere regard for its pedagogical approach. It then argues that we need to "raise the floor" on legal education by eliminating problematic performances of the Socratic method—those techniques deployed with power, fear, and hierarchy as its core features—across all courses and institutions. While admittedly isolated and waning in their usage, these harmful teaching techniques still frustrate and marginalize students and teachers. Eliminating problematic Socratic performances opens space to instead study more rigorously whether the remaining performances of Socratic teaching are effective, equitable, and inclusive.

Chapter 7 then proposes a set of shared institutional values to replace these problematic Socratic performances. It proposes Socratic techniques deployed to achieve student-centered, skills-centered, client-centered, and community-centered classrooms. These two chapters together are a call to center Socratic teaching around core values that render it more authentic. These proposals sit harmoniously as a foundational support for even more ambitious and transformative calls to reform legal education. More ambitious goals are undermined and thwarted by problematic performances of the Socratic method that compromise innovation and inclusion.

CONCEDING THE SOCRATIC METHOD'S PERSEVERANCE
AND PRAGMATIC POTENTIAL

The dominant approach to legal education has been to *add* innovation, such as clinical programs, experiential learning, formative assessment, and skills development, while simultaneously retaining the hallmarks of traditional legal education. The large lecture-hall Socratic course is not positioned to leave legal education any time soon, despite the steady chorus of critical voices over decades and the ongoing modern calls for curricular reform. Law schools continue to design their budgets, curricula, and student experiences around some substantial degree of case-based, Socratic law teaching in large lecture-style classrooms. Its efficiencies still anchor institutions in its scalability and its high faculty-to-student ratios.

The challenge for educators is to harness the Socratic method's strengths while avoiding its weaknesses. There are notable strengths to the Socratic method when performed inclusively and effectively, as Chapters 6, 7, and 8 collectively seek. Socratic teaching is efficient and scalable. It can be taught to a large lecture hall of students, using case-books that have been in publication for decades. It has robust volumes of existing teaching materials built around it, making its endurance economical. It is also replicable and sustainable, allowing faculty time for scholarship and service. It is comfortable for many professors because they were taught this way, and they have taught this way for decades.

From the student perspective, Socratic teaching also has some advantages for learning. It is repeated hundreds of times in different courses, offering the potential to reinforce important values and skills consistently across the curriculum. It is delivered to a large and diverse group of students, allowing for competing perspectives and critical inquiry. It uses real legal cases, so every Socratic exchange presents opportunities for meaningful classroom engagements that align with practice readiness, professional-identity formation, and cultural competencies. Every case contains at least two clients and an opportunity to engage in a Socratic exchange about what their objectives were and how the law met or did not meet these clients' objectives. Socratic exchanges can also reinforce how a client hired a lawyer, gathered relevant facts, and developed a strategy to meet the client's objectives. These exchanges can reinforce the locality of the case and how different communities are affected by its outcome. Socratic exchanges can help students learn to communicate legal outcomes to a client, particularly when the outcome is not favorable and leaves the client's objectives unfulfilled. From this repetition across casebooks and classes, students can thus learn incrementally to lawyer in a skills-centered and client-centered approach as part of a classroom community with other professionals.

These types of Socratic exchanges are dramatically different dialogues than those centered solely around an appellate court ruling or an abstract rule of law. These professional development opportunities are vital to law-practice readiness. They can begin from existing appellate casebooks and in large classrooms though, thus making the existing Socratic classroom an efficient and effective springboard to rapid curricular and cultural reform. These types of Socratic techniques are explored more concretely in Chapter 7. For now let's explore what components of the Socratic method we *are* trying to eliminate.

DEFINING PROBLEMATIC PERFORMANCES OF THE SOCRATIC METHOD

It is time to end the presumptive reverence and implicit immunity given to problematic performances of the Socratic method and instead invite rigorous review of its pedagogical value. Quite understandably, this is the first question I am asked when discussing Socratic-teaching reforms: "Are you talking about *my* Socratic teaching?" It is an important question to address head-on, as critiquing teaching is deeply personal, vulnerable, and potentially alienating. It can be perceived as an attack on beloved, accomplished, revered, and talented faculty colleagues.

Despite its acknowledged decline in traditional usage, Socratic teaching persists almost universally in core law school classes, such as first-year courses, bar courses, and large lecture courses.[1] It is far less often used in seminars, skills courses, and clinical teaching. Modern Socratic techniques do vary greatly by professor, class, and institution. For some the Socratic method remains a means of rigorous critical inquisition to develop analytic skills with clear hierarchies and power dynamics. Others use softer, gentler, and more approachable versions of the same technique. For others still, the Socratic method is just one teaching tool supplemented with other techniques such as group work, skills simulations, practice problems, and speakers.[2]

The following list provides a working definition of problematic Socratic performances. Note that these descriptors are about *how* material is taught, not *who* is teaching the material or *what* is being taught. These aspects of problematic Socratic performances are organized from the most problematic down to the least problematic. This organization likely also inversely progresses from the least commonly deployed to the most.

CHARACTERISTICS OF PROBLEMATIC SOCRATIC PERFORMANCES

- Wielding tools of **fear** and, to a lesser extent, **shame** to motivate student participation and underscore the inadequacies of the students while purporting to help them learn
- **Power-centered** teaching, with the professor leading the dialogue and holding all the answers centrally and unwaveringly—if not tauntingly—while students attempt to perform primarily for the professor and secondarily for their peers
- **Professor-centered** teaching, with a professor centered in the room and students engaging in serial participation with the professor, while positioned as subordinate absorbers of information as they bank new content
- **Heavily weighted summative** assessment motivating the full semester with little transparency of the performance metrics driving assessment or the relationship between those assessment criteria and Socratic teaching techniques
- Teaching rules and application in ways that are **abstract and timeless** and using materials that rarely need adapting across institutions or time
- Emphasizing **appellate** cases while obscuring facts, lawyering skills, and the context in which the case was decided

With these core criteria in mind, we return to the delicate question a law teacher may ask: "Are you talking about *my* Socratic teaching?" In a sense, the answer to all who employ the Socratic method in a traditional classroom—me included—is a more nuanced and conversationally inviting yes. There are aspects of problematic performances within all traditional Socratic teaching, whether it be the classroom design, the penultimate-exam emphasis, the absence of application exercises, or the sole use of appellate casebooks. The bottom three characteristics on the list of problematic Socratic performances have distinctly strong infrastructure because they align with the published books on the market, the rhythm of the academic semester, the technology of grade reporting, and so forth.

While most law teachers engage in some problematic performances of the Socratic method, a distinctly small subset of faculty wholly adopt these problematic performances with purpose and pride. For law teachers who strive to wield fear, shame, power, control, and hierarchy as intentional teaching tools, this chapter is more pointed. These professors often paradoxically hold an immunity, as they are feared by students and perceived as untouchable, with minimal accountability for the experiences of students in their classrooms. These classrooms hold and embrace *all* the listed characteristics. This type of systemic deployment of problematic Socratic performances is often compared to the famed Professor Charles Kingsfield.

John Jay Osborn's 1971 novel, *The Paper Chase*, famously depicted a first-year student at Harvard Law School, tangling with the esteemed and highly regarded contracts law professor, Charles Kingsfield. The story follows the student's journey through his social, academic, and professional struggles during law school and his eventual ascension from classroom humiliation and shame to the upper echelon of the classroom hierarchy. The book was later produced as a film, for which John Houseman, the actor depicting Professor Kingsfield, won an Academy Award for Best Supporting Actor.[3] The film remains iconic law school lore, highlighting the challenges and pressures of law school.

Professor Kingsfield is generally regarded as a *legendary* example of Socratic teaching, although perhaps never as a *good* example of Socratic teaching. His character embodies a distinct archetype of the US law professor.[4] Kingsfield, an older, White, male professor, is presumed brilliant and receives instant, deep, and enduring respect. He holds immense power in the large lecture-hall classroom in the traditional and enduring "sage on the stage" model of teaching. Kingsfield represents a performance of the Socratic method that uses tools of humiliation, degradation, mockery, and shame in masculinist ways that also reinforce and entrench racial and gender hierarchies. It is a performance of the Socratic method in which the professor wields power over students instead of wielding knowledge to empower students.

Kingsfield endures as a caricature of problematic Socratic performances. He boasts that his treatment of students is for their own good and, from his intellect, students would be transformed from a "skull full of mush" into "thinking like a lawyer." Christopher Langdell's Socratic method positions the teacher as the expert and conductor of the Socratic exchange, leaving students disempowered and unable to seek their own wisdom and clarity in understanding the law from the expert's mastery and knowledge.

This approach to teaching is distinctly disingenuous as Socratic dialogue. Indeed, Langdell's interpretation of the Socratic method as a tool for legal education "bears little resemblance to the actual ideas of Socratic dialogue." Langdell's Socratic method teaches students to revere the rules they study and submit to them. This leaves legal education "intrinsically justif[ying] the existing legal order and the social authority of the state."[5] Any efforts to question the rules or the cases must inherently derive from students drawing on another case or another rule. It is exactly this view of power dynamics that Socrates sought to upend, not entrench, through dialogue and inquiry. Kingsfield-esque professor-student hierarchies distort how and what law is taught. Problematic Socratic performances reinforce law as a system and structure *over* students. It teaches the law but allows little room to challenge the law's origins or justness. This perpetuates the legal and cultural status quo and reinforces the gendered and racialized critiques previously described.

Through supportive mentoring and assessment techniques to guide faculty, our institutions should seek to eliminate these problematic performances that proudly and unabashedly deploy fear, shame, power, hierarchy, and control. In sum the breadth and depth of the critique differs for all of us, but an element of problematic performances likely lingers in nearly all Socratic-style classrooms. The roots of this call to action sit in the same rationale regardless—adaptively responding to the sustained calls for reform from inside and outside of our institutional walls. We have robust cultures for critiquing scholarship collegially, professionally, and productively. The same culture and growth mindset can support teaching. This proposal is not just about the ghost of Kingsfield, though. Problematic performances affect *who* teaches law, *how* law is taught, and *what* law is taught. It affects teachers, students, and institutions. This shift is about making space for innovation, accountability, and inclusion. This begins with ending the presumptive reverence and implicit immunity given to Socratic teaching.

ENDING THE PRESUMPTIVE REVERENCE AND IMPLICIT IMMUNITY GIVEN TO SOCRATIC TEACHING

This chapter is an invitation to evaluate and assess Socratic teaching on its merits, grounded neutrally along with other teaching techniques.

The Socratic method has its role in legal education, but it is not presumptively worthy of the esteem that it receives in all its performative iterations. I have argued elsewhere that this is a call to "cancel Kingsfield," and other scholars have likewise argued that it is time to "dethrone" the case method.[6] Legal education inexplicably immunizes Socratic classrooms from explaining to students how these classrooms are designed, structured, and assessed. This is likely because the intentionality of design, structure, and assessment is simply not consciously developed by most faculty. This intentionality is likely not developed because faculty are systemically replicating the status quo of how *we* were taught using the Socratic method as the sole teaching tool.

Socratic teaching likely persists with such little transformation more by inertia and pragmatic economics than proven efficacy or intentional pedagogical certainty. Some data bear this out. When surveyed about *why* professors are still using the Socratic method, they reported believing it was the most effective (90 percent), comfortable to the faculty using it (59 percent), what *they* experienced in law school (32 percent), or that they wanted to align with their colleagues (4 percent).[7]

But when faculty report that Socratic teaching is the "most effective," I posit that this statistic is a concrete and vivid reflection of the presumptive reverence described in this chapter's thesis. I am deeply skeptical that this statistic reflects that rigorous support exists documenting that the Socratic method is the most effective teaching technique for *learners*. If so, this statistic seems woefully and profoundly out of touch with the documented accounts of students engaging in this method, as described in Chapter 1. This statistic more realistically communicates that the Socratic method is the most effective teaching technique *for faculty*, given the intense demands on their time to publish and serve in institutions, communities, and the legal profession, as also captured in Chapter 1. Half of faculty surveyed report that they use the Socratic method because it is "comfortable" to *them*. This begs the question of whether it should be comfortable for the *faculty* or comfortable for the *learners?* Effective teaching should be both. Chapter 8 maps a path for faculty communities to keep the aspects of Socratic teaching that are comfortable for them while making the technique more effective for all students.

Speaking to my experience, I use Socratic teaching in my doctrinal courses. Candidly, I am not sure it ever occurred to me at the outset of my teaching career that I *could* do anything else. Early on I was keenly aware that I was being reviewed and evaluated exclusively by colleagues who taught using traditional Socratic teaching techniques. Of the surveyed colleagues, 4 percent likewise reported that they use the Socratic method because it aligns with their colleagues. I suspect that this 4 percent is also likely early in their teaching careers. Over time they will continue the technique because it is "effective" for them and "comfortable" to them.

The idea that faculty are deploying a teaching technique solely because it is how *they* learned or what their colleagues are doing, however, is deeply limiting. This perpetuation of the status quo without further rigorous examination compromises the diversity of law schools because the mimicry of Socratic teaching is distinctly styled around a White, male norm. With Kingsfield reflecting an archetype of a Socratic professor, however problematic or outdated that archetype is, his shadow indeed looms large and harms women, faculty of color, and others in law teaching because expectations construct reality.[8]

This presumptive reverence to Socratic teaching techniques that align with limited archetypes of teaching in turn undergirds the well-documented "presumptive incompetence" plaguing women faculty, faculty of color, and nontraditional faculty.[9] The gendered and racialized context of an older, White, male professor holding power and control of a classroom translates very differently when deployed by faculty of color, women, and even young professors. Thus, even isolated or segmented problematic Socratic performances are still likely to harm law teachers because they create lasting norms and expectations for how law teaching looks and sounds.

In many cases the presumptive reverence given to Socratic teaching has been further reinforced through legal education's deeply bifurcated and hierarchical power and pay structures that value innovation less than traditional Socratic teaching. Dean Darby Dickerson's powerful critique of caste within legal education is insightful here.[10] Dean Dickerson reveals an inversion, whereby the top of academic castes is generally traditional Socratic faculty relying on century-old teaching techniques. The bottom is more likely to hold innovators in experiential learning, legal writing, and clinical lawyering, deploying more student-centered, skills-centered, client-centered, and community-centered practices.

Many students also expect Socratic teaching to be professor-centered and power-centered because that is what they see in campus visits, movies, and popular culture. Socratic teaching still wields a deep "presumptive reverence," whereby students internalize this technique as "good" teaching and what law school "should" be.[11] If students expect Socratic teaching, and faculty expect Socratic teaching, and that is all that motivates it, we are giving full immunity to the technique without examining its effectiveness or holding it accountable to responding to existing critiques. Law teachers are thus left seeking to conform and thrive within existing institutional norms systemically reinforced by both faculty and students alike.

Instead, we need to demonstrate affirmatively how this technique is effective, equitable, and inclusive if we are to replicate it over six or eight semesters. To study Socratic teaching, we first must remove it from its pedestal as legal education's gold standard, immune from accountability for its harms and inadequacies, and instead open space for innovation and experimentation. Its reverence should be validated and measured by lining it up with the best educational practices. The effect of this pivot will be to reboot dialogue and innovation. This call is for accountability but also a license to collaborate, innovate, and grow with intentionality. Here are three concrete ways to remove the reverence and implicit immunity given to traditional Socratic teaching.

Embed syllabi transparency regarding Socratic goals, participation expectations, and assessment metrics.

A simple and straightforward starting point is to bring clarity and transparency to course syllabi as to how the Socratic method aligns with legal education pedagogy and classroom learning outcomes. Most students genuinely have no concrete understanding of the purpose of the Socratic method or its goals.[12] Syllabi are intended to introduce students to the course, teaching philosophy, course-learning outcomes, and measures of assessment. Faculty can include specific guidelines and language in their syllabi, describing the technique and situating it within the course more broadly.

To not explain how students' classroom engagement is structured from class to class is instead problematically relying on an embedded and implicit reverence to the Socratic technique, particularly given that law teachers do use it in such divergent ways. For example, law teachers might be using the Socratic method to prepare for practice, to build advocacy and professional skills, or to test the boundaries of the material. Other courses, such as legal research and writing, clinics, and experiential learning are much more candid with their students about how classroom engagement is structured and why it is structured that way.

Silence on the role of the Socratic method assumes that students can figure out what this teaching technique is on their own and what successful engagement and performance entails. The reality is that some

Box 1. Sample Explanation of the Use of the Socratic Method in the Course

I use the Socratic method as a tool for class participation. The Socratic method positions students as active contributors, engaging, analyzing, and thoughtfully evaluating the material and how it affects our communities and lives. It also can contribute to your professional development as you work on legal reasoning, public speaking, and rule-based application skills. We all approach the Socratic method transparently and collaboratively. All students are on call. When on call, relax as best as you can, and remember that this is a conversation and a dialogue, role-playing the practice of law. The key to Socratic participation when not on call is to recognize that your classmates are presenting key concepts and rules, not your professor. Listen carefully and take notes while your classmates participate. We are all committed to the same goals—learning precise legal rules, testing their boundaries, and bridging these rules into practice readiness.

students have an advantage in their existing understandings of the Socratic method. Others may find it pedagogically dissonant to their culture, as described in Chapter 2. This type of communication with students will help them engage with the material more equitably and more fairly. The material in the subsequent chapters might help you develop more consciousness to the use of this technique. Once you understand why you use the Socratic method, and how it relates to your specific course-learning outcomes, add transparency in your course syllabus, articulating how and why you use the Socratic method, and how students can engage with it successfully. Box 1 contains the language that I use in my syllabus.

Evaluate student Socratic performance explicitly and fairly.

Students likewise need to concretely know what strong Socratic participation looks like and how you plan to assess it. This is a vital step to add transparency and accountability. If Socratic-style teaching is occupying nearly every class session and not being evaluated at all, that raises deep questions about course design and whether the teaching techniques align with students acquiring competencies in the course's stated learning outcomes. No evaluation of Socratic engagement means that students have no explicit tethering of the technique to work that is graded, assessed, and

---

Box 2. Sample Language on Assessing Socratic Performance

For every class I record a score for class participation for all students. You will receive a ✓+ when your participation exceeds expectations, a ✓ when your participation meets expectations, and a ✓– when participation is below expectations. A ✓+ means that you are actively pushing the classroom dialogue forward and contributing to the dialogue. Contributing to the dialogue is not the same as having all the answers. It is okay—and indeed quite normal—to have some uncertainty as you work through your reasoning and analysis. You should expect to get a ✓+ every four to five classes when you are on call. I will spread the on-call participation opportunities around equally, out of fairness. Scores of ✓+ are not linked to the volume of your participation. Being a good class contributor also involves carefully listening to your classmates' contributions. A ✓ means that you are engaged and thoughtfully involved in class. You are listening carefully to your classmates' participation, asking questions when needed, and acting as a professional would in a meeting-style setting. A ✓– means you were late, unprepared, distracted, distracting, or disrespectful. This denotes conduct that would be outside the bounds of a professional practice setting.

---

measured. Silence on whether and how you assess Socratic participation can also be a fertile environment for implicit biases to take over if you are just deploying an amorphous "bump" for "good" class participation.

You can hold yourself accountable to using effective assessment practices by building the terminology and criteria that surround your Socratic participation assessment criteria directly in your syllabus. Box 2 contains the language that I use in my syllabus. There are many ways to approach this. Focus on developing an assessment metric that values all student participation, not just the hyperparticipation of a few. If class participation is just framed as a "bump," faculty might inadvertently incentivize a flurry of "gunners" who try to dominate in the accumulation of class participation points. These goals can be accomplished by grounding the assessment metrics in the context of lawyering norms, which value both speaking and listening skills. With any of the measurement tools you use, you can consider making this scoring available to students in a real-time online gradebook or during conversations in office hours.

You can also find opportunities early on in your course to lend transparency to the kinds of Socratic participation you value. For example, you could send class-wide emails after the first few classes, communicating what you identify as successful aspects of Socratic participation (e.g., students knew the facts, procedural history, and rule well; students thought on their feet adeptly; or students knew the definitions of key terms). In select teachable moments, you could break character with the Socratic method to debrief how students are doing and how they can improve. For example, when students get stuck in an exchange, address transparently why they are stuck. Has the professor moved from examining the students' knowledge of an underlying case to the application of concepts to new factual scenarios or has the professor moved to analysis or synthesis of the rules? The students' anxiety over appearing prepared might undermine their processing of a professor's line of questions.

If an exchange goes well, incentivize students to critique favorably. For example, "I thought that was a good case discussion. What did you all think of how student X did?" The goal is to develop shared terminology about what characteristics reflect strong Socratic participation to you. These techniques help communicate expectations and goals to students. This, in turn, gives all students a fair chance to meet those expectations.

Be accountable for addressing student feedback.

To end the implicit immunity given to Socratic teaching, Socratic teachers must be accountable to assessing the effectiveness of student learning in a Socratic classroom. In course evaluations ask students explicitly to assess your use of the Socratic method as a teaching tool. Was it effective? Were students able to engage effectively? Did they feel included? Did they have the tools they needed to succeed? Look critically for connections between Socratic performance and exam performance in your grading. Does successful Socratic participation predict exam success? If not, probe why. Where you are not achieving effective results, be open to seeking out support. Institutions need to incentivize such rigorous reflection and growth.

Institutional Support for Inclusive Socratic Teaching

Institutional leaders can help cultivate more accountable and transparent Socratic classrooms. It can be far more efficient to host an introduction to the Socratic method during orientation to demystify the process and position all students to engage with it transparently and successfully. Likewise, schools can also have institutional best practices to transparently articulate on course syllabi the teaching methods used in the course and the rationale for each. Schools can create and share templates, models, and best practices for managing class participation grading in a Socratic course. Institutions can have faculty identify techniques to improve Socratic teaching by hosting workshops and trainings.

Institutions can systemically monitor course evaluations of all faculty, not just pretenure faculty, to identify and respond to student concerns. They can host listening sessions, where students can provide feedback on their overall learning experiences, and leaders can listen and learn. Institutions can prepare an annual report based on student feedback of general institutional trends in teaching. What is working well for students at your institution? What would students like more of? What are they frustrated by? This will, in turn, yield more effective course evaluations, if students understand that their course evaluations are considered reflectively. It will also mitigate the defensiveness that individual faculty might display if the feedback comes in the aggregate to the institution. Finally, schools can provide support to faculty, looking to strengthen their Socratic teaching, such as conference attendance, structured mentoring relationships, guest speakers at faculty meetings, awards and recognitions, and marketing excellence in teaching. Assessment techniques are explored further in Chapter 8. They are noted here as a tool to discontinue the presumptive reverence attached to the Socratic method, instead making space for rigorous study of student experiences. They move toward institutional and individual accountability for delivering effective learning.

. . .

Removing the presumptive reverence and implicit immunity given to problematic Socratic performances will spark greater authenticity and experimentation. Problematic performances can obscure the client, the community, the student, and lawyering skills at the exaltation of "thinking like a lawyer" in the abstract. This risks compromising all institutional diversity and inclusion goals. As "Becoming Gentlemen" concluded decades ago, the problem is in "institutional design."[13] This chapter repositions the Socratic method in our institutions and demystifies its usage. These proposals seek stronger innovation in and accountability for teaching to achieve shared goals that meet the needs of modern learners.

Chapter 7 proposes a set of shared institutional values to frame the Socratic method, modernize it, and align it with other curricular reforms. The call for developing shared values and responsive approaches is not about me or you. It is about our students, our institutions, and the profession. Our students are not well. Many are struggling. Many are not thriving. They are entering a profession itself riddled with wellness concerns and dissatisfaction. It is in their interest and for their wellness that we have a shared institutional and professional obligation to modernize, adapt, and meet their needs inclusively and equitably. Critical scholars have instead championed classrooms that build on lived experiences and problem-solving. They have sought classrooms that "build ... trust, collaboration, engagement, and empowerment ... rather than reinforc[e] the competition, individual achievement, alienation, passivity, and lack of confidence that now so pervade the classroom."[14] Once we end the presumptive reverence and implicit immunity, we are liberated to innovate and grow.

CHAPTER 7

Identifying the Shared Values That Shape Socratic Classrooms

This chapter proposes a set of shared institutional values for Socratic classrooms. As Chapter 6 describes, law teachers generally engage students with the Socratic method with little transparency or purposefulness. Instead, they tend to rely on the presumptive reverence that this teaching technique receives. With added curricular conformity, Socratic teachers are largely immune from accountability for monitoring classroom effectiveness. While this teaching technique reflects conformity with colleagues, law teachers actually deploy the Socratic method more like a string of independent contractors, with little collaboration across institutions or fields. Law teachers are not explicitly taught how to use the Socratic method effectively or how to avoid common pitfalls. Few conferences or training programs work to systemically refine this skill or to modernize it to meet the needs of today's law students. Yet modern law students are more diverse than they were historically, and they are increasingly strained in the costs—financial, psychological, and physiological—of law school.

In stark contrast to Socratic classrooms, legal research and writing courses, clinics, experiential learning, and externship placements *do* share more collaborative and unified terminology, goals, and values, even across divergent content and styles. Broad, shared pedagogical norms drive these genres of courses.[1] These norms have been cultivated through thriving professional communities of scholars and teachers working together to develop and refine best practices. These communities in turn foster growth, transparency, and innovation in these classrooms.

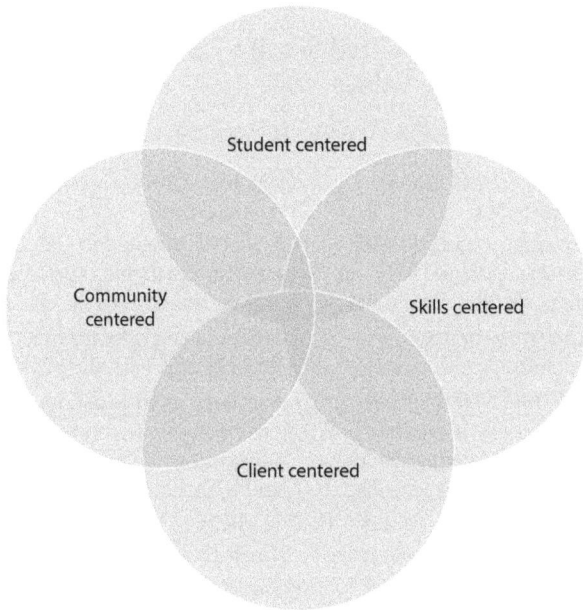

FIGURE 2. Inclusive Socratic teaching values. Illustration by the author.

While the day-to-day structure of Socratic classrooms might look the same—appellate casebooks, summative exams, professors at the podium, students on call, and so on—the pedagogical values and goals can vary widely. Students might attend one Socratic class that is deeply hierarchical, fear inducing, and abstract. Another Socratic classroom might deploy dialogue more collaboratively and interactively, with two-way exchanges between teacher and student, widespread student engagement, and real-world applications of legal rules. While the values, techniques, and tone change across Socratic classrooms, perhaps the most unifying aspect aligning all Socratic classrooms is the lack of transparency that generally frame these classrooms' stated goals, performance metrics, and curricular connections.

Socratic teachers, like their cross-curricular peers, need a set of shared values that drive their teaching in alignment with larger institutional and professional goals. To achieve these goals, this chapter proposes adopting shared Socratic teaching values that are student, skills, client, and community centered, as depicted in Figure 2. Cultivating a set of shared values would make Socratic teaching more effective and inclusive for

Box 3. Building a Shared Set of Socratic Teaching Values

STUDENT-CENTERED SOCRATIC TEACHING

PROBLEMATIC SOCRATIC PERFORMANCES	STUDENT-CENTERED SOCRATIC TECHNIQUES
• Students follow the professor-led Socratic dialogue, with one student performing at a time.	• Students bring unique, multifaceted, and dynamic experiences and perspectives to the classroom.
• Students are primarily motivated to read for class out of fear of being on call.	• Students engage with one another and with the professor.
• Students largely leave their perspectives and experiences out of core case discussions.	• Students' lived experiences and perspectives are central to their acquisition of legal knowledge and their basis of inquiry.
• Students rarely understand how they are performing in class.	• Students receive feedback to direct their own success.
• Students are not explicitly told the connection between Socratic engagement and exam success.	• Students understand how the Socratic method fits within the trajectory of legal education and how it helps them perform in this class and prepare for practice.

SKILLS-CENTERED SOCRATIC TEACHING

PROBLEMATIC SOCRATIC PERFORMANCES	SKILLS-CENTERED SOCRATIC TECHNIQUES
• Students are taught to think like a lawyer by progressing through many rules with a heavily weighted summative exam to assess the ability of students to rapidly analyze issues.	• Formative assessments move students incrementally through the development of both substantive rules and lawyering skills.
• There is little mention of the underlying skills that lawyers deploy in the cases, only the rules and outcomes that resulted.	• Teaching and assessments are packaged around sensitization to lawyering skills such as research, writing, advocacy, fact gathering, client counseling, and cultural competence.
• Thinking like a lawyer is the narrow classroom objective, not learning to be a lawyer more broadly.	

CLIENT-CENTERED SOCRATIC TEACHING

PROBLEMATIC SOCRATIC PERFORMANCES	CLIENT-CENTERED SOCRATIC TECHNIQUES
• Appellate cases compose the body of course materials. • Discussion of the client objectives and client counseling shaping the trajectory of a case is absent or sparse. • Clients are instead introduced to students outside of Socratic courses in clinical, simulation, and experiential courses.	• Socratic exchanges explore the role of clients in the case and the work of lawyers using legal rules to advance the clients' objectives. • Case discussions progress from a client engagement through to trial and then to appeal. • Every case studied is a chance to advise clients responsively. • Exams and assignments position students in active lawyering roles on behalf of clients.

COMMUNITY-CENTERED SOCRATIC TEACHING

PROBLEMATIC SOCRATIC PERFORMANCES	COMMUNITY-CENTERED SOCRATIC TECHNIQUES
• Students study cases from appellate casebooks, neglecting their time, context, or community. • The perspectives introduced in the materials tend to center White, heterosexual, male, and privileged lenses without acknowledging or reckoning with these dominant perspectives. • Learning to lawyer within a community occurs in clinics, externships, and student employment. • Students rarely feel connected to an identifiable learning community. They rarely discuss what it means to lawyer as part of a community.	• Students examine how the underlying rules apply in their communities and whether they adequately provide redress to real problems. • Students are empowered to consider whether the law reflects the values of their community. • Where the law does not reflect community needs or values, students consider reforms. • Learning environments are cultivated with the purpose of building welcoming and inclusive communities. • Students actively explore what it means to lawyer in a professional community.

both students and the profession. Shared values would leverage the repetition and volume of Socratic exchanges to better catalyze and support other components of the law school curriculum. These values can be customized and tweaked across institutions, but they should be relevant to advancing students in the legal profession.[2] These Socratic teaching values should be communicated transparently to students as classroom expectations. These values should be inclusive of all students. Integrating some combination of these shared values would yield more effective, equitable, and inclusive Socratic classrooms.

Integrating these shared values into the Socratic classroom systemically and purposefully would respond to long-standing critiques of the harmful effects and deficiencies of Socratic teaching.[3] Students can instead engage with the Socratic method on behalf of clients, within professional communities, and in collaboration with their peers, while unpacking how the law affects diverse clients and communities. Box 3 compares how deploying these shared Socratic values would shape a classroom that differs fundamentally from the problematic performances that characterize many Socratic classrooms.

Notably, many of these proposed, shared Socratic values also center and ground recent ABA accreditation reforms squarely in the curricular core. Student-centered and skills-centered Socratic teaching, for example, is a synergistic goal to cultivating professional-identity formation for students. The essence of professional-identity formation is students understanding the skills and values that shape the work of lawyers. The intersections of student-centered teaching, client-centered teaching, and community-centered teaching are likewise vital to addressing biases and acquiring the strong cultural competencies necessary to lawyer. This chapter next introduces each shared Socratic value in turn.

CULTIVATING STUDENT-CENTERED
SOCRATIC CLASSROOMS

Problematic performances of the Socratic method are professor and power centered, abstract, and removed from students' lived experiences. Instead, the Socratic method can be reframed *around* students. Student-centered teaching recognizes that students bring dynamic experiences and perspectives into the classroom. Our work as educators is to help our students layer core lawyering skills onto those existing identities and experiences, not to wipe the slate clean. Precisely *because of* the incredible range of diversity we have populating our large Socratic classrooms, it would be an extraordinary loss to *not* have students engage with one another and find their own voice in dialogue with others.

Students should also be the driving force directing how our courses are designed. Socratic teaching is not about marching from the first to the last chapter of a casebook. What do we actually want our students to be able to do at the end of the class? This is the vital starting point of designing a successful classroom. Students need to see how our Socratic classes tether to their skills classes, their clinical coursework, the bar exam, and their future career. This section offers two concrete action items to build student-centered Socratic classrooms. Inclusive Socratic teaching involves getting to know your students and designing the course around what you want *them* to know or do by the end of the course (not what content you want to teach). These are vital starting points. Much more can be done to expand and deepen these aspects of Socratic classrooms.

Inclusive Socratic Teachers Know Their Students

As a starting point, consider how much you know about your student community. While law teachers who have served in admissions and administrative roles may be uniquely savvy in this regard, consider whether most law teachers know these characteristics about their student communities.

- The average age of their students
- Their prior careers and degrees
- The percentage of full- or part-time students
- The geographic composition of their classroom community
- The percentage of racially diverse, gender diverse, or LGBTQ+ students
- The types of disabilities students in their institution face
- The financial-insecurity, housing-insecurity, or food-insecurity barriers that students in the institution generally face
- The parenting status of their students
- The military status of their students

Many law teachers slowly come to learn these points episodically and individually about some percentage of students as they come through office hours over time. Most of us do not know this information at the outset of a course or as we come on board in new institutions. Likewise, other broader insights into how adult learners thrive, how to teach for all learning styles, and generational differences in learning are also important for law teachers to keep pace with modern law students. If learning is not effective, the teaching is likely not effective, so we must understand how our students learn.

Inclusive teachers consistently deploy this type of knowledge to build their learning communities.[4] The best law teachers engage deeply in getting to know their students.[5] Clarity, intentionality, and specificity about who our students are should be a regular part of effective and inclusive law teaching. Socratic teachers should not hide behind being "bad with names" or "bad with faces" as an excuse to avoid getting to know each unique cohort of students.[6]

Law teachers' awareness of student attributes entering the course "is essential for creating environments where all students can meet learning goals."[7] The Law School Survey of Student Engagement (LSSSE) is a vital partner in this work and provides the embedded infrastructure and know-how.[8] For example, 2021 LSSSE data revealed that 29 percent of our students were concerned about housing and eviction, 63 percent were struggling to pay bills, and 40 percent struggled with food security.[9] These accounts offer a sobering wakeup call that we need to design our classes intentionally around the evolving needs of our students. Our students are changing, but our teaching methods are not. This merits study and action. Not understanding our students is a barrier to their effective learning, leaving us with a "lack of awareness of students' unseen burdens, including both the structural inequities that many students encounter in education and the personal feelings of doubt and fear that are cued in students by experiences on and off campus."[10]

Law teachers can get to know their students by deploying simple survey techniques before class begins. Law teachers can learn more about their students through orientation programming or small-group sessions. They can do it through LSSSE or other similar large-scale surveying. There are inefficiencies to all law teachers trying to do this individually. It is also important that institutional supports exist to help create the right culture, incentives, and efficiencies. To shape a Socratic classroom around student-centered learning requires institutional changes in values and visibility. Many institutional incentives toward scholarship and service can create powerful disincentives that work against student-centered teaching.[11] Institutions can further support such teaching by engaging in community surveying, disseminating community surveys for analysis, providing financial support for programming, and valuing the time invested in these activities.

HOW LAW TEACHERS CAN GET TO KNOW THEIR STUDENTS

- Survey students before the course begins to understand the unique attributes of your class section. Where are they from? What languages do they speak? What interests them about law school? Are they working? Did they work a prior career?
- Create an icebreaker game to help students get to know one another better and to help you meet them as a group.
- Use the students' identified pronouns and names.
- Host small group "meet and greets" in the first few weeks of the semester with your students.
- Host an introductory topical program before classes (e.g., a film viewing or current events discussion) to meet your students and allow students to meet one another.
- Create small-group learning exercises to interact efficiently with your students and to allow them to interact together throughout the semester.
- Mix up student groups to allow for robust student interaction beyond just working with students seated nearby.

HOW INSTITUTIONS CAN SUPPORT LAW TEACHERS IN GETTING TO KNOW STUDENTS

- Fund opportunities for meet-and-greet programs with 1L sections and upper-level classes.
- Provide admissions reports of evolving trends in the student community.
- Survey your student community using the Law School Survey of Student Engagement.
- Where LSSSE data exists at the institutional level, discuss its implications in forums with faculty. Work collaboratively to understand your student community and its unique struggles. Identify areas for growth as an institution.

- Value faculty time invested in student engagement toward performance evaluations and promotion metrics. For example, in the "Teaching" section of the annual performance review, institutions can ask faculty to identify what steps law teachers took to get to know their students and support them.

Inclusive Socratic Teachers Design Their Courses around Student-Centered Learning Outcomes

Student-centered teaching also includes designing our courses in reverse. We need to start by identifying clear learning outcomes in which we want students to achieve competency by the end of the course. Law teachers need to concretely identify the skills, knowledge, and values that they want students to have acquired by the end of the course. Reverse course design pushes law teachers to answer the vital and eminently student-centered questions: "Why are we doing this? What is the purpose? How will I use it in real life?" These questions necessarily demand teaching that is student, skills, client, and community centered and not simply exam or professor centered. This conceptual pivot, in turn, makes classrooms more equitable and effective.

That simple revelation in teaching is critical to cultivating a student-centered classroom, and it was a long time coming. Law teaching has predominantly relied on the Socratic method, with little emphasis on measuring the effectiveness of its results. There has been little intentionality in course design beyond marching through the various topics of the course sequentially along with the book. Law teachers generally take comfort in conformity by replicating how *they* learned the law decades earlier. These methods have supported the longevity and endurance of the traditional Socratic method, but they surely do not equate with effective, inclusive, or equitable classrooms.

The ABA standards governing accreditation were notably revised in 2014 to explicitly implement the concepts of reverse course design. The reforms require law schools to state learning outcomes and to measure student achievement of these identified outcomes.[12] Schools moved quickly to adopt learning outcomes at the institutional and course level. Law teachers developed a savvy understanding of what key words accurately captured measurable learning outcomes (e.g., analyze, apply, locate, advise) and which words did not (e.g., understand, learn). Beyond inserting some magic language on a syllabus and institutional website, though, these accreditation reforms did not systemically upend the content or techniques of traditional Socratic classrooms. Fully actualizing the benefits of outcome-based teaching through assessment is discussed further in Chapter 8. As a preview, we have notably misstepped by not looking institutionally at the *results* of those learning outcomes through an equity lens.

Law schools have been slower to really embrace meaningful reverse course design, and Socratic courses have been even slower yet (if at all). It has been largely perceived as a syllabus update, not a transformation in approach. This reluctance profoundly stifles necessary change. Paulo Freire's transformative work, *Pedagogy of the Oppressed,* tells us that "trusting the people is the indispensable precondition for revolutionary change." Education is not transformative when it is merely "banking" concepts, as educators "fill up" their students with knowledge.[13] Effective and transformative education positions students and teachers to work together. Such a mindset shift is critical to leverage the diversity of student experiences to make learning more engaging, effective, inclusive, and equitable.

Reverse course design, when implemented authentically, directs instructors away from a one-dimensional arc of course design, churning robotically through casebook chapters. Reverse course design instead directs instructors toward methodologically setting and achieving identified course goals built around the students. It provides a framework for law teachers to teach toward students achieving goals, not toward getting to the end of the casebook. Law teachers identify macrogoals for the course, break those goals down into smaller components, and then design learning activities, formative assessments, and summative assessments to support students in achieving each of those learning outcomes.[14] While casebooks are one component of reverse course design, students need far more transparency and clarity regarding the learning outcomes and their progression toward achievement. Reverse course design can efficiently and effectively map on to Socratic law teaching to make it more effective and more inclusive. Figure 3 visualizes this process.

Let's dig deeper into each part of this process as it relates to student-centered teaching in Socratic classrooms.

Identify large student-centered goals that focus on the big idea of the course or unit and then break those goals into smaller, well-defined learning outcomes.

Law teachers begin by identifying their student-centered learning goals. These learning goals state the knowledge, skills, and values that the

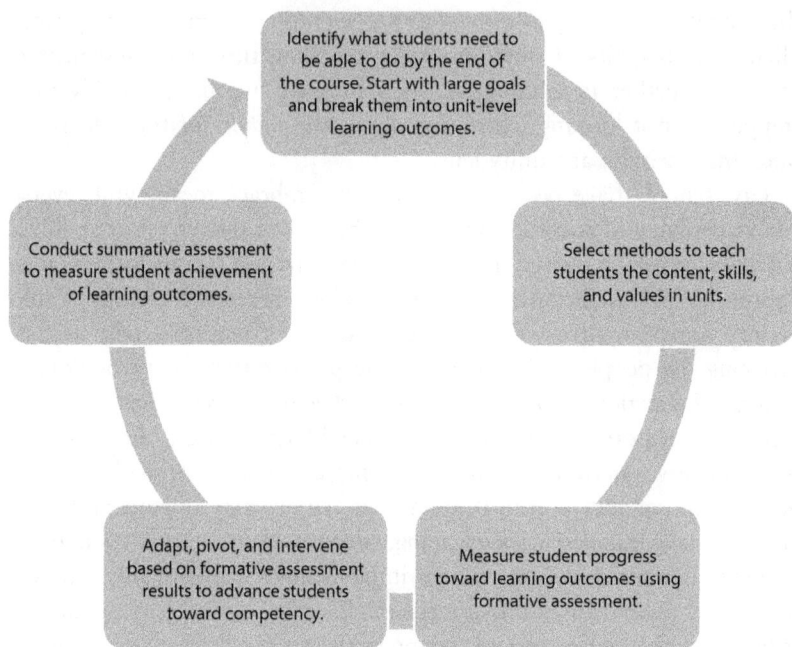

Identify what students need to be able to do by the end of the course. Start with large goals and break them into unit-level learning outcomes.

Select methods to teach students the content, skills, and values in units.

Measure student progress toward learning outcomes using formative assessment.

Adapt, pivot, and intervene based on formative assessment results to advance students toward competency.

Conduct summative assessment to measure student achievement of learning outcomes.

FIGURE 3. Reverse course design in Socratic law teaching. Illustration by the author.

teacher expects the students to have by course completion.[15] Socratic classrooms should not let "readiness for the bar exam" or "prepare for the final exam" sit clumsily as circular and unstated goals that do not serve student learning. Rather, Socratic teachers should identify concrete goals connected squarely to practice preparedness in the broadest sense. For example, a large student learning goal in a family law course might be to "advise clients in family law matters" or "predict likely outcomes in custody and property disputes." These larger goals help students bridge the course's relevance to law practice. In a Socratic classroom, stated goals provide vital purpose and transparency for students.

Next law teachers break down their large learning outcomes into subgoals. For example, break down a large goal like "advise clients in family law matters" to more manageable components, such as "explain to clients how the property distribution process works" or "counsel clients regarding the joint custody presumption and its effect on individual cases." Learning outcomes can also embed explicit commitments to diversity, equity, and inclusion in the law school class.[16] The law teacher can design their teaching around achieving these learning outcomes.

Students can then demonstrate their knowledge and skills through assessment tasks.[17]

Select teaching methods for achieving identified outcomes.

Law teachers should then decide which teaching format and activities they will use to help students achieve these stated competencies.[18] If a professor wants students to be able to advise clients about the property distribution process in divorce, then that might occur in a Socratic exchange, drawing out the legal advice from cases X and Y. It might also occur in a group client-counseling simulation after the cases. It might occur in a "goldfish bowl" role-play, where select students model client counseling on this topic for the rest of the class. Client emails, client-meeting role-plays, and legislative debates, for example, can bring students to higher-order tasks than just "remembering" or "understanding" the rules. Most existing casebooks have this type of content embedded already through practice problems. Technology can help replicate assignments annually and provide feedback without burdening the law teacher in a large course (e.g., model answers, pop-up answers, peer review).

Measure student performance of identified learning outcomes.

Students need formative assessments to help them monitor their growth in acquiring the identified knowledge, skills, or values stated in learning outcomes. These methods can take multiple shapes and forms, such as quizzes, exams, essays, assignments, and projects.[19] They need not all involve individual professor-student feedback. Notably, Socratic teaching and the final course exam have historically been the dominant—if not exclusive—assessment methods in Socratic classes. Socratic teaching itself *can* provide formative assessments if performed fairly and transparently and if the teacher is willing to do the work of providing feedback, which is different than just continuing the Socratic questioning throughout the semester. Using Socratic teaching as formative assessments requires fair distribution of on-call turns and active management of the roster. More abstract "hide the ball" versions of questioning students are quite unlikely to give students any meaningful assessments, instead leaving them feeling contorted and confused. Techniques deploying fear and humiliation similarly skew assessments entirely, rendering this technique performative and distracting only.

Simply stated, if the Socratic method is a form of assessment, students need to know how they are performing with it.

Rarely do Socratic law teachers candidly and transparently engage students regarding how their Socratic participation moves them toward competence in the course's stated learning outcomes, even though law teachers might unconsciously observe the growth. Students in Socratic classrooms often understand only how they move from content unit A to content unit B in a course (e.g., from intentional torts to negligence). Rarely, however, do they see how their learning outcomes are progressing from a skills-acquisition standpoint. Law teachers do not generally narrate the learning process in this way or use formative assessments in such explicit ways.

Instead, with the transition from unit to unit, consider explicitly ratcheting up expectations for the progression of Socratic participation as well. For example, students studying intentional torts in August of their first year might only be able to extract a rule from a case and work on their objective understanding of that rule. By midsemester, however, those same students might be expected to apply a medical malpractice rule to a new set of facts. In unit A expectations might be framed around case comprehension. The next unit might include higher expectations regarding identifying the procedural disposition of a case. The following unit might expect students to start delivering legal conclusions to the client in oral or written form. This is especially so for first-year classes, where there is critical foundational work to do.

There are several concrete ways to provide students with transparent formative feedback. Weekly or periodic emails to students about class performance broadly can be a helpful tool to use the Socratic method as an assessment tool. Messages, particularly in a first-year course, might progress as follows throughout the semester:

1. Congratulate the students on completing their first round of the Socratic method. Encourage students to try to relax into the dialogue, having gotten those jitters out of the way.

2. Nudge students toward listening carefully to the rhythm and sequencing of the Socratic exchanges to stylize their case briefing practices adaptively.

3. Challenge students to progress toward applying concepts to future clients. Who will benefit from these rules? Who will be harmed by them?

4. Close out the semester by moving Socratic exchanges toward rigorous client counseling that defines and deploys strong termi-

nology from the field, makes predictions with degrees of certainty and procedural context, and considers law-reform proposals.

5. Explicitly grade students in their Socratic performance in the classroom learning management systems, even with simple metrics like "met expectations" or "exceeded expectations."

Notably, though, if the Socratic method of teaching is both an approach to deliver the content and an approach to measure competencies, then faculty are doubling down on the effectiveness of this technique to both teach to those learning outcomes and assess the achievement of those learning outcomes. This is circular and flawed under the principles of reverse course design.

If the Socratic method and perhaps a midterm are the primary formative assessment techniques deployed, then law teachers need to help students see how the Socratic method relates to the exam as the selected teaching technique. This can be simple and obvious. For example, if students are engaged with a new hypothetical after learning a case, law teachers might simply say, "Hypotheticals like these are what your final exam will look like as well." This adds vital transparency connecting the teaching method to the assessment method. If your assessment techniques are a midterm and a final exam, help students see how, if at all, the midterm differs from the final exam. Is it a "dry run" of the exam? Is it an incremental step in the learning continuum? Law teachers should then adapt their teaching methods to this formative feedback.

Adapt in response to formative assessment.

Formative assessment works in both directions. It is a way for students to gauge their mastery of the material. It also provides law teachers with vital feedback about the effectiveness of their teaching methods. Rarely do law teachers use it to shape their own teaching though. This is especially so if midterms are intended to play a formative assessment role. Because most midterms are more often delivered as a practice run of a final exam *for students,* this is often just modeling what summative assessment would be like. This just previews the anxiety of summative assessment. It does not necessarily provide meaningful feedback to students or law teachers. Instead, techniques such as practice problems, multiple-choice questions, group work, or bar exam questions are more likely to provide meaningful feedback to students and law teachers.

Conduct summative assessment.

Reverse course design ends with summative assessment, measuring whether students have met the stated learning outcomes. Chapter 8 addresses this further. The key point here is that summative assessment should not be a tool to just rack and stack students. Rather, it should be a tool to measure students against the full suite of learning outcomes that you designed your course around. Many savvy law teachers have added thoughtful learning outcomes to the course, but they have not adapted their summative assessment practices to measure achievement. By the final exam, students might be able to evaluate the strengths and weaknesses of the law in a policy question. Students might also be prepared to create something with the course content, like a jury instruction or client email, thus reaching a higher order of learning. The key guidance is to add transparency to the selected assessment methods and the relationship between them.

Deploying these methods of reverse course design yields more student-centered teaching, which makes Socratic classrooms more effective, equitable, and inclusive.[20] The principles of reverse course design can also move Socratic teaching toward more skills-centered, client-centered, and community-centered approaches, in addition to being explicitly student centered. This Socratic-teaching value need not be revolutionary or burdensome. It simply creates transparent expectations as to what students should be able to do at the end of the course and how their teachers intend to get them there. The Socratic method should not lurk in the shadows of outcome-based teaching.

CULTIVATING SKILLS-CENTERED SOCRATIC CLASSROOMS

Socratic classrooms can also be shaped in skills-centered ways. It is not enough for students to "remember" and "understand" rules of law when they leave courses. They should be able to *do* some select practical tasks with those skills or at least understand which practical skills are part of that field. In a large lecture-style bar course, skills-centered Socratic approaches might simply be about skills sensitization as compared to skills mastery. Even using existing course materials, the Socratic method can do more to bring active legal cases to life beyond abstract discussions of rules of law.

Too many performances of the Socratic method are not helping our students prepare for law practice. Rather, if skills such as oral communication, interpreting and understanding legal materials, and compiling facts are consistently cited as more valuable to practicing attorneys, we can liberate our Socratic classrooms and redirect them. Studies instead emphasize critical competencies like "creativity/innovation, problem solving, practical judgment, listening, strategic planning, organizing, business development, working with others, integrity/honesty, stress management, self-development, and the ability to 'see the world through the eyes of others' as vital lawyering skills."[21] Workplace skills also rank high in value, including confidentiality, punctuality, integrity, respectfulness, and listening skills.[22] Thus, the evolving legal profession compels us to think differently about how we prepare our students.

Instead, many existing Socratic approaches are merely rule-based and outcome-based only.[23] Yet each case has skills inherently packed into it for easy discussion, sensitization, and exploration. Consider some of these lawyering skills to emphasize for students in Socratic dialogue:

- Why did the client contact an attorney? What obligations did the attorney-client relationship create, such as client intake, retainer letters, attorney fees, ethical duties, and attorney-client privilege?

- What obstacles might have prevented prospective clients from contacting a lawyer, such as access to justice barriers, legal marketing, or the economics of law practice?

- What legal authority would the lawyer have found at the outset of the case? What was the source of the legal authority (e.g., constitutional law, statutory law, regulations, case law, etc.). Was the law favorable to the client? If it was not favorable, what advocacy strategies might have helped the lawyer achieve change (e.g., storytelling, procedural maneuvers, negotiation tactics, changed political, social, or economic conditions)? How should the lawyer advise the client regarding the likelihood of success?

- How did the case progress through procedural steps? Did a jury or judge decide the issues? Did the case litigate or settle? What motions were filed and why? How did the lawyers' understanding of the facts progress over time?

- How was the case resolved? Did it meet the client's objectives? How should the lawyer advise the client of the results, particularly if unfavorable? What rights does the client have next, if any?

Think about the transformative potential of each Socratic case dialogue reframed in a skill-based approach, using Box 4 to stimulate thinking.

Box 4. Reframing Socratic Dialogue Using a Skills-Based Approach

Instead of a sequence of abstract Socratic questions, the same content can be framed around a sequence of skills-centered Socratic questions. These modifications reframe and refocus the existing cases and materials that law teachers use already, which meets instructors where they are in both their style and comfort level. These modifications yield several benefits for students. They sensitize students to the skills that will make them successful lawyers. They also promote transparency in class performance expectations.

Instead of	*What are the facts of the case?*
Try	• What facts led the parties to hire a lawyer?
	• What facts were missing or unknown to the lawyer at the outset?
	• What tools would the lawyer use to uncover or prove the facts that we now read in an appellate casebook?
To sensitize students to	• Client-intake skills
	• Client-interviewing skills
	• Client-counseling skills
	• Fact-gathering skills
	• Attorney-client ethics
	• Discovery skills

• • •

Instead of	*What is the issue in the case?*
Try	• What did the parties want to get out of the case?
	• What legal theories helped each side pursue its objectives?
	• What uncertainty did the law present in seeking each side's desired outcome?
	• How did the trial court resolve that uncertainty, and on what sources did it rely?
	• How did each side want the appellate court to resolve the uncertainty, and on what sources did it rely?

To sensitize students to	• Legal research skills
	• Hierarchy of authority
	• Case strategy
	• Case theory
	• Issue framing
	• Client-counseling skills
	• Attorney-client ethics

• • •

Instead of	*What was the court's holding?*
Try	• Who prevailed at the trial court level?
	• What options are available to the losing party?
	• What standard of review governs on appeal?
	• How does the possibility of appeal shape the client counseling for the prevailing party?
	• What resources will an appeal take?
	• What considerations might shape whether to appeal?
To sensitize students to	• Standards of review
	• Client counseling
	• Law-practice management
	• Legal processes

Reframing Socratic techniques around skills yields several benefits. Skills-centered techniques make the Socratic method about lawyering instead of about the professors and their power to control the dialogue. This is more inclusive for all students to engage in and to build their professional identity. Skills-centered Socratic teaching is more responsive to professional calls for reform at every level. These techniques also align Socratic courses with the curricular reforms and innovations happening elsewhere in our institutions, such as experiential learning courses, seminars, and clinics. Skills-centered teaching can thus catalyze other aspects of the curriculum.

Skills-centered teaching transforms the professor-student relationship to avoid the "banking" approach.[24] Instead, student and teacher are collaborators working to solve problems together. A skills-centered Socratic method could also do *more* than sensitize students to skills. For example, Bridge to Practice books and other skills supplements help students create documents representative of the field and perform core tasks in the field.[25] This previews the practice of law more authentically and accurately than the typical "it depends" context of a Socratic dialogue. Skills-centered materials avoid overstretching faculty by not "reinventing the wheel." Instead, law teachers can deliver prevetted materials with model answers, grading guidelines, and built-in classroom credibility. For example, torts students can complete a mock deposition of a witness in a malpractice case.[26] Students can draft jury instructions, discovery requests, demand letters, contracts, or complaints to apply the substantive content that they have learned. They can write letters to clients or draft opening statements. They can participate in mediations or negotiations. The Multistate Performance Test from state bars can be an excellent resource for these assignments and assessments.[27] Skills-centered Socratic teaching need not be onerous, but it can be transformative.

Skills-Centered Socratic Teaching Aligns with Bar-Licensure Pivots

A skills-centered approach to Socratic teaching further aligns with both the practice of law and the trajectory of the bar exam as well. The Testing Task Force of the National Conference of Bar Examiners has adopted "Foundational Concepts and Principles" and "Foundational Skills" as the substantive underpinning of its NextGen bar exam.[28] The "Foundational Concepts and Principles" are composed of a combination of traditional bar subjects (e.g., civil procedure, torts, contracts) and the foundational lawyering skills attorneys need (such as research, writing, analysis, fact investigation, client counseling, and negotiation). This revamped test requires less bulk rule memorization and, instead, more higher-order rule applications and work-product creations. The bar exam tests minimal competency in these areas in an integrated way. Students need to show their knowledge of the substantive concepts and principles and then apply that knowledge, using "Foundational Skills" to *do* a representative lawyering task.

This shift in methodology is intended to align with changes in legal education synergistically, "building on the success of clinical legal education programs, alternative dispute resolution programs, and legal writing and analysis programs." The bar exam no longer assumes that the first few years of practice are when new attorneys learn to lawyer. A skills-centered Socratic course is thus more effective in preparing students both for practice and for the bar. It is important that law schools and bar examiners align in their expectations of competencies for the licensure of new attorneys or at least provide candor to new graduates where they do not align.[29]

Skills-Centered Socratic Teaching Aligns with a Changing Profession

Momentum for skills-centered Socratic teaching also comes from the profession. Employers want students to have more robust competencies. The legal profession has encouraged legal education to devote less focus on memorizing rules for heavily weighted final exams. Rather, the profession seeks graduates with more sensitization to communicating, interpreting and understanding legal materials, and compiling facts.[30] Practicing attorneys consistently cite these skills as more valuable than banking large volumes of rules.

As introduced in Chapter 5, the Institute for the Advancement of the American Legal System identified twelve building blocks to develop minimally competent lawyers. These building blocks include an understanding of the threshold concepts of law as well as legal processes and sources of law. They identified how lawyers should be able to interact with clients, identify issues, conduct research, interpret legal materials, communicate, and see the "big picture." They also focused on *how* lawyers work, emphasizing professionalism, workload management, stress management, and self-directed learning.[31]

These building blocks chart a course forward for legal education, deploying skills-based learning, even in a Socratic classroom. Skills-centered techniques are more effective pedagogically because students are regularly applying, analyzing, and examining how rules work in practice. This promotes higher learning competencies. The goal of a Socratic classroom should not be focused so narrowly on filling a "brain full of mush" with common law rules and compelling their application on heavily weighted final exams. Indeed, modern lawyers candidly acknowledge that in practice it would be nearly malpractice to rely on the cache of legal rules learned in law school. Professor Beth Hirschfelder Wilensky empowers us to teach authentically to the work of real lawyers by aligning our teaching with the common skills lawyers use in practice.[32] Law teachers invested in skills-based Socratic teaching can problematically be swimming upstream relative to other institutional values and incentives. The Socratic method has its strengths, but it can also be an impediment to reform if legal education innovates around it without integrating the Socratic teaching method with the other curricular innovations.

Law schools can notably do more as institutions to support skills-centered Socratic teaching too. Faculty-hiring criteria and tenure processes often do not value robust practice experience.[33] Tenure and sabbatical processes tend to value rigorously traditional legal scholarship produced independently. Schools might instead allow interested faculty to pursue more practice-oriented writing, such as amici briefs, policy papers, and legislation. Service sabbaticals can also be impactful for faculty to work in nonprofits and the public sector for a term, thus allowing them to diversify and refresh their practice experience. Law schools can also offer training, mentoring, awards, and recognitions for faculty teaching in a skills-centered structure.

There are also exciting opportunities for law teachers to collaborate with the local bar or other members of the community to introduce skills. For example, I have done a dental malpractice deposition simulation with lawyers to teach my students about fact gathering, the adversarial process, and lawyering strategy.[34] This is skills, client, and community centered. Likewise, there is space for the ongoing development of new teaching materials, books, and tech tools to support skills-centered Socratic teaching.[35] Professor Aníbal Rosario Lebrón argues further that the use of nontraditional materials is a vital aspect of building a nonhierarchical classroom.[36] He invites us to think more expansively about the kinds of materials we use to engage our students holistically, including TV, blogs, videos, novels, news, and more. Skills-centered classrooms align with the needs of students and the practicing bar alike.

CULTIVATING CLIENT-CENTERED SOCRATIC CLASSROOMS

Socratic classrooms should also be client centered. This is intertwined with skills-centered classrooms. Instead of placing law teachers and their existing expertise as the center of Socratic exchanges, clients can reshape existing teaching materials in dynamic ways. Clients are the foundation of lawyering, and they need to hold a more visible place in the curriculum to authentically reveal what attorneys do.[37] This technique also makes teaching, in turn, more student, skills, and community centered. In practice lawyers do not acquire skills to hold in the abstract. Lawyers acquire knowledge and skills to represent a diverse cross-section of clients, such as individuals, organizations, entities, and governments. This knowledge acquisition and these fundamental skills should likewise be marshaled *to a client-centered end* in our teaching pedagogy too. For example, "Model Rule of Professional Conduct 1.1" requires that each lawyer develop competency in "the legal knowledge, skill, thoroughness and preparation reasonably necessary *to represent clients.*"[38] Legal education should share this foundational anchoring of learning and skills acquisition toward client-centered ends.

Every case in existing casebooks reflects at least two clients and an opportunity to engage in a Socratic exchange about what the clients' objectives were and how the law met or did not meet those objectives. From this repetition across casebooks and classes, students can be sensitized to client-centered lawyering, which inherently cultivates stronger cultural competencies within the profession.[39] Socratic exchanges can center clients in cases by examining how clients came to hire lawyers, what obligations lawyers have to their clients, and how lawyers developed a legal strategy to meet the clients' objectives. Centering clients in Socratic dialogues shows students how to communicate legal outcomes to clients, particularly when the outcome is not favorable and leaves the clients' objectives unfulfilled. This is a valuable skill that all law teachers should be helping their students acquire and cultivate to prepare them for practice.

This teaching technique aligns integrally with skills-centered teaching. It is also more student centered in its transparency. It diffuses traditional classroom hierarchies by centering clients. Client-centered Socratic exchanges are dramatically different than abstract ones centered around a court holding or the law. They are vital to law practice and will become increasingly relevant to the bar exam too. Box 5 identifies a few actionable techniques for applying this recommendation.

Client-centered teaching should carry into client-centered assessment, as discussed further in Chapter 8. When taking traditional issue-spotting exams, students are often weighed down by perennial questions such as these: How much time should I spend on each issue? How should I organize my answer? How should I handle weak or fatal claims? Using a client-centered lens in exam rubrics yields stronger exam rigors because it gives students a purposeful lens through which to conduct analysis. The essay exam assessment metric can be packaged

Box 5. Cultivating More Client-Centered Socratic Classrooms

Begin Socratic case exchanges by asking who hired a lawyer and why, instead of "What are the facts of the case?"

This simple reframing of a standard introductory Socratic question positions the client as the center of the case instead of the professor. It helps students see why clients hire lawyers. It also compels students to connect the law more actively to the clients' original objectives. Clients do not ask questions like "Can I prove proximate causation?" They ask questions about what they can do in response to a harm they have suffered or a challenge they are navigating in their lives. Students have to actively bridge the law to the clients' objectives, just as lawyers do. This is both skills-centered and client-centered thinking. It also yields more student-centered classrooms and fosters a greater sense of belonging because students are sharing a common and transparent objective when lawyering on behalf of clients.

Use classrooms to visualize opposing client representations.

Every case presents the opportunity to depict two clients in an adversarial proceeding. Use the visual layout of your classroom to create teams every time you discuss a case. Call on a student across the room to represent the opposing party. This seizes the layout of the large classroom as a tool to visualize client representations. It actively brings competing arguments to life as the competing legal arguments ping-pong across the classroom. This is also more student centered and community centered because students are lawyering in teams.

Invite co-counsel to represent the same client.

Have students located proximally to the on-call student act as co-counsel, representing the same client. Allow those proximal peers to support the primary on-call student in representing the same client, like a lawyer would do with a difficult case. If the on-call student gets stuck, consider allowing co-counsel to confer by conversing and strategizing with peers, so all students can regroup before the dialogue with the professor resumes. This technique allows the on-call student to achieve the client-centered task with support and avoids students one-upping others vis-à-vis the law teacher. Instead, students work collegially with their co-counsel to advance their client's case.

Flip the Socratic dynamics by positioning the professor as client and the student as lawyer.

Law teachers generally ask questions driven by published appellate cases and their holdings. This leaves students perceiving the flow of the Socratic dialogue as directed by their teacher's intellect and expertise or the appellate court's published opinions. Instead, the law teacher can frame the same questions as the client's questions. The students answer questions to explain what the court did, why it did what it did, and what it means to the client. These types of discussions better prepare students for practice, level the classroom power dynamics, and cultivate a shared purpose. This approach centers clients instead of law teachers, while still relying on the law teacher's expertise and classroom management.

Replace abstract hypotheticals by applying legal rules with hypotheticals that center a client.

Law teachers often turn to discussing hypotheticals after they finish teaching a legal rule. The purpose of these hypotheticals is to test the application of the rule. What are the rule's boundaries? What are some of the nuanced exceptions to the rule? Instead of abstract what-if questions to wrap up a case or unit discussion, package hypotheticals around business generations within a law-practice setting. After the class role-plays representing the clients depicted in the casebook, faculty can introduce the same hypotheticals as new clients who contact the same lawyers with different factual scenarios. What advice would students give these new clients who present added factual or procedural nuances? What is their predictive legal advice based on the legal authority they just studied? How is their advice shaped by the underlying opinion? This technique easily repackages existing casebook practice problems with a more engaging and effective client-centered delivery.

Assess client counseling on the exam.

Our assessment methods should align with our teaching methods. Client-centered Socratic dialogue should accompany an expectation that students advise clients on the final exam. Like the Socratic exchanges, this is a subtle, yet transformative, modification. Most essay exams give students scenarios for which they are expected to predict the legal outcomes. Perhaps it is implied that these are clients the students are representing, but explicitly communicating this expectation lends more purpose and transparency to exam performance. If students perceive exam performance as a task in which they abstractly predict conclusions, it is easy to see why students might answer with conclusory and cursory writing. If students instead understand the same exam prompts as advising clients, they will be more likely to discuss rules, rationales, and predictions with depth and detail. Appendix A provides a sample grading rubric that assesses client counseling.

around how *clients* would perceive an answer instead of leaving students thinking they are writing to meet the idiosyncratic preferences of the law teacher.

In Chapter 8 and Appendix A, I share a grading rubric that includes a client-centered assessment metric that can translate into any style of essay exam or subject area. It tells students transparently to analyze claims with a depth and thoroughness that supports a client's understanding of the law. This includes tethering arguments to the parties that will raise them. Instead of the passive answer that "it will be argued," students should explicitly name the party that will raise the argument or counterargument. This includes telling the client what the rule is and perhaps why it is what it is, especially when the claim is contrary to the client's expectations or objectives. If there are strategic reasons why one claim or course of action is better than another, students should advise the client accordingly. Thus, if students spot four causes of action arising from the same set of facts, they should explain which is the best claim and why. It also directs students to situate the legal analysis in a procedural, evidentiary, and litigation-based context—not just who will win, but when and how this might occur in the process. Many law faculty might implicitly value these savvy and sophisticated aspects of a strong exam answer. Including a client-centered component directly in the assessment rubric lends more transparency to students, allowing all students to perform equitably and ensuring that the style and emphasis of class discussions aligns with the method of assessment.

The effects of this shift toward client-centered Socratic teaching are transformative. A client-centered Socratic approach is more inclusive and inviting because it calls all students to action and participation as attorneys and as professionals instead of as isolated "skulls full of mush" (as Professor Kingsfield stated) in dialogue with the lone professor positioned at the podium. Students grow more proficient at reading cases when reading with the perspective of clients. After spending multiple semesters using their casebooks as staged client representations, they will be even more prepared to represent real clients in their clinics and externship settings. Thus, this teaching approach catalyzes other pedagogical innovations, such as clinics, simulations, and experiential-learning courses.[40] Students also envision themselves within the field more meaningfully and concretely, thus cultivating their professional identity. The professor becomes a facilitator or a "guide on the side," helping students learn to be lawyers. These techniques work with existing materials, class sizes, and room layouts. They engender a more interactive and purposeful class dialogue, which counters the competitive and individualistic approaches that can leave students detached or dejected.

CULTIVATING COMMUNITY-CENTERED SOCRATIC CLASSROOMS

Socratic teaching can also be grounded in the local and global community, the professional legal community, and all the other meanings of community in between. Community-centered Socratic classrooms avoid abstract "in the air" discussions and better prepare students for practice. Community-centered classrooms are also about the relationship between the doctrine and communities instead of the professor and the student. Let's consider some concrete ways to develop these different dimensions of community-centered Socratic classrooms.

The Community of Legal Professionals

To better align with shifts in legal education, Socratic classrooms can be styled more intentionally toward building professional identity, helping students see how they are entering a professional community with other lawyers, and cultivating a strong sense of self. Professional identity examines "what it means to be a lawyer and the special obligations lawyers have to their clients and society."[41] It is about the values, principles, and practices that are foundational to lawyering. In February 2022 the American Bar Association's Council of the Section of Legal Education and Admissions to the Bar amended Standard 303 of the accreditation standard requiring law schools to "provide substantial opportunities to students for the development of a professional identity."[42]

Socratic classrooms can be styled more intentionally to meet this accreditation standard by building professional identity and helping students see themselves joining a professional community of attorneys. This aligns with skills-centered and client-centered Socratic methods because many aspects of current approaches to Socratic teaching are actually *distorting* the practice of law for students. Professor Beth Hirschfelder Wilensky argues in "Dethroning Langdell" that our pedagogy practice needs to be accurate in informing students about what they will do as lawyers; otherwise, our pedagogy is inauthentic.[43] Our Socratic pedagogy must therefore authentically align with the practice of law.

The new accreditation standard requires schools to provide "frequent opportunities" for professional-identity development "during each year of law school and in a variety of courses and co-curricular and professional development activities."[44] The requirement for professional-identity formation should be implemented throughout various courses and not as an isolated program because of the reflection and growth that goes into such cultivation. Community-centered Socratic classrooms would help support students on their journey to becoming ethical and competent members of their profession.

This students-as-lawyers model also aligns with the NextGen bar exam. The bar exam is moving squarely toward measuring student readiness for practice too. A shift in Socratic teaching is thus an efficient way to achieve alignment. Reframing the Socratic classroom to model a professional legal community is prudent structurally and symbolically. Students learning skills and representing clients are also inherently role-playing as part of a community. The Socratic classroom offers important and abundant opportunities to model lawyering within the legal community. Faculty can tease out the ethical complexities and professional demands embedded in existing case coverage consistent with the skills-centered and client-centered Socratic method. This in turn might also improve the overall wellness of students as they study law in Socratic classrooms with people and their interests centered.

HOW LAW TEACHERS CAN BRIDGE STUDENTS
INTO THE LEGAL PROFESSION

- Take students to the courthouse to observe a case in your field. A judge or judicial panel might even bring a real case to your law school, as we did annually at the University of Louisville.[45]
- Have students interview lawyers to find out more about what their practice in the field looks like.
- Bring in a panel of lawyers in your field.
- Have students write reflections on how the field in which you are teaching aligns with their professional values, interests, and goals.

The Community

Law is also distinctly a service profession. Socratic teaching "in the air" is not effective at preparing students to practice. The Socratic classroom should prepare students to apply concepts in their community. Paradoxically, large Socratic classes are quite effective classes to incorporate community-centered teaching. With the largest number of students, they offer the most voices and perspectives to draw on. Yet Socratic classrooms tend to deploy appellate casebooks generally devoid of any grounding in a particular community.

A perspectiveless, abstract appellate framing leaves unexamined the underlying hierarchies and power structures of the law's effects on others. Inclusive Socratic teaching compels student engagement in exploring how legal doctrine shapes various communities and what further reforms best meet community needs. Tethering Socratic classrooms to the local community would also better prepare students for community-based law clinics, externships, community service, and community-engaged scholarship, as well as foster student engagement and wellness.

More community-centered classrooms also must be buttressed and reinforced by institutional norms, values, and incentives.[46] Even faculty who are experienced in their fields of practice may not have practiced law in the community in which they eventually teach due to the geographic breadth of the job market. Most faculty have likely not practiced directly in all their teaching areas. Over time, faculty also grow further removed from practice experience. Thus, institutions may need to consider carefully how they value community engagement as service and how they can support faculty engagement in ways that align with annual reviews, performance evaluations, and tenure criteria.

HOW LAW TEACHERS CAN MAKE SOCRATIC CLASSROOMS MORE COMMUNITY CENTERED

- Regularly discuss local news stories that raise issues of importance to your class. Consider what neighborhoods, businesses, groups, and individuals might be affected. Consider the role that lawyers have played and will play in the issues.
- Conduct mock legislative debates about pending bills of interest in your field or about disputed areas of law. Brainstorm a list of possible stakeholders or constituencies and have students role-play in the debate.
- Have students research a bill of interest pending in your local or state legislative body, thus practicing their research skills, statutory interpretation, and community-centered application.

- Bring in community speakers to highlight seminal local cases.
- Make classroom time available for students to bring in current events for discussion.
- Host a community tour related to your field. For example, in my torts class, I co-led a "toxic torts" tour in the community with an environmental law professor. On a lighter note, I also took my torts class axe-throwing (!!!) and organized a discussion on liability with the facility's owner.[47]

Diverse Community Perspectives

The inclusive Socratic classroom also explores the application of legal concepts to diverse communities. Preparation for the practice of law demands this.[48] Law schools have obligations to demonstrate concrete commitments to diversity and inclusion pursuant to existing accreditation standards.[49] These obligations, explored more in Chapter 8, need to be rooted in the full substantive study of law, not just niche seminars and ad hoc programs. The effects of laws on diverse communities must be centered in classrooms in the curricular core to have inclusive law schools.

Embracing this shared Socratic value begins with recognizing that existing Socratic approaches, if left unchecked, risk privileging the voices of a narrow few. Community-centered Socratic teaching is a correction to the blind spots of traditional Socratic performances. Considering the law from the perspectives of all communities, to be effective, needs to be woven into the curriculum systemically instead of clumsily inserted as a miscellaneous add-on. Law teachers need not hold power and control over these discussions, but they do need to be facilitated and structured with clear ground rules for success.

These approaches work best when they engage the students, and they are grounded squarely in the practice of law, instead of politics or opinions. Notably, these approaches should incorporate *all* students and *all* faculty, thus mitigating the critique that diverse students are left to raise the perspectives of diverse communities. In a well-designed Socratic classroom, all students are regularly applying the doctrine to a broad cross-section of communities to evaluate and assess the rules.[50] Community-centered teaching holds a vital role in Socratic classrooms.

HOW LAW TEACHERS CAN PUT SOCRATIC
LEARNING IN CONVERSATION WITH *ALL*
COMMUNITIES

- Assign students to blog about a course topic from the perspective of a nonprofit or community stakeholder.
- Have students advise different community groups, civics associations, or constituencies about the effects of a law.
- Use publications by the Feminist Judgments Project, which rewrites iconic legal opinions to center feminist legal theory and publishes these rewritten opinions by field, to consider alternate perspectives, contest understandings of how judicial opinions are drafted, or fill pedagogical gaps.[51]
- Position students to lead a legislative caucus to consider the pros and cons of a proposed law.
- Draft amendments to a particular law in response to critiques from constituents.
- Brainstorm grant proposals drafted by a nonprofit to try to reform an area of law (e.g., the abuse and neglect system in family law or domestic violence responses in criminal law).

. . .

Collectively, our Socratic classrooms can do more to catalyze reforms in legal education and to make learning more inclusive, effective, and engaging. This can begin with coalescing Socratic pedagogy around values that are student, skills, client, and community centered. Collaterally, these proposals can also foster more community in law teaching across our fields as well. We tend to think of law teaching in starkly hierarchical and siloed ways. The more we modernize Socratic teaching, the more we open space for intergenerational and interdisciplinary collaboration, mentoring, and innovation, thus building a community of Socratic law teachers committed to achieving shared goals. The recommendations presented in this chapter can all be achieved efficiently and pragmatically with existing resources and materials. These are just the beginning, however. Our students will benefit from our ongoing, collaborative dialogue about how to identify and implement these shared Socratic values successfully and sustainably.

CHAPTER 8

Measuring Effective, Inclusive, and Equitable Socratic Classrooms

Removing the Socratic classroom's presumptive reverence and implicit immunity compels us to then measure and assess the remaining Socratic techniques objectively as students, teachers, and institutions.[1] Legal education can strengthen how it measures and assesses Socratic teaching to ensure it is effective, inclusive, and equitable. Law teachers generally do little to self-critique or analyze the effectiveness of their teaching or their students' learning, even when using long-standing assessment metrics or tools such as exams or course evaluations. Rarely are any assessment tools used consciously for professional growth or development for either students or law teachers. High-stakes, summative law school exams are more often used to simply rack and stack students.[2] Teaching evaluations are used in wildly divergent ways, depending on the law teacher's status and seniority, as they are too often housed solely within the tenure, promotion, and contract-renewal processes, which are distinctly professor centered, not student centered.

Yet there are vital, student-centered reasons to measure and monitor learning to inform our teaching and our students' readiness to begin practicing law. Chapter 2 presents enduring critiques of Socratic classrooms that should compel our reflection on both the effectiveness and the equities of meeting learning outcomes. Attrition data are further insightful. For example, while White students were 62 percent of law school enrollment in 2016, they accounted for 49 percent of attrition in the first year. First-year law students of color began with 30 percent of total enrollment but accounted for a disproportionate 44 percent of law school attrition.[3] These students likely enrolled in only one legal research and writing course, and the remainder of their courses were likely traditional Socratic classes. These statistics call for measurement and inquiry into the equities and inclusiveness of Socratic classrooms.

By retooling existing feedback and assessment mechanisms, effective, inclusive, and equitable classrooms can be explicitly designed, measured, and refined. Effectiveness is about students meeting the stated learning outcomes. Inclusion is about students' sense of belonging and about meeting the needs of all learners. Equity is interrelated with effectiveness and inclusion. Equity requires that we provide the appropriate tools and supports to see *all* students through to competency and success, recognizing that all students enter with varying obstacles and starting points. This chapter focuses on pragmatic assessment pivots that work within standard budgets, capabilities, and infrastructure by examining existing tools of student learning, teaching, and institutional assessments. The first section is about how we assess our students' learning and how they assess our teaching. It considers the roles of all stakeholders—students, teachers, and institutions—in effective assessment. The second section is about bringing the accreditation norms that govern and incentivize our individual and institutional practices into alignment with stronger assessment practices.

ALIGN STUDENT-ASSESSMENT PRACTICES WITH SHARED SOCRATIC VALUES

Effective assessment is a loop whereby both students and law teachers acquire feedback to strengthen teaching and learning practices. Assessment should collect information for the purpose of ensuring that teaching is achieving effective student learning.[4] It moves law teachers from knowing what *they* did to knowing what their *students* can do. That realization can be transformative for many law teachers. Candidly, this realization can also be quite far removed from how law teachers generally think about assessment. Debra Moss Vollweiler describes how many law teachers confuse teaching and learning, concluding that professors give knowledge and students receive it rather than thinking about what students learned as a metric to understand what was taught effectively.[5] This section considers the role of students, teachers, and institutions in assessing student learning effectively.

Assessing Student Learning

Cultivating an effective, inclusive, and equitable Socratic classroom leads us to examine whether our practices align with the three steps of effective assessment of student learning:

1. Set goals for what students should be able to do when they finish the course.

2. Collect formative and summative feedback as evidence of whether students are achieving the identified goals.

3. Use the assessment content collected to take action toward improving teaching.[6]

The static nature of Socratic teaching over the past one hundred years of legal education is insufficient to justify its unmodified endurance. No teaching technique is immune from these baseline expectations of applying best practices in assessment.

Our students need us to think more boldly and responsively about assessment. Chapter 3 describes the general detachment, disappointment, and depression hovering over modern law students. Notably, when students described the *source* of their detachment and disillusionment, they often cited the competitive grading framework that dominates Socratic classrooms distinctly as one root of the malaise they experienced. They described how their otherwise strong connections to classmates and instructors were compromised by the values placed on rankings, curves, highest-grade awards, and elite job placements. Scholars have long called for a reexamination of law school assessment practices for a variety of reasons.[7]

Thus a vital starting place to achieving effective, inclusive, and equitable Socratic classrooms is to align our assessment practices with our shared Socratic values. Our methods of assessing student learning need to also be student, skills, client, and community centered. Legal education has three key areas for growth in assessing student learning in Socratic classrooms:

1. Align shared Socratic teaching practices with compatible Socratic assessment practices.

2. Normalize institutionalized and individualized action in response to the measurement of student competencies.

3. Implement accreditation standards that measure student-learning outcomes through an equity lens across our institutions.

Let's consider each in turn. Existing practices of summative and formative assessment in Socratic classrooms are mostly just about racking and stacking students, not meaningful assessments of student learning. The high-stakes summative final exam is a hallmark feature of the traditional Socratic classroom. Most Socratic classes give an issue-spotting final essay exam, in which students apply a set of rules and concepts to a fictional fact pattern, using analytic skills to predict results. While the traditional issue-spotting exam plays a limited summative assessment role, it is often clunky and flawed in implementation. Summative assessment, in concept, should be a final measurement tool, assessing whether students met the learning outcomes for the course. It should provide feedback to the student and teacher alike.

These exams are not currently aligned with student-centered, skills-centered, client-centered, or community-centered teaching practices. These exams are generally not student centered. Students find these issue-spotting exams generally frustrating and challenging for all the wrong reasons. It is hard for students to ascertain, either in advance or afterward, what denotes a strong exam versus a weak exam, given the range of content, order, and style of submissions. This is even more so if the professor does not provide a grading rubric or memorandum to explain the grading standards. Accordingly, students often feel like they are navigating the idiosyncrasies of teachers' respective styles instead of deploying a set of transferable and useful skills. Students are left simply starving for more information about expectations and models for success regarding exam performance. Absent this clarity, students work maddeningly hard, trying to succeed. Many students deploy "whisper networks," relying on upper-level students to advise them of what they understand each professor to want. Not all students have access to such informal networks, however, which can feed already existing inequities.

Nor are traditional, issue-spotting exams very well grounded in lawyering skills. Students are generally assessed on the volume of issue spotting and the rigors of legal analysis. These broad skills, however, are often deployed in the abstract. Students do not generally have to layer their analysis with any insights about client counseling, fact gathering, research, discovery, negotiation, or cultural competency. This reinforces the bifurcation that students already sense between their doctrinal courses and their skills courses, particularly in the first-year curriculum. Further, not only are traditional essay exams disconnected from lawyering skills, but they can also actually incentivize and indoctrinate students into poor lawyering and bar exam perform-ance skills. Traditional law school exams are often administered both with closed notes and tightly timed. These parameters often yield rushed, sloppy writing with imperfect language not at all grounded in its audience or purpose—two foundational hallmarks of effective legal writing.

Practicing lawyers instead value precision, accuracy, and polish, par-ticularly when writing for an audience such as a court or a client. Tradi-tional law school exams sometimes distinctly value a high-volume spew-ing of legal analysis. One colleague of mine, for example, memorably measured exam performance using a "clicker," like a nightclub bouncer would use counting patrons, to track the quantity of issues students flagged. One-dimensional measurement techniques undermine the judg-ment involved in students weighing the strengths and weaknesses of issues, the value of strategizing which claims best meet the client's objectives, and the consideration of resources that a lawyer would deploy in resolving multiple, competing claims.

The instructions given to students for the final exam are often sparse, which can undermine the equities of student performance. Likewise, only sometimes are assessment rubrics or grading guidelines provided by the law teacher in advance of the exam. As with Socratic teaching practices, these norms are likely a case of faculty replicating what they know and perpetuating the status quo more than a steadfast commit-ment to the effectiveness, wisdom, or intuitiveness of approaching issue-spotting exams with these parameters. The results, however, can exacerbate inequities and reward the students privileged enough to already know this insider information.

Finally, the traditional issue-spotting exam format is also often lacking in clients, context, and community. Students are rarely tasked with a specific lawyering role, an identifiable client, or a community within which to conduct legal analysis. Rather, students are often abstractly asked to "analyze all claims and defenses" or some similarly open-ended prompt. This distorts the law. The oft-stated goal of teaching students to "think like a lawyer" cannot occur without deploying substantive knowl-edge on behalf of clients within a profession and a community.

From the professor's perspective, grading these issue-spotting exams is also very tedious and time-consuming to maintain the necessary focus and rigor. The issue-spotting essay has few teaching rewards as a one-time, anonymous document. In contrast, grading final office memo-randa, advice letters, motions, briefs, or student papers such as those submitted in a writing course or seminar often reveal inspiring student growth and skills progression to the law teacher. Students submitting these alternate forms of assessment, in turn, are also preparing a more functional document that can be used in job searches and further refined for the future, which promotes a growth mindset and self-actualized learning. In sum most of the existing practices of assessing student learning through a summative final exam following a Socratic course are either entirely detached from teaching practices or only tethered in ways that are not transparent enough to all students.

The use of formative assessments is also emerging, expanding, and evolving in law schools, even in Socratic classrooms. We collectively have more room for growth and sophistication in how we conceptualize and use formative assessments in Socratic classrooms, however. For Socratic classrooms particularly, law teachers often conclude that deploying formative assessments is constrained by the class sizes. Law teachers are understandably generally overwhelmed by the prospect of grading fifty to one hundred of *any* type of formative assessment because of the intensities involved. Law teachers are generally hampered in their thinking, though, about formative assessment as an all-or-nothing proposition.

Likely because of these constraints, traditional Socratic classrooms often implement formative assessments by delivering a midterm, which is often positioned as a practice run intended to help students perform well on the summative final exam. While these goals and intentions are admirable, the effect of this approach often simply replicates twice over the same uncertainties and anxieties as the summative final without providing meaningful feedback to students or teachers.

The conversation about effective assessment practices thus raises threshold questions of what exactly these summative and formative issue-spotting exams are trying to accomplish for our students: Are exams trying to provide students with formative and summative feedback regarding whether they are approaching and achieving competency in course-learning outcomes? Are exams trying to provide students with summative feedback on their readiness for lawyering and measuring their practice readiness in the field? Are exams measuring student readiness to perform on the bar exam? Are exams giving law teachers feedback on their teaching, such that they can rework their teaching practices? Are exams trying to achieve some combination of these goals? Or are exams merely a tool to rack and stack students to facilitate all the other hierarchies of legal education?

If our exams are intended to be assessment tools to measure student-learning outcomes, it is unlikely we are collectively doing that effectively. Like most law teachers, I responded to the 2014 accreditation reforms by adding course-level learning outcomes to my syllabi. I also added more structured formative assessment to my courses. I worked hard to write the learning outcomes, studied Bloom's Taxonomy, consulted with my campus's Teaching and Learning Center, and followed all the advised best practices to get my learning outcomes placed in the syllabi. What I did not do—and I suspect I am in good company here—is change anything about my summative exam to position it more concretely as a tool to *measure achievement* of the learning outcomes that I worked so hard to draft and conceptualize. Rather, most traditional summative exams measure a narrower set of skills than the course emphasizes, staying tightly focused on analytic skills and the accuracy of legal rules.

Law teachers might alternatively or additionally cite the bar exam as the motivation for using traditional issue-spotting exams as the method of assessment in Socratic classrooms. Each state regulates admission to the legal profession by setting qualifications for licensure, generally including a bar exam.[8] The traditional law school curriculum is therein sustained by students taking a multitude of subjects to prepare for the bar exam. The gatekeeping function of the bar exam has historically left law schools reluctant to innovate.[9]

Even assuming the issue-spotting exam *might* help students cover a wide range of course content and prepare them to perform on the bar exam using basic written analysis skills, the strength of that justification diminishes as the National Conference of Bar Examiners proceeds with its NextGen exam. The NextGen format positions students *as lawyers* to perform a concrete task *for clients,* requiring students to layer on fundamental *skills* with foundational concepts of courses.[10] The test is moving away from largely rewarding bulk rule memorization across a range of practice areas, recognizing that legal competencies include mapping lawyering skills to substantive rules on behalf of clients.

The synergistic alignment of reforms to Socratic classrooms with forthcoming bar exam reforms is also important to advance diversity, equity, and inclusion goals. The bar exam plays an important gatekeeping role to the profession, although many contest its validity and appropriateness in this function. The bar exam has long been criticized for performing its gatekeeping function in ways that exclude along race, gender, and class lines because of both the exam itself and the externalities of what exam readiness demands. The ABA finally released passage rates for 2020 and 2021 by race, ethnicity, and gender. These data revealed the pass rates for first-time test takers by race: Asian, 90 percent; White, 88 percent; Native American, 78 percent; Hispanic, 76 percent; and Black, 66 percent.[11]

Because of how important this test is and because law school pedagogy did *not* actually prepare most students fully for the bar, graduates usually spend two intensive months preparing for the exam. Students are squarely advised to minimize all other "distractions" during this time, especially paid employment. Students are also advised to purchase preparation courses that add thousands of dollars to the cost of law school. These costs embed a privilege into bar performance, allowing the most-resourced students to follow the recommended course of study, while anyone with caregiving or employment responsibilities or unable to purchase the supplement course will likely enter the bar with lower odds of passing. The racial disparities revealed in the recent ABA data call for rigorous and prompt scrutiny of both the bar exam and legal education. Thus the time is now to likewise adapt our assessment practices. Changes to the bar exam liberate our traditional law school exam methods.

The combination of student frustrations, law teacher fatigue, bar reforms, and pedagogical misalignment all collectively lead us to reimagine what our classrooms' assessment practices are truly accomplishing. In practice it is much more likely that assessment practices are used in Socratic classrooms largely as a pure sorting and ranking tool. This is a very different purpose than measuring student learning, and students acutely sense the difference.

Best practices for summative assessment suggest that exams should be tied to institutional and course-level learning outcomes to measure student competencies. Learning outcomes identify what law teachers want students to know, understand, and do by the end of the class. Our summative exams should test the achievement of these outcomes. Thus, if we transform our Socratic classrooms to deliver the teaching in student-centered, skills-centered, client-centered, and community-centered ways, our exams should transform in turn.

Summative assessments should be a reinforcing process, whereby we validate whether teaching methods achieved learning outcomes for all learners. A few small adaptations can go a long way toward leveraging the exam to more effective ends. Making summative exams—like the Socratic classroom—more student, skills, client, and community centered aligns with shared classroom values. These adaptations need not be arduous; indeed, they might reduce grading burdens. Let's consider some concrete techniques that are scalable and readily implementable.

Student-Centered Assessment Practices

Student-centered assessment practices begin by transparently advising students what the format of assessment is. Transparency is vital for equity. Students should never walk into an exam unsure of how the exam is structured or designed. They should know what percentage of the exam is in essay format versus multiple choice versus other assessment metrics. They should know the relative weighting of questions, so they can allocate their time appropriately. Students should know very early in the course whether the final assessment is closed or open book, timed or take-home, and written or typed. These transparencies are vital to supporting student note-taking and course engagement.

Student-centered assessment practices further reveal to students what the assessment metrics are for the exam. A rubric is essential so that students know how they will be evaluated. Best practices are to align grading criteria with the same skills and values that informed your teaching and to make exams available for student review and discussion after completion. Most institutions and faculty do this already. This supports students' ownership of success and helps them inventory their skills and strengths and target areas for growth. This support is particularly important for first-year courses.

To help minimize the burdens of individual exam meetings, consider deploying some mitigating tactics that are student centered and burden lightening. I find it helpful to release the grading memo *before* grades are released because the students are uniquely eager to channel their anxieties into some productive tasks. Reading this memo starts to set expectations and promote student accountability. Before student meetings, consider having students complete a self-assessment of their work. This flips the burden on students to do the work of self-assessment first and strengthens the quality of the one-on-one consults from describing weaknesses to improving them. Finally, student-centered assessment practices work carefully with student affairs and disability-accommodations experts on campus to ensure that the exam is accessible to all students. For example, be sure all students understand the setting and characters in your exam equally regardless of their background. Reliance on pop culture characters or references can be whimsical, but it can also present challenges to comprehension.

Skills-Centered and Client-Centered Assessment Practices

Skills-centered assessment practices ground traditional exam questions in a realistic lawyering context with concrete skills framing the tasks. This need not be a dramatic transformation of existing practices. Simply repackage existing questions around a client letter, a client intake decision, a judicial opinion, legislative testimony, client emails, case memos to the file, complaints, jury instructions, and so on. A very simple repackaging from traditional issue spotting to writing a memo analyzing the strengths of the possible claims is a substantial improvement in context and purpose. The lack of context can be deeply problematic otherwise. Weaker exams might rightfully—yet mistakenly—be framed as if the students are writing for their law teacher and thus conclude that they do not need to define terms or provide much more than legal conclusions. Stronger exams might intuit that they should write by explaining and elaborating on all relevant points relating to the rules and analysis.

Client-centered assessment practices align closely with skills-centered ones. Use a broad array of "clients," such as plaintiffs, defendants, corporations, community organizations, legislative actors, and judicial chambers. This presents the full array of the legal community to students and is more inclusive overall. These framing devices position students engaging with assessments with purpose. Students are not just abstractly facing a beastly task; rather, they are working on behalf of clients to deploy the skills that they have learned to meet client objectives. This better aligns with shifts in the bar exam and with the ABA's focus on professional-identity formation. It also promotes stronger wellness practices and greater equities.

Community-Centered Assessment Practices

Finally, law teachers can tether the grading rubric to the practice norms of the legal community so students do not link the expectations of exam performance to their teachers' personal idiosyncrasies. Appendix A provides an example of this approach. Assessment rubrics build a student community that has shared terminology and expectations. Exam questions should also reflect diverse parties and communities.

Sustainable Formative Assessment Practices for Law Teachers

Law teachers can greatly liberate their thinking on formative assessment and its burdens on workloads generally. Authentic formative assessment

Box 6. Delivering Meaningful Feedback without Individualized Grading

Post an **annotated model answer,** in which you identify the components of a successful submission. Even better, instead of (or in addition to) assigning points to the assignment itself, assign points to the students' active effort in comparing their own answer to the annotated model answer. This promotes students' self-directed learning. It also builds a shared terminology regarding successful performance metrics, which supports equity and inclusion.

Provide a set of **self-guided assessment questions,** in which you help students look for required or expected components in their own work. For example, you could ask, "Did you state the rules before applying them in your legal analysis?" or "Did you use the facts from the fact pattern explicitly when you applied the rule?" Students can actively annotate their own submission, using the self-guided assessment questions. This promotes students' self-directed learning. To diffuse classroom hierarchies, you might even incentivize the rigors of this self-review by grading the self-assessment rather than the work itself.

Facilitate **peer review,** whereby students assess one another's performance. Most learning-management systems (e.g., Blackboard, Canvas, Sakai) facilitate this teaching technique within the basic assignment-submission settings. Peer review is commonly used outside of Socratic classrooms, such as in legal research and writing courses, so students may even have this skill set developed by the time you deploy it. Peer review has the collateral benefit of supporting a strong, student-centered learning community. It gives students the vital professional skill of learning to deliver feedback to a colleague. Peer review might further include working with the class to collaboratively build a shared grading rubric. This promotes student-centered learning, transparency, and equity.

Compile a **genericized compilation of typical student answers for revision.** Have small groups work together collaboratively, guide the class through revisions, or have students individually revise the text. I like to frame this around *This Is Spinal Tap*'s witty scene about taking the speaker volume to eleven. I often play the clip for students and direct them, in turn, to take this work I have selected for them to eleven! The implication is that the work was strong, but students should look for ways to improve it further.

Rely on **existing learning modules delivered by major law publishers,** with feedback embedded for students, such as the Center for Computer-Assisted Legal Instruction (CALI) exercises; Aspen's Connected e-Books, PracticePerfect materials, and Examples and Explanations

Series; or West Academic's Exam Pro Series, Concepts and Insights Series, and Acing Series.

Deliver a **broad performance matrix** instead of a penultimate grade or points. For example, try flagging benchmarks of "High Competency," "Competency," "Developing Competency," or "Below Competency" (preferably with an opportunity or requirement to resubmit if "Below Competency"). This approach prevents students from quibbling about grades while still providing outcome-based learning feedback. It is dramatically more efficient for law teachers to score and assess students against the learning outcomes instead of against one another.

is a necessary component of outcome-based teaching. It helps measure where students are on the path to achieving competency in learning outcomes. Learning outcomes are not supposed to be dropped in the course syllabi as an interesting course preview or trailer. Rather, they are supposed to *drive* teaching thoroughly and systemically. Formative assessment should thus operate both as a measuring tool and as a learning tool toward that end. Formative assessment needs to deliver feedback to students, but it need not require individual markings by the law teacher for every student. Box 6 offers some alternate methods of providing feedback.

When done effectively, strong assessment practices *are* student-centered practices. Testing substance through skills aligns further with bar exam–reform trajectories and gives students a stronger purpose as lawyers-in-training. Repackaging exams around a client-centered lawyering task lends more meaning, pivoting from the abstract to the purposeful act of lawyering. These adaptations are implementable with existing materials, faculties, and workloads. The next section explores how to evaluate effective teaching.

Normalize Institutional and Individual Action in Response to Student Assessments

Institutional infrastructure can further support law teachers in their effective use of assessments too.[12] Reviewing the steps to effective assessment framing this section, the words that might catch the most attention are "take action." As a teaching community, most of us added student-learning outcomes to our syllabi and then stopped there. Our Socratic teaching and testing practices marched on and endured. The measurement of student *achievement* of published learning outcomes—

both at the institutional and the classroom level—is not meaningfully happening. Without measuring the effectiveness of teaching practices, in turn, no action is happening in response to evidence. Legal education needs to strengthen the mechanisms by which assessment informs and modifies teaching, both at the classroom and the programmatic level.

Institutions need to value and support formative assessment as a pedagogical practice that informs teaching and does not just rank students. Effective formative assessment requires a culture of assessment that is authentic and holistic.[13] Efficiencies are vital here. All classes do not need to add all measures of formative assessment. Coordination is critical to avoid overburdening students and to support law teachers' workload distribution. Law faculty and staff are also already enduring fatigue and burnout. Any feasible curricular reforms must align with incentives to ensure their successful implementation. Most law schools have a standard teaching package that treats all courses as equal, with little differentiation given to what intensities sit in the course structure. Over time institutions might come to think in more specialized ways about equity in course coverage. For example, schools could provide a subset of first-year classes that are intensified around formative feedback, with smaller section sizes as the trade-off.

Schools might also pay a stipend to one colleague to serve as a 1L section coordinator to help provide consistency and intentionality in what formative assessments are offered in the first year. The section coordinator could also lead section-wide events, bringing cross-curricular content together and bridging into the community applications of course content.[14] These institutional management strategies would navigate the tension in not allowing curricular changes to exacerbate student wellness concerns through burdensome and tedious extra assignments or programs. Effective assessment needs to be sustainable for students and teachers alike.

Legal education can also move collaboratively toward developing more robust best practices in analyzing summative exam results so that exams play the assessment role that they should for courses, institutions, and students. This must include rigorous examination of grading curves. L. Danielle Tully's influential work, "What Law Schools Should Leave Behind," powerfully reminds us that the curve is a distraction from "equitable, consistent, and effective assessments that communicate to students and to their would-be employers where students excel and where they need to grow."[15] Tully calls for an abandonment of the curve because it is out of sync with the other transformative changes that we have made in legal education. Tully thoughtfully outlines how curves were implemented at a different time for a different purpose, and they are now out of sync and inequitable.

When the ABA moved to an outcome-based model, the curve became distinctly problematic. A learning-outcomes model is distinctly supposed to use formative assessment to measure student progress and hold faculty accountable for students meeting the learning outcomes. Yet rigid curve-based grading systems measure students based on their performance relative to their classmates, with a fixed capacity in each grading category. In a strict curved class, the number of students who can receive an A, B, C, or D is fixed by the number of students enrolled in the class. This skews and distorts students' understanding of whether they are meeting the competencies. Curved grading undermines the very goals of using learning outcomes if the summative assessment exam is used to assess competencies. Instead, grades should be tethered to criteria to evaluate student's competencies.[16] Institutional curves breed competition, which undermines community building, thwarts a sense of belonging, skews meaningful learning, and undermines inclusive classrooms.

Strict curves are also problematic because they immunize law teachers from providing meaningful feedback to students. This institutional grading practice allows law teachers to sincerely and accurately tell students that their performance was strong, but the students just could not receive a higher grade because those spots were "taken" in the curve distribution. This undermines the self-efficacy of students. Instead, over time, as the bar exam reforms crystallize, it makes more sense to use criterion-referenced grading that measures whether students have met the stated learning outcomes.[17] This criterion-based approach is more consistent, tethered, and grounded with effective assessment practices. Summative assessment should measure what students will have to do as lawyers, and it should position all students as capable of meeting the stated goals. More rigorous and collaborative discussions of equitable grading practices and evidence-based teaching practices will benefit all our institutions. There are much more robust conversations to have about equitable grading practices across our curriculum.[18]

ALIGN TEACHING-EVALUATION PRACTICES WITH SHARED SOCRATIC VALUES

While exams are the dominant assessment metric for student learning, course evaluations are the most dominant metric for assessing teaching. Traditional course evaluations rarely provide insights as to whether a

Socratic course was effective in meeting the stated learning outcomes or whether the course was inclusive. Rather, from the outset course evaluations are well documented to be infused with bias.[19] Course evaluations are often entirely generic to a school or campus, which all but ensures that they will provide no course-level information on customized learning outcomes. Institutions sometimes use peer faculty observations to measure the effectiveness of teaching as well. Neither course evaluations nor faculty teaching observations—as currently implemented—are particularly well suited for this purpose. These teaching-assessment tools can both suffer from a skew toward the status quo and reinforce biases.

These measurement tools are also distinctly hierarchical, carrying heavy weight at the beginning of one's career and virtually no weight later in one's career. Formative student assessments, such as those provided in legal research and writing and other skills courses, also tend to lower student evaluations. Because term faculty are more regularly reviewed than tenured faculty, this can also create an outsized weighting of student evaluations on term faculty. Senior and tenured faculty rarely have any feedback other than course evaluations, which are not systemically reviewed or analyzed by faculty. Pretenure faculty reviews are more often assessing whether the teacher aligns with the standards necessary for retention or promotion. Most peer-teaching evaluations occur in the context of promotion decisions, which again distorts their function and creates steep strata in whose teaching is subject to peer critique and whose is not.

Strengthening our use of existing evaluation tools is a good and an efficient place to start. Typical course evaluation questions inquire about the instructor's mastery of the material, preparation for class, availability outside of class, use of course materials, and provision of feedback. Yet course-level learning outcomes are generally far more concrete and specific to the field. This disconnect is a missed opportunity that could be efficiently and systemically improved with few administrative burdens or costs.

The approach to course evaluations in Socratic classrooms could instead, with the right infrastructure and support, measure students' perception of whether the course met the stated learning outcomes and whether the environment was inclusive. First, let's consider the alignment with learning outcomes. For example, consider learning outcomes for a first-year torts class as presented in the left-hand column of the following list. The proposed questions presented in the right-hand column of the list could provide meaningful feedback about the effectiveness of the teaching methods in getting students to competencies in the course outcomes.

PUBLISHED COURSE LEARNING OUTCOMES	COURSE EVALUATION QUESTIONS
Upon completion of Torts, students will achieve the following learning outcomes:	*On a scale of 1 to 5, assess your own competence in meeting each of the course's stated learning outcomes:*
Discern legally relevant facts from a client story to frame a negligence cause of action.	Did the course prepare you to discern legally relevant facts from a client story to frame a negligence cause of action?
Structure and argue plausible negligence claims arising out of client harms and assess the relative strengths and weaknesses of each claim.	Are you prepared to structure and argue plausible negligence claims arising out of client harms and assess the relative strengths and weaknesses of each claim?
Analyze each element of negligence through to a predictive legal conclusion by applying the rule to the facts.	Are you able to analyze each negligence element through to a predictive legal conclusion by applying the rule to the facts?
Understand tort cases in the context of the basic architecture of our civil litigation system (e.g., filing a complaint, discovery, motion practice, jury, appeal).	Did this course give you the content and materials needed to understand tort cases in the context of the basic architecture of our civil litigation system (e.g., filing a complaint, discovery, motions, jury, appeal)?
Contextualize tort claims in social, political, economic, and historical perspectives.	Are you able to contextualize tort claims in social, political, economic, and historical perspectives after completing this course?
Critically consider the policy implications of tort law from competing perspectives.	Can you critically consider the policy implications of tort law from competing perspectives following this course?

These questions, styled tightly around actual learning outcomes, would provide vital feedback on the effectiveness of teaching methods. While students are only one data source around our teaching, their perceptions of their *own* competencies are much more insightful to our effectiveness as teachers than the current approaches to course evaluations. If students identified, for example, that they do not agree that they had the content or materials to understand a tort case through the civil litigation system, then I would in turn act on that information. Perhaps the following year, I would revise my Socratic dialogues to add more rigor, change my readings to include materials more explicitly about the progression of tort litigation, add an assignment, or collaborate more with civil procedure colleagues. Or perhaps I would decide that I do not have the bandwidth to meaningfully achieve this learning outcome or that my institution's curricular structure does not support my ability to achieve this in the course. In that case I might remove the learning outcome in subsequent years. Notably, assessments need to be meaningful *and* sustainable. It is thus important that these techniques can work with existing materials. Because we are all already required to write learning outcomes, this is an efficient adaptation to get more meaningful evaluations regarding the effectiveness of our teaching.

Existing approaches to measuring classroom learning through course evaluations are also unlikely to capture meaningful feedback on diversity, equity, and inclusion in the Socratic classroom at all. Typical course evaluation questions are more often focused on whether the classroom is nondiscriminatory. While this is *also* necessary, it is not the same as cultivating an inclusive and equitable classroom that prepares all students to practice in our diverse communities.

Many course evaluations ask generic questions that could be understood as misguided. Consider the following common evaluation questions asked of students:

The instructor encouraged the inclusion of diverse perspectives.

The instructor was sensitive to issues of diversity encountered during the course.

Note the passivity of these evaluation questions. These common questions are often phrased passively, leaving it unclear whether the instructor had the obligation to include diverse perspectives or whether the instructor just had to encourage students to do so or whether the instructor just had to not misstep if others happened to introduce "issues of diversity." For example, asking if the instructor was sensitive to issues of diversity might be construed as a license to *avoid* discussing vital topics that reflect the law's impact on all communities. These types of questions only get at how the instructor *reacts* when students proactively offer diverse perspectives in the classroom. Chapter 1, however, reveals critiques of how students of color, LGBTQ+ students, and women students are often left to challenge the purported perspectivelessness of courses and the weight that students feel when pushed into this participation role. These questions remove vital accountability for the instructor's obligation to introduce diverse perspectives to foster an inclusive learning environment. These questions are notably more passive than holding the instructor directly accountable for selecting materials, assignments, and discussion points that foster inclusion.

Other typical questions that intend to get at diversity and inclusion likewise fail to pull the importance of diversity and inclusion down to the course level or situate it within students' readiness to join the legal profession, instead hovering in the abstract around viewpoints and differences. Consider common questions like these:

The professor treated all students fairly.

The instructor respected all viewpoints.

These questions are important to ensure that classrooms are nondiscriminatory. But they problematically position diversity in ways that can be perceived as untethered from the course content and readiness for the profession.

Course evaluations can do more to measure student achievement of learning outcomes and the inclusiveness of our classroom environments. Course evaluations can help assess the inclusivity of learning environments, if used intentionally and sincerely. Questions should position the instructor as accountable for creating an inclusive classroom. Evaluation questions addressing diversity, equity, and inclusion can also be framed through the lenses of clients, community, and skills, to better support students in training to join the legal profession.

The threshold inquiry to frame the measurement of inclusion is why inclusion is important to your course and your field. Inclusion in the abstract is hard to measure. Think about the kind of work that lawyers do and with whom they interact. Reflect on who your students are and what perspectives they bring to the class. This can help inform what ideas, content, or perspectives students might need to prepare them for practice. Focus particularly on *measurable* outcomes. How do you want your students to interact with one another, with the profession, with clients, and with the community?

With that mindset evaluation questions about inclusion should instead address whether the *professor* and the *course* directly provided instruction that facilitated diverse perspectives to cover the full range of the subject matter as needed to prepare for practice. For example, students might rank on a scale whether they had the tools they needed to be successful in the course or whether they felt like they were part of the classroom. Questions relating to diversity should get at the materials provided and the assignments given. Sample questions, presented in the following list, might instead tether the professor and the classroom to the professional reasons for diverse course coverage:

COMMON COURSE EVALUATION QUESTIONS	SUGGESTED REVISIONS
✗ The professor treated all students fairly.	✓ The instructor's assigned materials demonstrated how the subject matter affects all communities.
✗ The instructor respected all viewpoints.	✓ The assignments reflected a diverse set of clients, issues, and applications to prepare me for a range of client representations and practice settings.

Institutional supports also need to align with teacher-level queries. Law school institutional supports can bring vital standardization, expertise, and collaboration to the tasks of evaluating teaching and learning. Institutional practices can better support faculty in designing effective course evaluations and in strengthening expertise on how to use formative and summative assessment in classrooms and institutions. As explored previously, most course evaluations are precanned at the institutional level. While the opportunity to add questions might be available, few faculty seize this opportunity or have the expertise to draft effective questions. Nor are the institutional incentives there to do it either. Institutional leaders can help faculty customize evaluation questions effectively. Institutional leadership might work to develop a repository of questions that can support faculty in measuring the inclusivity and effectiveness of their classrooms.

Institutional norms should also systemically value course evaluations more equitably. Law teachers with renewable contracts, for example, are more dependent on course evaluations, less able to direct faculty governance, and often overwhelmingly women and faculty of color.[20] This can lead to weightier course evaluations for some and feed student perceptions of power imbalances. Standardization regarding how and why course evaluations are used can help level hierarchies. For example, annual review materials might ask faculty to identify the learning outcomes that they have for each class and evaluate opportunities for growth in meeting those learning outcomes. This could include a question about any obstacle that hindered success in meeting the stated learning outcomes to help identify what additional institutional supports are needed.

Likewise, leadership might also ask faculty in the annual review process what steps they are taking to monitor both the inclusivity of their classrooms and the achievement of student-learning outcomes. This would help demonstrate institutional support for inclusion and for the achievement of learning outcomes across the entire student body. This would also embed a layer of standardized accountability, institutionally communicating that *all* law teachers can and should continue to grow and improve year to year, not just pretenured faculty or term faculty. Law schools can also cultivate an equitable culture of self-evaluation beyond course evaluations. They can tether course evaluations to course-level learning outcomes and institutional ones.

Thoughtful and effective teaching evaluations also require context and community. Reflection is hard in isolation. Rather, group analysis of teaching practices will often be more beneficial and constructive than individual analysis. What are our institutions doing well? Where can we grow as a teaching community? We all have blind spots and room for growth in our teaching. Diversifying and expanding opportunities for meaningful feedback and self-assessment will produce more meaningful results.[21] Leaders might also present an annual summary on systemic strengths and areas for growth institutionally after reviewing the course evaluations globally. Schools could also deploy more 360-degree observation opportunities to collaborate intergenerationally and nonhierarchically. Institutions might also consider what awards and recognitions support teaching. Awards might emphasize innovations or inclusion. This is a chance for faculty to work toward building shared institutional identity in law teaching. It is an opportunity to see the institution from a student perspective. True self-evaluation must seek a "searching self-reflection, with no fear of retribution regardless of revelation."[22] Our institutions can do much more to promote self-reflection and growth in both Socratic learning and teaching.

MEASURE LAW SCHOOL LEARNING OUTCOMES THROUGH AN EQUITY LENS

The accreditation processes can further support inclusive and equitable law schools and classrooms. The classroom-level and institutional-level reforms described in this text need larger structural supports and incentives. Stronger accreditation oversight within ABA standards can hold law schools more accountable for both *what* is taught and *how* it is taught. Accreditation is a powerful tool to yield systemic reforms in legal education and to raise teaching and learning standards. Yet historical accreditation reforms have missed an important alignment. Accreditation reforms to improve inclusion, like pedagogy reforms, cannot happen around the perimeter while leaving the architectural center of legal education untouched. Rather, accreditation standards need to build a bridge between institutional commitments to diversity, equity, and inclusion and the measurements of learning outcomes within the curricular center of legal education.

Legal education moved to an outcome-based approach to law teaching in 2014, marking a transformative shift. ABA Standard 302 requires all law schools to establish learning outcomes in at least these four areas:

1. Knowledge and understanding of substantive and procedural law
2. Legal analysis and reasoning, legal research, problem solving, and written and oral communication in the legal context
3. Exercise of proper professional and ethical responsibilities to clients and the legal system
4. Other professional skills needed for competent and ethical participation as a member of the legal profession[23]

Standard 314 also requires schools to embed formative and summative assessment in the curriculum to measure student learning, improve student learning, and provide students with feedback.[24] These reforms marked completion of a six-year review of the accreditation standards, yielding modest steps to align with an outcome-based measurement across other disciplines in earlier years.[25] These reforms also moved legal education toward more experiential education consistent with other professional programs.[26] Previously, law school accreditation had focused only on the input and output of law schools, including the resources invested, bar-passage rates, and job-placement data.[27] A handful of iconic publications in prior decades had nudged law schools toward curricular reform, but they had not yielded formal revisions to accreditation standards.[28] This shift to outcome-based teaching as an accreditation standard reflected that the historical model of teaching content and relying solely on summative assessment was outdated and ineffective.[29] These reforms pushed law schools to better prepare students for practice with experiential content, formative assessment, and outcome-based teaching.[30] These reforms were not embraced by all.[31]

These accreditation reforms stirred law schools to be more intentional in their teaching and curriculum design. Notably, though, the Standard 302 learning outcomes also doubled down on the longevity of the traditional curriculum, while giving schools an opportunity to differentiate, innovate, and promote distinct values *beyond* the curricular core, which was envisioned to still dominate.[32] As a practical matter, Standard 302's baseline learning outcomes have led to few changes in the curricular design or approach within traditional Socratic classrooms. Rather, they have predominantly led to learning outcomes posted on school websites and on course syllabi.

At the institutional level, ABA Standard 315 requires schools to measure the degree of student competency in meeting the identified institutional learning outcomes. This programmatic measurement *should* then yield curricular changes to meet identified student needs. The examples provided in the ABA standards for measuring the program include methods such as student portfolios, student evaluations, capstone courses, bar-passage rates, job-placement rates, and surveys of practitioners.[33]

Yet effective implementation of outcome-based learning requires measurement in all classrooms, *especially* those dominating the first-year and bar exam courses. Law schools *should* be working to understand which students are failing, leaving, or transferring and where and why those losses occur. Are there trends that merit institutional response? Who is thriving and succeeding in the courses? Who is struggling? Are some student communities uniquely struggling in the courses or institutions relative to others? If so, why? Answering these questions requires institutional expertise, collaboration, and innovation.[34] This work is not easy, but it is essential. Decades of critical theorists have revealed how law schools march onward with traditional Socratic teaching techniques, while knowing that these methods are not always working inclusively, equitably, or effectively. Accordingly, the measurement of learning outcomes must be accompanied by an equity and inclusion lens to measure the effectiveness of teaching techniques and assessment methods. Box 7 provides further reading and resources for supporting schools in this vital program work.

Box 7. Resources for Measuring Learning Outcomes through an Equity Lens

A few critical publications provide guidance on how to do the broader program work required to successfully couple achievement of learning outcomes with inclusive teaching and assessment practices. The go-to manual on learning outcomes in legal education is Lori Shaw and Victoria VanZandt's *Student Learning Outcomes and Law School Assessment: A Practical Guide to Measuring Institutional Effectiveness* (Durham: Carolina Academic Press, 2015). Many other thoughtful resources help schools and law teachers work through identifying and measuring the achievement of learning outcomes:

Andrea Curcio, "A Simple Low-Cost Institutional Learning-Outcomes Assessment Process," *Journal of Legal Education* 67, no. 2 (2018): 489–530.

Janet W. Fisher, "Putting Students at the Center of Legal Education: How an Emphasis on Outcome-Measure in the ABA Standards for Approval Might Transform the Educational Experience of Law Students," *Southern Illinois University of Law Journal* 35, no. 2 (Winter 2011): 225–47.

Marie Summerlin Hamm, Benjamin V. Madison III, and Ryan P. Murnane, "The Rubric Meets the Road in Law Schools: Program Assessment of Student Learning Outcomes as a Fundamental Way for Law Schools to Improve and Fulfill Their Respective Missions," *University of Detroit Mercy Law Review* 95 (Spring 2018): 343–92.

Melissa N. Henke, "When Your Plate Is Already Full: Efficient and Meaningful Outcomes Assessment for Busy Law Schools," *Mercer Law Review* 71 (2020): 529–84.

Anthony Niedwiecki, "Law Schools and Learning Outcomes: Developing a Coherent, Cohesive, and Comprehensive Law School Curriculum," *Cleveland State Law Review* 64, no. 3 (2016): 661–713.

Lori A. Roberts, "Assessing Ourselves: Confirming Assumptions and Improving Student Learning by Efficiently and Fearlessly Assessing Student Learning Outcomes," *Drexel Law Review* 3 (2011): 454–84.

Debra Moss Vollweiler, "Don't Panic! The Hitchhiker's Guide to Learning Outcomes: Eight Ways to Make Them More Than (Mostly) Harmless," *Dayton Law Review* 44 (July 2018): 17–52.

These works are just a sample of the guidance and support available. These works collectively remind us that assessment is a *process,* not a task. It is ongoing. They remind us that assessment—when done right—yields action. They walk readers through the processes to assess learning at the institutional and classroom level. These influential works also collectively critique the American Bar Association for not providing more concrete guidance of expectations, a point that merits further development of accreditation resources, given the volume of works guiding law schools through this process now.

Existing accreditation approaches are simply not enough as implemented.[35] Reforming legal education's accreditation processes could bring an important reconciliation, positioning diversity, equity, and inclusion as *both* a programmatic goal with emphases in admissions, recruiting, mentoring, and programming *and* a curricular goal, analyzing equity and inclusion in achieving learning outcomes. Measuring learning outcomes with an equity and inclusion lens is a stronger path of accreditation because it strengthens teaching and bridges diversity, equity, and inclusion goals into the curriculum, where it further belongs. These accreditation pivots would also align with stronger assessment practices.

. . .

With revamped teaching practices come the alignment of our assessment practices. This chapter outlines improved practices that are scalable and sustainable within existing budgets, resources, and assessments. These proposed changes to course assessments, course evaluations, and accreditations proposals can better catalyze the Socratic classroom in ways that build more effective, inclusive, and equitable institutions.

Raising the Floor on Legal Education

This book is a call to action for legal education. Socratic classrooms—for better or worse—continue to dominate our institutions. These classrooms deliver the curricular core to our students across our institutions, particularly in their first year. While many scholars thoughtfully and fairly call for the end of Socratic teaching, this book pragmatically declares that we cannot afford to wait for all law teachers to reimagine their teaching style before we act. These calls to "raise the ceiling" on legal education in more transformative ways are vital and essential to heed and to ignite our momentum toward reform. In the interim, as these seeds of change take root, we need to "raise the floor" on legal education to hold ourselves accountable for achieving learning outcomes and fostering inclusive experiences in our traditional Socratic classrooms.

In many corners of legal education, clear and intentional pedagogies drive the classroom, such as in clinical classrooms, legal research and writing classrooms, and experiential learning courses. These courses have explicit and universal pedagogical tethers to practice readiness, skills acquisition, client-centered lawyering, and more. The Socratic classroom at one time was also an innovative and purposeful pedagogy. Today, however, Socratic classrooms are much more likely to dominate our curricula simply because that is how *we* were educated, and our budgets, staffing models, and workloads are structured around this model. The endurance of Socratic classrooms is currently more of a lesson in curricular conformity than curricular purpose. We have allowed our institutions to grow structurally dependent on these large, lecture classrooms with appellate casebooks and high-stakes summative exams. For that reason, whether we want to or not, we need to revisit these classroom pedagogies explicitly and objectively to catalyze learning for all students and to align with the needs of modern legal education and law practice.

Our adherence to this teaching approach, one hundred years later, is no longer innovative or purposeful—nor is it transparent. Most students, to the extent they learn anything about the Socratic method and how it works, learn it in orientation and law school–preparation programs and through privileged whisper networks of students. Rarely do our syllabi or teaching materials explicitly tell students why we are using the Socratic method, how to participate when on call, how to participate when not on call, or how Socratic engagement connects to the course exam, the bar exam, or practice readiness. There is often a similar lack of transparency regarding the summative assessment high-stakes issue-spotting exam. Lacking transparency, students are often overcome with anxiety while navigating the Socratic classroom and its summative exam.

What *is* well documented, however, is the ongoing threads of scholarly critique that contest the effectiveness of core features of the Socratic method as a teaching tool. Qualitative and quantitative accounts, dating back to Lani Guinier, Michelle Fine, and Jane Balin's influential work, "Becoming Gentlemen," have documented how women students, students of color, nontraditional students, and others have found Socratic classrooms to be alienating, perspectiveless, abstract, and harmful. These accounts are consistent, enduring, and unified over decades of authors. The accounts of student experiences are likewise searing and problematic.

Critical theorists for more than fifty years have issued calls to action in response to these Socratic-classroom critiques. Critical theorists have identified institutional structures and hierarchies as the site for action. It is not that *students* need to change. Rather, our *institutions* need to change. Existing approaches risk stifling discussion of the law and its transformative potential. They can constrain student learning rather than ignite it. From feminist theory to critical legal studies to critical race theory to LatCrit to queer theory, all these theories align in sourcing many of legal education's harms in the Socratic classroom and its embedded hierarchies. These scholarly communities made great strides in transforming the curriculum through seminars, clinics, and revitalized teaching materials and continue to leave their impactful mark on legal scholarship and law reform. They have yielded improvements in law school hiring practices, student support systems, and institutional culture. These scholarly communities' calls for reforms of Socratic teaching, however, have not yielded as much transformation as the robustness of the critique would suggest. The Socratic classroom persists despite these calls for reforms. Legal education reforms are largely happening around the curricular core.

Yet there is no compelling reason to fear reform of traditional Socratic classrooms when legal education and the legal profession are considered pragmatically. Our students—across the board—are struggling in unparalleled ways with wellness issues. They are entering our institutions just as happy and just as prone to wellness issues as the general population. Within months, however, they are more unhappy and more prone to issues such as substance abuse than even other professional school peers. Socratic courses dominate the first year, so these classrooms are a vital starting point. Further, the profession too is struggling with wellness concerns and an overall professional malaise. In sum the unwell law students of today go on to become the unwell lawyers of tomorrow. With that perspective in mind, we have nothing to lose by innovating.

The time to reform Socratic classrooms is now. Inclusive education cannot happen around the margins. We cannot be satisfied with innovative seminars, thoughtful mentoring programs, and lunchtime workshops because they leave the curricular core unmodified, which is the dominant locus shaping the bulk of students' time, energy, and grade-point averages. Inclusive institutions cannot be erected solely around the margins. Rather, all classrooms and pedagogies must align in delivering inclusive legal education.

Thus, the evidence is abundant, aligned, and informative. It is time to cultivate inclusive Socratic classrooms. This begins by ending the presumptive reverence and implicit immunity given to Socratic classrooms. Socratic classrooms need to be evidence based, just like other corners of education. This begins by ending problematic performances of the Socratic method. Socratic classrooms that are power centered, professor centered, abstract, perspectiveless, and assessed with an opaque, high-stakes, summative exam can be ineffective and harmful. While this version of Socratic teaching has waned, it does still exist, and it forms a curricular floor that needs elevating in all our institutions.

This book issues a call to action to build more inclusive Socratic classrooms by identifying shared teaching values. This book proposes that these shared values include student-centered, skills-centered, client-centered, and community-centered Socratic classrooms. This book provides a roadmap of where to start and how to achieve this vision. Notably, these proposals are distinctly pragmatic, scalable, and achievable. They can work with existing budgets, teachers, casebooks, and curricula.

Implementing these proposals, however, does require vital institutional support. **Law schools as institutions** can support and lead this overarching call to action for inclusive Socratic teaching in the following ways:

- Host spotlights on teaching practices and institutional values *during* faculty meetings to ensure that all faculty engage. One prompt for discussion could be this question: "When instructors describe Socratic teaching as the 'most effective' teaching technique, what do we mean? Most effective at what?"

- Celebrate successful innovations in teaching using social media, blogs, and publications, just as you would celebrate publications. These shout-outs can be circulated by students and colleagues to build awareness and community.

- Reward faculty who innovate and build inclusive and equitable learning environments.

- Facilitate intergenerational and 360-degree support for teaching, recognizing that experienced teachers have much to offer new teachers, just as new teachers have much to offer experienced teachers.

- Align professional development work plans and annual-review reporting with your institutional pedagogical values.

IMPLEMENTING STUDENT-CENTERED SOCRATIC TEACHING

This book proposes that our Socratic classrooms align in being student, skills, client, and community centered. A student-centered Socratic classroom begins with knowing our students. Our students are changing from year to year and from institution to institution. They are of a different generation than Langdell's law students. They are more diverse than ever. They are taking on an exorbitant debt. Student-centered teaching also includes designing our classrooms with our students' learning outcomes in mind instead of teaching from the beginning of the casebook to the end. The ABA made vital shifts toward outcome-based learning models, but most Socratic classrooms have changed their syllabi only or perhaps added a midterm. There is much more work to do in implementing learning outcomes to measure and assess student learning.

Law teachers can incorporate this proposal for a student-centered Socratic pedagogy in at least the following concrete ways:

- Learn preferred pronouns and pronunciations of all students' names.
- Survey students in each course to understand components of their lived experiences and perspectives.
- Prepare introductory activities, such as icebreakers or meet-and-greet programs to meet your students.
- Monitor data from the Law School Survey of Student Engagement and similar research for trends in enrollment patterns and experiences.
- Deploy diverse teaching techniques to meet the needs of all learners.
- Engage in reverse course design to add transparency and intentionality to teaching techniques and assessment methods.
- Explain the relationship between published learning outcomes and Socratic teaching explicitly to students. Some content and context that would be useful to give students include the following:
  - Describe how your use of the Socratic method helps students get closer to achieving the learning objectives you have set for the course.
  - Give students some examples of categories of questions that you might ask in your Socratic dialogue and how those questions relate to course goals.
  - Develop shared language and terminology to govern the criteria for a strong Socratic performance.
  - Suggest readings regarding successful Socratic participation. For example, Heidi K. Brown has particularly useful materials in *The Introverted Lawyer,* offering thoughtful guidance on how students should prepare for Socratic dialogue. Brown offers further strategies for overcoming challenges in Socratic participation in *Untangling Fear in Lawyering.*

- Be transparent about how students should grow in their engagement with the Socratic method as their skills improve, from the beginning of the semester to the end.
- Manage on-call participation fairly, actively, and equitably.
- Create other opportunities for participation, such as discussion boards.
- Hold accessible office hours. Consider a variety of individual, group, online, and in-person options.

Law schools as institutions can further support and incentivize institutional shifts toward student-centered Socratic teaching in at least the following ways:

- Have all students record an audio file of the correct pronunciation of their full name so that faculty can use this to facilitate inclusive course participation without students having to repeat it every class.
- Capture preferred pronouns and chosen names consistently from all students and communicate them systemically to the faculty for each course.
- Present annual reports that introduce trends and shifts in each new class of students and discuss how these students might differ in their experiences, perspectives, and demographics from prior years. For example, examine the changes a higher or lower population of international, diverse, part-time, out-of-state, or older students would necessitate.
- Celebrate students and their learning in blogs, social media, and reports.
- Provide financial stipends to appoint a section coordinator to sequence assessments and programs.
- Identify the unwritten rules shaping law school success and ensure that these rules are communicated transparently and equitably.
- Train law teachers in reverse course design.

IMPLEMENTING SKILLS-CENTERED SOCRATIC TEACHING

Socratic teaching can also transform to be more skills centered. Practicing lawyers want our graduates to have more practice-ready skills. The bar exam wants our students to apply substantive knowledge using foundational legal skills. Students want more context and perspective in their Socratic classrooms. All these constituencies point toward embedding more skills in the Socratic classroom. This need not be to achieve skills *mastery*. To achieve skills *sensitization* alone would be a huge measure of improvement. Implementing a skills-centered Socratic method involves simply changing the structure of questioning and the format of assessment.

Law teachers can cultivate skills-centered Socratic classrooms in at least the following ways:

- Frame Socratic exchanges such that students are in the roles of party counsel to build professional identity and to add purpose to the teaching technique.
- Incorporate Socratic exchanges that sensitize students to the skills deployed in practice so students can envision what practicing lawyers in the field do day-to-day (e.g., issue identification, research, procedural motions, communication, and client counseling).
- Embed select practice-oriented assignments, such as discovery, research, negotiation, or client counseling, in the course.
- Package the exam format around a specific lawyering skill, such as client letters, jury instructions, or complaints.

Law schools as institutions can cultivate more skills-centered Socratic classrooms in at least the following ways:

- Work with the local bar and involved alumni to maintain a current and robust understanding of what employers want from your graduates. Include all sectors broadly, not just private firms, and focus on what skills are considered strengths and weaknesses for your graduates.
- Discuss transparently and openly the hiring priorities for new faculty. Consider whether the institution is undervaluing practice experience as a paradoxical disqualifier for law teaching.
- Consider the value given to interdisciplinary publications and coauthored pieces, particularly when the scholarly writings position faculty to acquire new skills, engage with community partners, and apply new concepts.

- For faculty lacking practice experience, consider the possibility of making service-based sabbaticals available to freshen and expand practice skills while also serving the community.

- Encourage innovation and collaboration among faculty. A section coordinator for 1L sections could work to diversify the skills to which 1Ls are exposed without overburdening students.

IMPLEMENTING CLIENT-CENTERED SOCRATIC TEACHING

Socratic teaching would also be more inclusive when delivered in client-centered ways. The Socratic classroom presents numerous opportunities for repetition to reinforce lawyering skills. Every case presents at least two possible clients for our students to represent and advise. Transforming our Socratic questioning around who these clients are, what their objectives are, how the precedent met or did not meet these objectives, and how the lawyer represented them to achieve their objectives are simple ways to get the same Socratic content out while bringing it to life in engaging and real-world ways for students. This can carry over to the assessment metrics deployed on the exam as well, to likewise bring the high-stakes, summative assessment to life around clients.

Law teachers can support client-centered Socratic teaching by taking the following steps:

- Style Socratic questioning around the clients embedded in the case.

- Enlist Socratic peer support as co-counsel, thus empowering struggling students.

- Frame existing hypotheticals and practice problems around a client representation.

- Assess final exam performances using rubrics measuring the client-centered delivery of legal substance.

IMPLEMENTING COMMUNITY-CENTERED SOCRATIC TEACHING

Finally, Socratic teaching can also be community centered. Law teachers are building learning communities, whether intentionally or not. The core tenets of inclusive classrooms include holding law teachers responsible for cultivating a sense of belonging and equipping all students with the tools to succeed. Community-centered Socratic classrooms also bring lawyering to life within communities.

Law teachers can cultivate community-centered Socratic classrooms in the following ways:

- Foster a sense of belonging in the classroom.
- Get mid-semester feedback on the classroom learning environment.
- Role-play students as lawyers in the professional community.
- Update materials to address current events in the community.
- Contextualize cases in communities, thinking critically and comprehensively about how rules affect various communities.

Law schools as institutions can further support community-centered Socratic teaching in the following ways:

- Reduce hierarchies institutionally to cultivate a mission-driven law school community that flattens and softens faculty-staff and faculty-faculty hierarchies.
- Value scholarship in collaboration with others in the profession or the community.
- Host collaborative programming and trainings to build institutional knowledge around inclusive and equitable teaching and assessment practices.
- Provide funding for meet and greets in the community, speakers, and other programming that integrates the law school with the community.

ALIGNING ASSESSMENT PRACTICES

Once we have built a pedagogy around inclusive Socratic classrooms, from there we need to align our existing assessment practices and eventually build new ones. This includes reforming how we deploy summative issue-spotting exams, course evaluations, teaching evaluations, and accreditation. Socratic classroom assessments need—at a bare minimum— greater transparency regarding assessment criteria, tethering to our Socratic teaching practices and grounding in clear lawyering roles and skills. We also need to revamp the effectiveness of our long-criticized student-evaluation procedures. These student evaluations can be one tool—among others—used to assess whether students perceive that they have achieved our stated learning outcomes for the course. They can also be an effective and efficient starting place regarding whether our classrooms are indeed inclusive learning communities.

Socratic law teachers can align their assessment practices with their teaching pedagogy in some of the following ways:

SUMMATIVE AND FORMATIVE ASSESSMENT PRACTICES

- Update the learning outcomes in your Socratic courses to explicitly embed the shared Socratic classroom values and teaching goals that you have developed and solidified, as recommended in Chapter 7.
- Evaluate your formative and summative assessment practices to determine whether you are measuring the full breadth of your revamped learning outcomes or measuring only issue spotting and analysis in the abstract.
- Ground assessments in skills, clients, and communities to give students purpose and to catalyze their professional-identity formation. Package existing exam questions around relevant lawyering work products (e.g., jury instructions, client letters).
- Explicitly connect your assessment criteria to the published learning outcomes (which ideally connect to the bar exam or to law practice) to reveal their relevance.
- Systemically rely on published grading rubrics that candidly articulate performance expectations and promote equity and transparency. Where possible, ground these rubrics in the language and framing of professional practice norms rather than individual idiosyncrasies. This decenters the law teacher and promotes more equitable grading practices.
- Frame summative exam questions and formative assessments around an assigned lawyering role for students to play that is realistic in its application (e.g., counsel, legislative aide, elected official, nonprofit director).
- Annotate a strong exam submission to help students develop a shared terminology of success and to promote equity in performance.

- Stay current on research developments surrounding best practices in assessment techniques, just as you stay current in your subject-matter fields.

TEACHING-EVALUATION PRACTICES

- Use existing course evaluations to assess whether students perceive themselves to have met the stated learning outcomes.
- Measure whether you created an inclusive learning environment.
- Assess whether students had all the tools needed to succeed in meeting your learning outcomes for the course.
- Analyze evaluation responses systemically for professional growth at all phases of your career, recognizing that they do have weaknesses and imperfections.

Law schools as institutions are integral partners and provide vital efficiencies in supporting these efforts. Here are some concrete steps that institutional leaders can take to implement more equitable assessment practices that foster more inclusive and effective learning environments:

SUMMATIVE AND FORMATIVE ASSESSMENT PRACTICES

- Manage the burdens of formative assessment across the institution, with careful work plans that support law teachers engaged in rigorous formative assessment work.
- Identify at course registration the types of assessment practices that will be deployed in a course to support students' self-directed learning.
- Revisit mandatory grading curves and institutional practices to ensure alignment with institutional learning outcomes and best educational practices.
- Design templates to support faculty in assessing the grade distribution in their courses, including what faculty should look for regarding equitable grading practices and the steps they should they take if they notice disparate outcomes.

TEACHING-EVALUATION PRACTICES

- Invest all faculty and staff—not just term faculty or institutional specialists—in the work of building an equitable and inclusive institution.
- Conduct an institutional overhaul of course-evaluation questions that capture diversity, equity, and inclusion outcomes or create a repository of questions that law teachers can add to their course evaluations. For example:
  - Did your instructor give you the tools you needed to succeed?
  - Did your instructor facilitate the participation of all students fairly?
  - Did your instructor have a clear structure to the course?
  - Did you know what your instructor expected of you?
- Review course evaluations for law teachers of *all* ranks and status for institutional trends.
- Identify thematic trends in student course evaluations across the institution to identify law school–wide strengths and weaknesses.
- Measure achievements of institutional learning outcomes with an equity lens.
- Develop and deliver responsive pedagogy programming to address institutional opportunities for growth in law teaching and to build a community committed to growth.
- Evaluate peer teaching observation practices to ensure that they do not stifle innovation or incentivize the status quo. Standardize categories of assessing, for example, the types of teaching techniques used and the breadth of student engagement.
- Cultivate a comprehensive culture of self-evaluation at all career stages, not just pretenure or term faculty.
- Report trends and patterns in transfer students and withdrawals annually.
- Conduct standardized exit interviews for departing students at graduation, transfer, or withdrawal to understand trends and opportunities for growth.

Legal education needs to begin by deploying existing student- and teaching-assessment tools for their true purpose—action—not the racking and stacking of students or the perpetuation of faculty hierarchies. We need to take the ABA's focus on learning outcomes and apply an equity lens to whether our students are achieving competencies in meeting our learning outcomes. This call to action sits at both the classroom level and the institutional level.

The legal academy can play a critical role in standardizing and incentivizing reforms to law school assessment practices. Given the existing conformities and uniformity in legal education, systemic change to strengthen assessment practices can be scaled and implemented efficiently. Legal education can act in at least these concrete ways:

- Invest in conferences and knowledge generation regarding best assessment practices that are effective and equitable.
- Strengthen the norms surrounding published casebooks and teaching materials so they are organically more student, skills, client, and community centered, without law teachers generating add-ons or assigning supplemental materials.
- Revise ABA Standard 206 to bridge the monitoring of diversity, equity, and inclusion explicitly into classroom learning.
- Add an equity lens to ABA Standard 302 to examine the achievement of learning outcomes with a vigilance to remedying any identified inequities.

While this book contains numerous concrete ideas for implementing a student-centered, skills-centered, client-centered, and community-centered Socratic classroom, perhaps more important, it seeks to engage a profession-wide dialogue on what it will take to build and retain inclusive Socratic classrooms. This book focuses on building a Socratic pedagogy. Numerous other scholars have developed thoughtful resources that align synergistically with this proposed pedagogy, far too many to cite here. Appendix B provides representative examples of additional materials that support inclusive teaching and assessment practices.

We need to hold our Socratic classrooms accountable because some groups of students are finding it harmful and no groups of students are thriving enough to justify retaining the status quo. Our institutions are gloriously more diverse than they used to be, although there is much more work to do. The profession has fifty years of critical legal scholarship—across various theoretical strands—that reveal a plan for action going forward. It is time to heed these unform and consistent calls. Just as we saw during the COVID-19 global pandemic, a little collaboration and relationship building can empower professors to try new things.

This book is for any law teacher who uses the Socratic method. It is a call to action. Legal education has innovated around its curricular core for long enough. The Socratic classroom is not going anywhere rapidly or systemically in legal education, even if it *should* be abandoned. It is thus time to build a community of law teachers committed to inclusive Socratic teaching, so all Socratic classrooms achieve effective, inclusive, and equitable student learning.

Essay Exam Assessment Criteria

This appendix contains models of essay exam assessment rubrics that I use in all doctrinal classes. I attach them to the syllabus at the outset of the course, consistent with principles of reverse course design. The first section is the grading rubric that I use for essay answers. Components A and B (issue spotting and analysis) likely align with most exam criteria used by most Socratic faculty, whether explicitly or implicitly. Component C, which is also excerpted in Chapter 7, asks students to deliver the content using client counseling skills. These assessment materials align with the teaching techniques shaping Socratic classrooms as described throughout this book. They decenter the law teacher's subjective perspective from the grading and reframe exam writing for students more objectively around the law-practice setting.

The general grading criteria that appear in the second section preview for students what kinds of characteristics—from the perspective of a law-practice setting—differentiate an A exam from a B exam and so on. This excellent assessment material originated from a model developed by the North Carolina Center for Teaching and Learning, with Professor Ruth McKinney of the University of North Carolina School of Law and Professor Mary Beth Beazley of Ohio State Law School as the original authors. Notably, both documents originated in legal writing classrooms, where clients are centered, skills are central, and learning communities are purposeful. I have adapted this resource to an exam context. The underlying approach and substance are entirely credited to Professors McKinney and Beazley, and I thank them for their generosity in permitting me to adapt and reproduce this content.

. . .

ASSESSMENT CRITERIA FOR ESSAY EXAM RESPONSES

This grading sheet identifies the criteria that I will use in grading your essay exams. Part A is a critical component because it confirms your subject-matter mastery in this course particularly. Part B is a critical lawyering component to develop across all subject matters. Part C is critical to preparing you to advise real clients in the practice of law, particularly clients who likely have limited resources and minimal legal knowledge.

A. Issue-Spotting Claims and Defenses

CRITERIA

- Spots relevant legal issues triggered by the facts presented, including claims and defenses.
- Avoids discussing any claims not presented by the facts.
- States accurate legal rules that govern each cause of action and each element, using precise terminology.
- Reaches a clear legal conclusion on all elements and claims.
- Identifies the source of authority governing the legal rules, being careful to distinguish between cases, statutes, and constitutions; federal and state legal sources; and uniform acts, restatements, and adopted rules.
- Articulates counterarguments, as appropriate.
- Explains jurisdictional splits, as relevant.

INSTRUCTOR REMARKS

B. Legal Analysis

CRITERIA

- Analyzes the legal rules by applying the law to the facts provided in the fact pattern accurately and explicitly.
- Shows the reasoning that leads to the stated conclusion fully and completely.

INSTRUCTOR REMARKS

C. *Client-Centered Framing*

CRITERIA

- Organizes analysis clearly and thoughtfully to maximize client understanding.
- Explains in a client-centered manner why the rule is what it is, particularly when the outcome is counter to the client's expectations or objectives.
- Explains *who* specifically will raise each claim and counterclaim.
- Grounds legal analysis of each legal claim in the appropriate level of coverage, given the strength of the claim and consistency with client resources and objectives.
- Advises the client of why particular claims may be advantageous or disadvantageous, particularly where multiple claims are analyzed.
- Explains the result to the client in a procedural, evidentiary, and litigation-based context: not just who will win, but when and how this might occur in the process.

INSTRUCTOR REMARKS

GENERAL GRADING CRITERIA

The following descriptions will give you some idea of the reasons behind each grade:

A exams would make a supervising attorney feel confident about relying on your work with little or no corrections or interventions. A client would be pleased that you prepared for all possible counterarguments and legal obstacles that the case would likely encounter. The reader would understand *what* the law is, *how* it applies to the case, and, where appropriate, *why* the law is what it is or why it is as uncertain as it is. A exams may

- be easy to read owing to strong large-scale organization, clarity, and focus;
- have missed no major causes of action or misstated any major rules of law;
- have further analyzed the minor or more subtle legal issues in the fact pattern;
- connect fact and law seamlessly to reason to legal conclusions;
- be based on a close, accurate, and thorough reading of the facts; and
- ground legal advice in a sophisticated understanding of how a case proceeds through the legal process.

· · ·

B exams would make a favorable impression on the intended audience. They would communicate that you know the law and legal analysis well. A supervising attorney would enjoy watching your growth and would feel confident that, with guidance, you will be a very good attorney. The work product might require some "gap filling" to thoroughly address all issues, to refine the precise terminology, or to tighten the analytic structure. The intended audience would generally understand the law, the conclusions, and the legal advice with strong clarity. B exams may

- be similar to, but lack the thoroughness, power, or polish of an A paper;
- have generally hit the big issues and stated the law accurately but missed some of the minor nuances and complexities;
- be generally well organized but may require the reader to reread certain sentences or paragraphs before fully grasping your point, or the exams may use excessive space to make minor points;
- state defensible legal conclusions, but further clarity may be necessary to understand the reasoning in all its contours; and
- explain the "what" and "how" of the law but may leave the client with further follow-up questions regarding why the result is as you suggest it is or why the other side might prevail.

· · ·

C exams would leave the intended audience uneasy about relying unguardedly on your work or unclear on how you produced the work. A supervising attorney might pick up some interesting points of law from the work but would feel compelled to rethink the legal reasoning or closely research your legal rules further. However, a supervising attorney would likely see sufficient promise in your work to decide to invest time and energy in supervising your future assignments more closely. C exams may

- present some good thoughts but contain little organizational structure;
- fail to identify all relevant issues fairly raised by the facts;
- misstate or omit important facts;
- misstate some propositions of law relevant to the facts;
- rely on legal doctrine whose relevance is not immediately apparent or that is not relevant to the facts provided;
- fail to accurately or appropriately explain the meaning of the law discussed; or
- present legal analyses that do not follow the logic of the legal doctrines learned in the course or that are not internally coherent from beginning to end.

. . .

D exams would not be acceptable to a supervising attorney or to the client. They may provide a few cases or ideas from which they could begin on their own but would be wholly undependable standing alone. A supervising attorney would need to rework the document or assign it to a different associate. Both a judge and a supervising attorney might question the reliability of future work. D exams may

- significantly misstate the facts, legal doctrine, or major issues;
- significantly fail to use the facts from the exam hypothetical or legal authorities within the argument, present significant conclusions with little or no support, or fail to include significant arguments or major legal issues; or
- contain so many organizational or analytic errors as to inhibit the reader from following your thoughts.

. . .

F exams show a fundamental lack of grasp of the legal doctrines studied in the course and a failure to adequately apply those doctrines to the facts presented. An F represents the judgment of the professor that you should retake the course to show sufficient mastery of the subject. In addition to the deficiencies of D exams, F exams may

- demonstrate consistent lack of knowledge or misapplication of legal doctrine;
- demonstrate a failure to closely read or understand the legal relevance of the facts;

- exhibit poor organization, inconsistent legal analysis, and conclusions that do not follow from the premises of the argument; or
- spend significant time discussing issues not fairly raised by the facts.

. . .

These tools collectively offer students transparency about assessment criteria. Inherently student-centered, transparency advances equity, removing reliance on implicit and unstated performance expectations. These assessment criteria offer a bridge from inclusive Socratic teaching to aligned summative assessment. They explicitly reveal that the content covered in the course and the methods of coverage that drove the full semester of Socratic exchanges were not just the whims of the professor. Instead, the course was designed around exam performance, which itself was styled on law practice and applied skills mastery.

Additional Resources

Many valuable resources are available to law teachers and law schools to help them reform their classrooms and institutions for greater equity and inclusivity. In writing this book, I perceived a gap in how to distinctly create an equitable and inclusive Socratic classroom. This appendix contains sources for further reading and guidance on the broader themes underlying the Socratic teaching strategies, such as building inclusive teaching and assessment practices and student-centered, skills-centered, and community-centered classrooms. Each entry is annotated with a short description of its contents to help you identify which resources will best support your priorities and efforts.

GENERAL RESOURCES

Lisa Bliss, Susan L. Brooks, and Chaumtoli Huq, "Creating Online Education Spaces to Support Equity, Inclusion, Belonging, and Wellbeing," *John Marshall Law Review* 14, no. 2 (2021): 1–40.

Outlines how to create an equitable and inclusive online learning community.

Sean Darling-Hammond and Kristen Holmquist, "Creating Wise Classrooms to Empower Diverse Law Students: Lessons in Pedagogy from Transformative Law Professors," *Berkeley la Raza Law Journal* 25, no. 1 (2015): 1–67.

Reports on eleven interviews of professors whom students identified as "transformative" and experienced in creating environments in which all students were positioned for success.

Nicole P. Dyszlewski, Raquel J. Gabriel, Suzanne Harrington-Steppen, Anna Russell, and Genevieve B. Tung, eds., *Integrating Doctrine and Diversity:*

Inclusion and Equity in the Law School Classroom (Durham: Carolina Academic Press, 2021).

Collects practical advice from more than forty law faculty for implementation by law faculty on best practices to integrate Diversity, Equity, and Inclusion (DEI) principles into legal education in the first year.

Howard E. Katz and Kevin Francis O'Neil, *Strategies and Techniques of Law School Teaching* (Philadelphia: Wolters Kluwer 2009).

Outlines casebook-selection, course-design, syllabus-drafting, classroom-management, exam-drafting, and exam-grading techniques.

"Law Deans Antiracist Clearinghouse Project," Association of American Law Schools, accessed October 30, 2023, www.aals.org/antiracist-clearinghouse/.

Provides resources for leading law schools with antiracist practices and builds a community of leaders committed to this work and methods for auditing existing practices.

L. Danielle Tully, "What Law Schools Should Leave Behind," *Utah Law Review* 22, no. 4 (2022): 837–70.

Advocates that law schools must leave behind "the faculty caste system, high-stakes final exams, and mandatory grading curves to build a more equitable, inclusive, and just profession."

INCLUSIVE TEACHING PRACTICES
Student-Centered Practices

Anne M. Coughlin and Molly Bishop Shadel, "The Gender Participation Gap and the Politics of Pedagogy," *Virginia Law Review Online* 108 (February 2022): 55–71.

Counsels against using cold calls to teach some complex and emotive subjects because students need to be able to opt out, just as lawyers can decline certain cases.

Gerald F. Hess, "Collaborative Course Design: Not my Course, Not Their Course, but Our Course," *Washburn Law Journal* 47, no. 2 (Winter 2008): 356–87.

Provides a roadmap to involve students actively in course-design decisions, such as course goals, learning materials, teaching methods, assignments, and evaluations, using principles of self-determination theory and learner-centered teaching.

Cassandra L. Hill, "The Elephant in the Law School Assessment Room: The Role of Student Responsibility and Motivating Our Students to Learn," *Howard Law Journal* 56, no. 101 (2013): 447–504.

Identifies strategies to involve and motivate students in their own learning, a necessary part of understanding both teaching and learning.

Aníbal Rosario Lebrón, "If These Blackboards Could Talk: The Crit Classroom, a Battlefield," *Charleston Law Review* 9 (2015): 305–33.

Proposes an approach to pedagogy that builds a horizontal, nonhierarchical classroom, including numerous examples of how to structure the classroom to invite critical dialogue.

Molly Bishop Shadel, Sophie Trawalter and J. H. Verkerke, "Gender Differences in Law School Classroom Participation: The Key Role of Social Context," *Virginia Law Review Online* 108 (February 2022): 55–71.

Argues that addressing gender inequality in law schools can help make the entire field of law more equitable. Notes that asking for volunteers (as opposed to cold-calling) can exacerbate gender imbalances in law classrooms and gives recommendations for ways to lower the social costs of participating in class for women.

Amy H. Soled and Barbara Hoffman, "Building Bridges: How Law Schools Can Better Prepare Students from Historically Underserved Communities to Excel in Law School," *Journal of Legal Education* 69, no. 2 (2020): 268–96.

Proposes strategies for how law professors can build bridges to support students from underserved communities.

Skills-Centered Practices

Chad Christensen, "Preparing Law Students to Be Successful Lawyers," *Journal of Legal Education* 69, no. 2 (2020): 502–24.

Focuses on teamwork, collaboration, and cultural competencies as areas in which scholars, law students, and law firms identify as areas for growth in legal education.

Clifford S. Zimmerman, "Thinking beyond My Own Interpretation: Reflections on Collaborative and Cooperative Learning Theory in the Law School Curriculum," *Arizona State Law Journal* 31 (1999): 957–1020.

Explains cooperative and collaborative learning theory and provides guidelines for how to incorporate it into first-year writing assignments.

Community-Centered Practices

Tiffany Atkins, "Amplifying Diverse Voices: Strategies for Promoting Inclusion in the Law School Classroom," *Second Draft: Legal Writing Institute* 31 (Fall 2018): 10–14.

Describes concrete strategies for amplifying the voices and experiences of diverse communities in the classroom.

Anastasia M. Boles, "The Culturally Proficient Law Professor: Beginning the Journey," *New Mexico Law Review* 48 (2018): 145–72.

Advises faculty members on how they can deliver culturally proficient instruction to students through training, bias mitigation, and recognition of microaggressions.

Jeannie Suk Gerson, "The Socratic Method in the Age of Trauma," *Harvard Law Review* 130 (2017): 2320–47.

Describes techniques to use the Socratic method to put all students in active and productive dialogue to make the classroom a space "to confront problems that feel urgently alive."

Sonia M. Gibson, "What's (Race in) the Law Got to Do with It: Incorporating Race in Legal Curriculum," *Connecticut Law Review* 54 (2022): 923–52.

Helps professors navigate discussions about race and equity in the classroom.

Chris Chambers Goodman, "Retaining Diversity in the Classroom: Strategies for Maximizing the Benefits That Flow from a Diverse Student Body," *Pepperdine Law Review* 35 (2008): 663–704.

Identifies strategies to retain, promote, and value the diversity within our law school communities.

Jennifer Jolly-Ryan, "Disabilities to Exceptional Abilities: Law Students with Disabilities, Nontraditional Learners, and the Law Teacher as a Learner," *Nevada Law Journal* 6 (2005): 116–55.

Describes legal education's failure to provide equitable learning environments for students with disabilities and proposes teaching strategies to foster a more inclusive learning environment.

Erin C. Lain, "Racialized Interactions in the Law School Classroom: Pedagogical Approaches to Creating a Safe Learning Environment," *Journal of Legal Education* 67 (2018): 780–801.

Defines "racialized interactions" in law school classrooms and outlines some "best practices and practical tools for professors to help students navigate and learn from these interactions while maintaining psychological safety."

Stevie Leahy, "Fostering Equity and Inclusion across the Gender Spectrum in the Law School Classroom," *Villanova Law Review* 65 (2020): 1105–17.

Introduces law teachers to the dynamics of sex and gender in the law school classroom and proposes concrete ways to cultivate equitable and inclusive classrooms for all students across the gender spectrum.

Vernellia R. Randall, "Increasing Retention and Improving Performance: Practical Advice on Using Cooperative Learning in Law Schools," *Thomas M. Cooley Law Review* 16 (1999): 201–78.

Describes how traditional legal education pedagogy differs from cooperative learning. Articulates the benefits of cooperative learning and strategies for implementation.

Sophie M. Sparrow and Margaret Sova McCabe, "Team-Based Learning in Law," *Legal Writing* 18 (2012): 153–208.

Discusses "Team-Based Learning" as a way to use the case-dialogue method (Socratic teaching) to introduce students to essential lawyering skills, particularly communication.

Palma Joy Strand, "We Are All on the Journey: Transforming Antagonistic Spaces in Law School Classrooms," *Journal of Legal Education* 67 (2017): 176–210.

> Provides concrete strategies to integrate principles of equity and inclusion into traditional law school classrooms and argues that "making space for and eliciting diverse voices, diverse experiences, and diverse perspectives is fundamental to [the] evolution [of legal education]."

Bonny L. Tavares, "Changing the Construct: Promoting Cross-Cultural Conversations in the Law School Classroom," *Journal of Legal Education* 67 (2017): 211–41.

> Explains why cross-cultural awareness is important in legal education pedagogy and outlines "how to create an effective and safe classroom for conducting cross-cultural discussions by assessing the classroom climate, establishing a respectful and approachable relationship with students, and developing the cultural literacy and emotional knowledge to lead cross-cultural conversations with sensitivity and openness."

Cara Cunningham Warren, "Achieving the American Bar Association's Pedagogy Mandate: Empowerment in the Midst of a 'Perfect Storm,'" *Connecticut Public Interest Law Journal* 14 (2014): 67–105.

> Outlines an empowerment teaching framework that synthesizes adult-learner theory, cognitive-learning theory, and self-regulated–learning theory to build learner-centered classes and community-building practices.

INCLUSIVE ASSESSMENT PRACTICES

Meera E. Deo, "A Better Tenure Battle: Fighting Bias in Teaching Evaluations," *Columbia Journal of Gender and Law* 31 (2015): 7–43.

> Describes the effects of bias in student evaluations and analyzes options to eliminate, modify, or supplement them.

Barbara Glesner Fines, "Competition and the Curve," *UMKC Law Review* 65 (1997): 879–915.

> Advocates that law schools discontinue curves and instead rely on norm-referenced grading to promote a more effective learning environment.

Anne D. Gordon, "Better Than Our Biases: Using Psychological Research to Inform Our Approach to Effective, Inclusive Feedback," *Clinical Law Review* 27 (2021): 195–252.

> Proposes practical steps to reduce bias in providing feedback.

DeShun Harris, "Let's Talk about Grading, Maybe: Using Transparency about the Grading Process to Aid in Student Learning," *Seattle Law Review* 45 (2022): 805–52.

> Describes grading as one of the least transparent parts of law school and proposes concrete processes to improve communication about grades and grading.

Paula J. Manning, "Word to the Wise: Feedback Intervention to Moderate the Effects of Stereotype Threat and Attributional Ambiguity on Law Students," *University of Maryland Law Journal of Race, Religion, Gender and Class* 18 (2018): 99–138.

Suggests how law teachers can "combat the negative consequences of stereotype threat and attributional ambiguity by using a social-psychology based intervention known as 'wise feedback.'"

Sophie M. Sparrow, "Describing the Ball: Improve Teaching by Using Rubrics— Explicit Grading Criteria," *Michigan State Law Review* 2004 (2004): 1–55.

Advises law faculty step-by-step on how to create rubrics and why they help strengthen student learning.

Notes

INTRODUCTION: LEGAL EDUCATION'S CURRICULAR CONFORMITY

1. See Prentiss Cox, "1L Curricula in the United States: 2023 Data and Historical Comparison" (research paper, University of Minnesota Law School, 2023), https://ssrn.com/abstract=4450371.

2. Tracie Marcella Addy et al., *What Inclusive Instructors Do* (Sterling, VA: Stylus, 2021), 4.

3. Jess M. Krannich, James R. Holbrook, and Julie J. McAdams, "Beyond 'Thinking Like a Lawyer' and the Traditional Legal Paradigm: Toward a Comprehensive View of Legal Education," *Denver University Law Review* 86, no. 2 (2009): 382, https://digitalcommons.du.edu/cgi/viewcontent.cgi?article=1414&context=dlr.

4. Christopher M. Ford, "The Socratic Method in the 21st Century" (master's thesis, United States Military Academy, 2008), 1–2, www.westpoint.edu/sites/default/files/inline-images/centers_research/center_for_teching_excellence/PDFs/mtp_project_papers/Ford_08.pdf; Tenielle Fordyce-Ruff, "Research across the Curriculum: Using Cognitive Science to Answer the Call for Better Legal Research Instruction," *Dickinson Law Review* 125, no. 1 (2020): 6–7; David R. Barnhizer, "The Purposes and Methods of American Legal Education," *Journal of the Legal Profession* 36, no. 1 (March 2011): 10–11; Bruce A. Kimball, "The Langdell Problem: Historicizing the Century of Historiography, 1906–2000s," *Law and History Review* 22, no. 2 (Summer 2004): 57–140; see also Michele R. Pistone and John J. Hoeffner, "No Path but One: Law School Survival in an Age of Disruptive Technology," *Wayne Law Review* 59, no. 2 (Fall 2013): 207–10; and Ruta K. Stropus, "Mend It, Bend It, and Extend It: The Fate of Traditional Law School Methodology in the 21st Century," *Loyola University Chicago Law Journal* 27, no. 3 (1996): 451–55.

5. Danielle M. Conway, Bekah Saidman-Krauss, and Rebecca Schreiber, "Building an Antiracist Law School: Inclusivity in Admissions and Retention of Diverse Students; Leadership Determines DEI Success," *Rutgers Race and the Law Review* 23, no. 1 (2021): 1–38; Alexa Z. Chew and Rachel Gurvich, "Saying the Quiet Parts Out Loud: Teaching Law Students How Law School Works," *Nebraska Law Review* 904 (2022): 887–904.

6. Catherine A. MacKinnon, "Mainstreaming Feminism in Legal Education," *Journal of Legal Education* 53, no. 2 (June 2003): 212.

7. Rachel Gurvich et al., "Reimagining Langdell's Legacy: Puncturing the Equilibrium in Law School Pedagogy," *North Carolina Law Review Addendum* 101 (2023): 120–21, 146.

8. *ABA Annual Reports,* American Bar Association, 2020, www .abarequireddisclosures.org/Disclosure509.aspx.

9. See, for example, Ford, "Socratic Method," 4.

10. Ford, "Socratic Method," 4.

11. Joshua Krook, "The Real Socratic Method: Law Schools Fail to Understand Why Socrates Asked So Many Questions," *New Intrigue,* September 24, 2017, https://newintrigue.com/2017/09/24/the-real-socratic-method-law-schools-fail-to-understand-why-socrates-asked-so-many-questions/#_ftn22.

12. Carrie Menkel-Meadow, "Taking Law and _____ Really Seriously: Before, during and after 'The Law,'" *Vanderbilt Law Review* 60, no. 2 (2007): 562.

13. Beth Hirschfelder Wilensky, "Dethroning Langdell," *Minnesota Law Review* 107, no. 6 (2023): 2708.

14. Krook, "Real Socratic Method."

15. Lucille A. Jewel, "Silencing Discipline in Legal Education," *University of Toledo Law Review* 49, no. 3 (Spring 2018): 659.

16. Bennett Capers, "The Law School as a White Space," *Minnesota Law Review* 106 (2021): 34.

17. Jewel, "Silencing Discipline," 661; Menkel-Meadow, "Taking Law."

18. Elizabeth Mertz, *The Language of Law School: Learning to Think Like a Lawyer* (Oxford: Oxford University Press, 2007), 31–39.

19. Stephen C. Halpern, "On the Politics and Pathology of Legal Education," *Journal of Legal Education* 32, no. 3 (September 1982): 383–94.

20. See Elizabeth Mertz, "Teaching Lawyers the Language of Law: Legal and Anthropological Translations," *John Marshall Law Review* 34, no. 4 (September 2000): 113–14; Edward Rubin, "What's Wrong with Langdell's Method, and What to Do About It," *Vanderbilt Law Review* 60, no. 2 (2007): 613; Gary Shaw, "A Heretical View of Teaching: A Contrarian Look at Teaching, the Carnegie Report, and Best Practices," *Touro Law Review* 28, no. 4 (November 2012): 1242–43; Deborah L. Rhode, "Missing Questions: Feminist Perspectives on Legal Education," *Stanford Law Review* 45, no. 6 (1993): 1554; Rubin, "What's Wrong," 610.

21. See, for example, Pistone and Hoeffner, "No Path but One," 222.

22. See Lani Guinier, Michelle Fine, and Jane Balin, "Becoming Gentlemen: Women's Experiences at One Ivy League Law School," *University of Pennsylvania Law Review* 143, no. 1 (November 1994).

23. Menkel-Meadow, "Taking Law," 561.

24. See, for example, William M. Sullivan et al., *Educating Lawyers: Preparation for the Profession of Law,* Carnegie Foundation for the Advancement of Teaching, 2007, 56, http://archive.carnegiefoundation.org/publications/pdfs/elibrary/elibrary_pdf_632.pdf; Rubin, "What's Wrong," 662–63; and Minna J. Kotkin, "Clinical Legal Education and the Replication of Hierarchy," *Clinical Law Review* 26, no. 1 (Fall 2019): 287–306.

25. Melanie Hanson, "Average Law School Debt, Education," Education Data Initiative, June 15, 2023, https://educationdata.org/average-law-school-debt (calculating that the average cost of tuition has increased $42,600 and then adjusting for inflation, which is a $34,956 increase).

26. Hanson, "Average Law School Debt."

27. *The Cost of Women's Success,* Law School Survey of Student Engagement, 2019, https://lssse.indiana.edu/wp-content/uploads/2015/12/LSSSE-AnnualSurvey-Gender-Final.pdf (reporting that 19 percent of women leave law school more than $160,000 in debt, compared to 14 percent of men, and 7.9 percent leave owing more than $200,000, compared to 5.5 percent of men). See Chris Guthrie and Emily Lamm, "The Aid Gap," *Journal of Legal Education* 69, no. 1 (Fall 2019): 123–37.

28. Hanson, "Average Law School Debt."

29. Teri A. McMurtry-Chubb, *Strategies and Techniques for Integrating Diversity, Equity, and Inclusion into the Core Law Curriculum: A Comprehensive Guide to DEI Pedagogy, Course Planning, and Classroom Practice* (Philadelphia: Wolters Kluwer, 2021), 64–65, 54–55 (comparing to how "unlike the Indigenous, Black, Chicanx, and Asian American studies movements that occurred on undergraduate campuses, legal education has not experienced a significant social movement within the physical structures of law school buildings that has led to the inclusion of people of color centered interventions into the canon").

30. Students for Fair Admissions (SFFA) v. University of North Carolina (UNC) and SFFA v. Harvard College 600 U.S. 181 (2023).

31. *ABA Approved Law Schools,* American Bar Association, 2022, www.americanbar.org/content/dam/aba/administrative/legal_education_and_admissions_to_the_bar/Questionnaires/2022/2022-aba-standard-509-data-overview-final.pdf; *Statistics,* American Bar Association, February 10, 2023, www.americanbar.org/content/dam/aba/administrative/legal_education_and_admissions_to_the_bar/statistics/2023/2022-jd-non-jd-enrollment.xlsx; *American Bar Association Required Disclosures on Faculty Resources,* American Bar Association, 2022, www.abarequireddisclosures.org/Disclosure509.aspx.

32. Forty-one law schools withdrew from the *U.S. News and World Report* rankings between November 2022 and the spring of 2023. "List of Law Schools Withdrawing from *U.S. News and World Report* Rankings Participation," Spivey Consulting, November 19, 2022, www.spiveyconsulting.com/blog-post/list-of-law-schools-withdrawing-from-us-news-rankings/. The *U.S. News and World Report* instead relied on data disclosed to the ABA to calculate the rankings of the schools that did not respond. Robert Morse et al., "Methodology: 2023–2024 Best Law Schools Rankings," U.S. News, May 10, 2023, www.usnews.com/education/best-graduate-schools/articles/law-schools-methodology.

33. See Sue Liemer, "The Hierarchy of Law School Faculty Meetings: Who Votes?," *UMKC Law Review* 73, no. 2 (2004): 351–418 (surveying voting rules for legal research and writing, library, and clinical faculty).

34. L. Danielle Tully, "What Law Schools Should Leave Behind," *Utah Law Review* 22, no. 4 (2022): 842, 848. Tully explains how law faculty are generally tiered around "casebook, clinical, legal writing, academic success, and law librarians" (847).

35. See, for example, Darby Dickerson, "President's Message: Abolish the Academic Caste System," American Association of Law Schools, accessed July 17, 2021, www.aals.org/about/publications/newsletters/aals-news-fall-2020/presidents-message-abolish-the-academic-caste-system; see also Rachel López, "Unentitled: The Power of Designation in the Legal Academy," *Rutgers University Law Review* 73, no. 3 (Spring 2021): 923–32.

36. Capers, "White Space," 17.

37. Robert Kuehn, "Shifting Law School Faculty Demographics," Best Practices for Legal Education, January 5, 2022, https://bestpracticeslegaled.com/2022/01/05/clinical-legal-education-by-the-numbers/.

38. "Law School Enrollment by Race and Ethnicity (2019)," Enjuris, accessed June 20, 2021, www.enjuris.com/students/law-school-race-2019.html.

39. Laura Bagby, "ABA Profile of the Legal Profession: Diversity and Well-Being," 2Civility, August 13, 2020, www.2civility.org/aba-profile-of-the-legal-profession-diversity-and-well-being/.

40. "Law School Enrollment."

41. Miranda Li, Phillip Yao, and Goodwin Lui, "Who's Going to Law School?," *UC Davis Law Review* 54, no. 2 (December 2020): 614.

42. "Various Statistics on ABA-Approved Law Schools," American Bar Association, accessed June 20, 2021, www.americanbar.org/groups/legal_education/resources/statistics (citing 2020 enrollment data that 7,598 women of color enrolled, compared to 4,827 men of color, out of 38,202 total 1L students); "Law School Enrollment."

43. NALP Foundation for Law Career Research and Education and the Center for Women in Law. *Women of Color: A Study of Law School Experiences (2020)*. 2020. www.nalpfoundation.org/product-page/women-of-color-a-study-of-law-school-experiences.

44. "Law School Enrollment."

45. See, for example, Kathryn Rubino, "Black at Harvard Law School Is the Instagram Account You Need to Read Right Now," Above the Law, June 24, 2020, https://abovethelaw.com/2020/06/black-at-harvard-law-school-is-the-instagram-account-you-need-to-read-right-now; and Capers, "White Space," 21 (summarizing how only 9 percent of White students report feeling uncomfortable on campus, while 25 percent of Black students and 18 percent of Latinx report feeling uncomfortable).

46. NALP Foundation, *Women of Color*.

47. *2020 Diversity and Exclusion: 2020 Annual Survey Results*, Law School Survey of Student Engagement, September 29, 2020, 9, https://lssse.indiana.edu/wp-content/uploads/2020/09/Diversity-and-Exclusion-Final-9.29.20.pdf.

48. See Elizabeth Bodamer, "Do I Belong Here? Examining Perceived Experiences of Bias, Stereotype Concerns, and Sense of Belonging in U.S. Law Schools," *Journal of Legal Education* 69, no. 2 (2020): 456, 474–76.

49. Carliss N. Chatman and Najarian R. Peters, "The Soft-Shoe and Shuffle of Law School Hiring Committee Practices," *UCLA Law Review* 69, *Discourse* 2 (2021): 15–16.

50. "Law School Enrollment"; *2019 Report on Diversity in U.S. Law Firms,* National Association for Law Placement, December 2019, 16, www.nalp.org /uploads/2019_DiversityReport.pdf.

51. Bagby, "ABA Profile."

52. Chris Chambers Goodman and Sarah E. Redfield, "A Teacher Who Looks Like Me," *Journal of Civil Rights and Economic Development* 27 (2013): 114.

53. Kuehn, "Shifting Law School Faculty."

54. Deborah Archer et al., "The Diversity Imperative Revisited: Racial and Gender Inclusion in Clinical Law Faculty," *Clinical Law Review* 26, no. 1 (August 2019): 128. ("Overall, White faculty continue to hold nearly 8 out of 10 clinical faculty positions.")

55. Meera E. Deo, "Trajectory of a Law Professor," *Michigan Journal of Race and Law* 20, no. 2 (2015): 457, 445–46 (citing 2009 numbers before the American Association of Law Schools stopped releasing data), 446.

56. Davida Finger, "CLEA Statement on Anti-racist Legal Education," Best Practices for Legal Education, April 22, 2021, https://bestpracticeslegaled. com/2021/04/22/clea-statement-on-anti-racist-legal-education.

57. Kuehn, "Shifting Law School Faculty."

58. Chatman and Peters, "Soft-Shoe and Shuffle," 5, 10, 16.

59. American Association of Law Schools, "Highlights from the American Law School Dean Study," *ABA Journal,* 2021, www.abajournal.com/files /Deans_Study_Short_Report.pdf; Stephanie Francis Ward, "Diversity Increases with Law School Deans, According to New AALS Study," *ABA Journal,* April 4, 2022, www.abajournal.com/web/article/diversity-increases-with-law-school-deans-according-to-aals-study.

60. American Association of Law Schools, "Highlights."

61. Dara Purvis, "Legal Education as Hegemonic Masculinity," *Villanova Law Review* 65, no. 5 (January 2021): 1145–54.

62. See, for example, Kathryn M. Stanchi, "Who Next, the Janitors? A Socio-feminist Critique of the Status Hierarchy of Law Professors," *UMKC Law Review* 73, no. 2 (2004): 469; and Purvis, "Legal Education."

63. See Elizabeth Olson, "Women Make Up Majority of U.S. Law Students for First Time," *New York Times,* December 16, 2016, www.nytimes.com/2016/12/16 /business/dealbook/women-majority-of-us-law-students-first-time.html; "Law School Rankings by Female Enrollment (2019)," Enjuris, accessed November 13, 2023, www.enjuris.com/students/law-school-female-enrollment-2019.html.

64. Kuehn, "Shifting Law School Faculty."

65. *ABA Approved Law Schools.*

66. Deborah Jones Merritt and Kyle McEntee, "Gender Equity in Law School Enrollment: An Elusive Goal," *Journal of Legal Education* 69, no. 1 (Fall 2019): 103–5, 106–8, 106.

67. Merritt and McEntee, "Gender Equity," 108 (reporting a 66 percent versus 60 percent factor), 109 (finding that 86 percent of women cite this factor compared to 78 percent of men), 110. See *Cost of Women's Success,* 8 (reporting that 21 percent of men scored a 161 or above on the LSAT, compared to 16 percent of women, and 51 percent of women reported undergraduate grade-point averages above a 3.5, compared to 40 percent of men), 111 (calling for more data collection on gender differences).

68. Karen Sloan, "ABA Votes to Keep Law School Standardized Test Requirement," Reuters, February 6, 2023, www.reuters.com/legal/legalindustry/aba-votes-keep-law-school-standardized-test-requirement-2023-02-06/.

69. Susan Ehrlich Martin and Nancy C. Jurik, *Doing Justice, Doing Gender: Women in Legal and Criminal Justice Occupations* (Thousand Oaks: Sage, 2006), 124; Richard H. Chused, "The Hiring and Retention of Minorities and Women on American Law School Faculties," *University of Pennsylvania Law Review* 137 (1988): 548.

70. Chused, "Hiring and Retention," 548.

71. Kuehn, "Shifting Law School Faculty" (analyzing archived American Bar Association reporting data).

72. *ABA Annual Reports.*

73. See Ann C. McGinley, "Reproducing Gender on Law School Faculties" *BYU Law Review* 99, no. 1 (2009): 99–156; Paula Monopoli, "Gender and the Crisis in Legal Education: Remaking the Academy in Our Image," *Michigan State Law Review* 5 (2012): 1745–75; Christopher J. Ryan Jr. and Meghan Dawe, "Mind the Gap: Gender Pay Disparities in the Legal Academy," *Georgetown Journal of Legal Ethics* 34, no. 3 (2021): 567–611. See also, for example, Yolanda Flores Niemann, Gabriella Gutiérrez y Muhs, and Carmen G. González, eds. *Presumed Incompetent II: Race, Class, Power, and Resistance of Women in Academia* (Denver: University Press of Colorado, 2020), 3 (citing 2016 data from the National Center for Education Statistics, published in 2018).

74. Ruth A. Robbins, Kristen M. Tischione, and Melissa H. Weresh, "Persistent Structural Barriers to Gender Equity in the Legal Academy and the Efforts of Two Legal Writing Organizations to Break Them Down," *Villanova Law Review* 65, no. 5 (2021): 1161.

75. Robert R. Kuehn, Margaret Reuter, and David A. Santacroce, *2019–20 Survey of Applied Legal Education,* Center for the Study of Applied Legal Education, 2020, www.csale.org/#results (identifying new faculty as those with three years or less experience).

76. Just under one-third (29 percent) of clinical faculty have tenure or a form of tenure, 21 percent have traditional tenure or tracks toward it, and 8 percent have "clinical tenure" (known as programmatic tenure) or are progressing toward it. Another third (33 percent) have long-term presumptively renewable contracts, and just over a third have long- or short-term contracts. Robbins, Tischione, and Weresh, "Persistent Structural Barriers," 1162.

77. Kuehn, "Shifting Law School Faculty," note 37.

78. Robbins, Tischione, and Weresh, "Persistent Structural Barriers," 1161n99.

79. Archer et al., "Diversity Imperative Revisited," 128–30n65.

80. Robbins, Tischione, and Weresh, "Persistent Structural Barriers," 1163n99 (concluding based on the Association of Legal Writing Directors and Legal Writing Institute Survey reports that traditional tenured faculty begin with an average of $108,089, and legal research and writing faculty begin with an average of $84,909). Those data likely dramatically underreport the disparities.

81. Jewel, "Silencing Discipline," 676n11.

82. Robbins, Tischione, and Weresh, "Persistent Structural Barriers," 1165, 1164 (citing the Standards 405[c] and [d] policies that "explicitly exempt clinicians and legal research and writing faculty, segregating faculty by security of positions based on the subject matter they teach").

83. See Meera E. Deo, *Unequal Profession: Race and Gender in Legal Academia* (Redwood City: Stanford University Press, 2019).

84. McGinley, "Reproducing Gender."

85. See Meera E. Deo, "Investigating Pandemic Effects on Legal Academia," *Fordham Law Review* 89, no. 6 (2021): 2467–95; and Arlie R. Hochschild, *Second Shift: Working Parents and the Revolution at Home* (New York: Viking Penguin, 1989).

86. See Deo, *Unequal Profession.*

87. See Capers, "White Space," 7.

88. Julia H. Chang, "Spectacular Bodies," in Niemann, Gutiérrez y Muhs, and González, *Presumed Incompetent II,* 261.

89. Laura M. Padilla, "Presumptions of Incompetence, Gender, Sidelining, and Women Law Deans," in Niemann, Gutiérrez y Muhs, and González, *Presumed Incompetent II,* 117–19 (noting that women have led many top-ten law schools and further analyzing the data of first Latina, Native, and Asian American deans).

90. "Deans by Ethnicity and Gender: Listed Alphabetically," Mississippi College School of Law, accessed November 12, 2023, https://lawdeans.com /results.php?s=15 (calculated from reported figures from Rosenblatt's Dean Database: Black women, 13.50 percent; Hispanic/Latina women, 3.02 percent; Asian Pacific Islander women, 1.51 percent; Native American women, 1.01 percent; Asian American women, 0 percent).

91. Padilla, "Presumptions of Incompetence," 119.

92. Candice Norwood, "More Black Women Are Leading U.S. Law Schools and Changing the Conversation on Race and Gender," *19th News,* February 8, 2022, https://19thnews.org/2022/02/black-women-law-school-deans/.

93. Robbins, Tischione, and Weresh, "Persistent Structural Barriers," 1161.

94. W. C. Kim and Renee Mauborgne, "Tipping Point Leadership," *Harvard Business Review* 50, no. 4 (2003): 52.

95. See, for example, Alice Ristroph, "The Curriculum of the Carceral State," *Columbia Law Review* 120, no. 6 (2020): 1631–1708; McMurtry-Chubb, *Strategies and Techniques;* Conway, Saidman-Krauss, and Schreiber, "Antiracist Law School"; Capers, "White Space, 45"; Nicole P. Dyszlewski et al., eds., *Integrating Doctrine and Diversity: Inclusion and Equity in the Law School Classroom* (Durham: Carolina Academic Press, 2021); Etienne C. Toussaint, "The Purpose of Legal Education," *California Law Review* 111 (February 2023): 1–70.

I. SOCRATIC CLASSROOMS DOMINATE LEGAL EDUCATION'S CURRICULAR CORE

1. Stephen C. Halpern, "On the Politics and Pathology of Legal Education," *Journal of Legal Education* 32, no. 3 (September 1982): 389 ("The power and control exercised by the instructor and the manipulation and intimidation of students which occur as a legitimate part of classroom 'teaching' tend to make students fearful, passive, intellectually uninteresting, and uncreative").

2. Margaret E. Montoya, "Silence and Silencing: Their Centripetal and Centrifugal Forces in Legal Communication, Pedagogy and Discourse," *Michigan Journal of Race and Law* 5, no. 3 (Summer 2000): 263–327.

3. See Bennett Capers, "The Law School as a White Space," *Minnesota Law Review* 106 (2021): 40–41 ("Certainly the 'dialogue' students are expected to master is a particular kind of dialogue, in a particular register").

4. Montoya, "Silence and Silencing" (explaining the importance of fighting negative misconceptions of silence).

5. "Law School Enrollment by Race and Ethnicity (2019)," Enjuris, accessed June 20, 2021, www.enjuris.com/students/law-school-race-2019.html.

6. "Law School Enrollment by Race and Ethnicity (2022)," Enjuris, accessed July 12, 2023, www.enjuris.com/students/law-school-race-2022/.

7. Elizabeth Bodamer, "Do I Belong Here? Examining Perceived Experiences of Bias, Stereotype Concerns, and Sense of Belonging in U.S. Law Schools," *Journal of Legal Education* 69, no. 2 (2020): 457.

8. Carmen G. González, *Women of Color in Legal Education Challenging the Presumption of Incompetence*, Federal Lawyer, July 2014, https://upcolorado.com/excerpts/PresumedIncompetent_FederalLawyer.pdf.

9. Carmen G. González and Angela P. Harris, "Presumed Incompetent: Continuing the Conversation," *Berkeley Journal of Gender, Law, and Justice* 29, no. 2 (Summer 2014): 183–94.

10. Martha Chamallas, "The Shadow of Professor Kingsfield: Contemporary Dilemmas Facing Women Law Professors," *William and Mary Journal of Race, Gender, and Social Justice* 11, no. 2 (2005): 199–206.

11. Darby Dickerson, "President's Message: Abolish the Academic Caste System," Association of American Law Schools, accessed July 17, 2021, www.aals.org/about/publications/newsletters/aals-news-fall-2020/presidents-message-abolish-the-academic-caste-system/.

12. Dickerson, "President's Message."

13. Kathryne M. Young, "Understanding the Social and Cognitive Process in Law School That Creates Unhealthy Lawyers," *Fordham Law Review* 89, no. 6 (2021): 2594–95.

14. Montoya, "Silence and Silencing."

15. See David Garner, "Socratic Misogyny: Analyzing Feminist Criticism of Socratic Teaching in Legal Education," *BYU Law Review* 2000, no. 4 (2000): 1614–27 (documenting studies at Yale in 1988, Stanford in 1988, Berkeley in 1989–90, and the University of Pennsylvania in 1994, along with studies conducted by the Law School Admissions Council in 1994 and by Taunya Lovell Banks).

16. Stephanie Wildman, "The Question of Silence: Techniques to Ensure Full Class Participation," *Journal of Legal Education* 38, no. 1 (March 1988): 151

(concluding that "silence, deference, and talk with no substance are not ways of survival in law firms, courtrooms, and legal life").

17. Lani Guinier, Michelle Fine, and Jane Balin, "Becoming Gentlemen: Women's Experiences at One Ivy League Law School," *University of Pennsylvania Law Review* 143, no. 1 (November 1994): 1–110.

18. "Lani Guinier," Harvard Law School, accessed March 25, 2022, www .hls.harvard.edu/faculty/directory/10344/Guinier; Guinier, Fine, and Balin, "Becoming Gentlemen," 21–32.

19. See, for example, Taunya Lovell Banks, "Gender Bias in the Classroom," *Journal of Legal Education* 38, no. 1 (March 1988): 141.

20. Guinier, Fine, and Balin, "Becoming Gentlemen," 6, 42, 68, 81.

21. Sari Bashi and Maryana Iskander, "Why Legal Education Is Failing Women," *Yale Journal of Law and Feminism* 18, no. 2 (2006): 392; Molly Bishop Shadel, Sophie Trawalter, and J.H. Verkerke, "Gender Differences in Law School Classroom Participation: The Key Role of Social Context," *Virginia Law Review Online* 108 (February 2022): 55–71.

22. Young, "Social and Cognitive Process," 2588–92 (interviewing students and documenting their sense of gendered and racialized disparities in class participation and noting that these "descriptions were virtually identical whether or not a professor used panels, cold calls, or a volunteer system"), 2590–91 (noting, however, that while "cold calls stood out as a particularly salient source of inequality, gendered and racialized classroom dynamics extended into other parts of the learning environment as well"), 2589–90.

23. Richard Delgado and Jean Stefanic, "Can Lawyers Find Happiness?," *Syracuse Law Review* 58 (2008): 248; Susan A. McMahon, "What We Teach When We Teach Legal Analysis," *Minnesota Law Review* 107 (2023): 2511–60.

24. Elizabeth Berenguer, Lucy Jewel, and Teri A. McMurtry-Chubb, "Gut Renovations: Using Critical and Comparative Rhetoric to Remodel How the Law Addresses Privilege and Power," *Harvard Latinx Law Review* 23, no. 2 (2020): 214, 216.

25. Berenguer, Jewel, and McMurtry-Chubb, 207, 215.

26. Duncan Kennedy, *Legal Education and the Reproduction of Hierarchy* (New York: New York University Press, 2004), 31 (reproducing a work previously published in 1983, with more critical commentary, an introduction, and an afterword); Joshua Krook, "The Real Socratic Method: Law Schools Fail to Understand Why Socrates Asked So Many Questions," *New Intrigue*, September 24, 2017, https://newintrigue.com/2017/09/24/the-real-socratic-method-law-schools-fail-to-understand-why-socrates-asked-so-many-questions/#_ftn22.

27. Joshua Krook, "The Real Socratic Method: At the Heart of Legal Education Lies a Fundamental Misunderstanding of Why Socrates Asked So Many Questions," *Griffith Journal of Law and Human Dignity* 5, no. 1 (2017): 35.

28. See Capers, "White Space," 40–41.

29. Kennedy, *Legal Education* (critiquing how students learn to categorize rules to fit certain situations).

30. Berenguer, Jewel, and McMurtry-Chubb, "Gut Renovations," 217.

31. Lucille A. Jewel, "Oil and Water: How Legal Education's Doctrine and Skills Divide Reproduces Toxic Hierarchies," *Columbia Journal of Gender and Law* 31, no. 1 (2015): 112–13.

32. Emily Zimmerman, "Do Grades Matter?," *Seattle University Law Review* 35, no. 2 (2012): 305–76.

33. "Are 1L Grades Really That Important in Law School?." J.D. Advising, accessed October 15, 2023, https://jdadvising.com/are-1l-grades-really-that-important-in-law-school/.

34. Halpern, "Politics and Pathology," 390.

35. See Capers, "White Space," 7, 11–12.

36. Teri A. McMurtry-Chubb, *Strategies and Techniques for Integrating Diversity, Equity, and Inclusion into the Core Law Curriculum: A Comprehensive Guide to DEI Pedagogy, Course Planning, and Classroom Practice* (Philadelphia: Wolters Kluwer, 2021), xviii.

37. Patricia Williams, *The Alchemy of Race and Rights: The Diary of a Law Professor* (Cambridge, MA: Harvard University Press, 1991), 35–36.

38. Mari J. Matsuda, "When the First Quail Calls: Multiple Consciousness as Jurisprudential Method," *Women's Rights Law Reporter* 11, no. 1 (1993): 8.

39. Dean Spade, "For Those Considering Law School," *Unbound* 6 (2010): 114–15.

40. Kimberlé Crenshaw, "Foreword: Toward a Race-Conscious Pedagogy in Legal Education," *Southern California Review of Law and Women's Studies* 4 (1994): 35–36, 38.

41. Kim Brooks and Debra Parkes, "Queering Legal Education: A Project of Theoretical Discovery," *Harvard Journal of Law and Gender* 27 (Spring 2004): 96–97.

42. Scott Ihrig, "Sexual Orientation in Law School: Experiences of Gay, Lesbian, and Bisexual Law Students," *Minnesota Journal of Law and Inequity* 14, no. 2 (1996): 555–59.

43. See Kelly Strader et al., "An Assessment of the Law School Climate for GLBT Students," *Journal of Legal Education* 58, no. 2 (2008): 225 (concluding that 11 percent of LGBTQ+ students reported feeling somewhat uncomfortable discussing LGBTQ+ issues in class).

44. Brooks and Parkes, "Queering Legal Education," 96–97.

45. Brooks and Parkes, "Queering Legal Education," 96–97.

2. SUSTAINED CALLS FOR CURRICULAR REFORMS

1. The following content on feminist influences on legal education is heavily rooted in my previously published chapter: Jamie R. Abrams, "Feminism's Transformation of Legal Education and Unfinished Agenda" in *Oxford Handbook of Feminism and Law in the U.S.*, ed. Deborah L. Brake, Martha Chamallas, and Verna L. Williams, 494–516 (Oxford: Oxford University Press, 2021).

2. Virginia G. Drachman, *Sisters in Law: Women Lawyers in Modern American History* (Cambridge, MA: Harvard University Press, 2001), 152.

3. "Our Founding Mothers," American University Washington College of Law, accessed July 17, 2023, www.wcl.american.edu/impact/history/.

Notes | 195

4. Grace Hathaway, *Fate Rides a Tortoise A Biography of Ellen Spencer Mussey* (Philadelphia: Winston, 1937), 130.

5. Jamie R. Abrams and Daniela Kraiem, "Banding Together: Reflections on the Role of the Women's Bar Association of the District of Columbia and the Washington College of Law in Promoting Women's Rights," *Modern American* 4, no. 2 (Fall 2008): 42–56.

6. Mary L. Clark, "The Founding of the Washington College of Law: The First Law School Established by Women for Women," *American University Law Review* 47 (1998): 656.

7. Abrams and Kraiem, "Banding Together."

8. Deborah L. Rhode, "Missing Questions: Feminist Perspectives on Legal Education," *Stanford Law Review* 45, no. 6 (1993): 1547 (quoting the dean of Harvard Law School reassuring alumni that women's presence in law school was unlikely to "change the character of the school or even its atmosphere to any detectable extent"). See Lani Guinier, "Of Gentlemen and Role Models," *Berkeley Women's Law Journal* 6, no. 1 (1991): 93–106 (explaining that women of color should be hired not to *become gentlemen* but to add race and gender); Stephanie Wildman, "The Question of Silence: Techniques to Ensure Full Class Participation," *Journal of Legal Education* 38, no. 1 (March 1988): 149 (describing women's class participation as "Ladies Day").

9. David Garner, "Socratic Misogyny: Analyzing Feminist Criticism of Socratic Teaching in Legal Education," *BYU Law Review* 2000, no. 4 (2000): 1613, 1614.

10. Elisabeth Hayes, "Insights from Women's Experiences for Teaching and Learning," *Effective Teaching Styles: New Directions for Continuing Legal Education* 1989, no. 43 (Fall 1989): 58.

11. Carrie Menkel-Meadow, Martha Minow, and David Vernon, "From the Editors," *Journal of Legal Education* 38 (March–June 1988): 1–2.

12. See Kate E. Bloch, "A Rape Law Pedagogy," *Yale Journal of Law and Feminism* 7, no. 2 (1995): 307–40 (noting that many criminal law instructors do not teach about rape laws, or they teach them differently from other rules).

13. See, for example, Barbara Allen Babcock et al., *Sex Discrimination and the Law: Causes and Remedies* (Boston: Little, Brown, 1975); Kenneth Davidson, Ruth B. Ginsburg, and Herma Hill Kay, *Text, Cases, and Materials on Sex-Based Discrimination* (Saint Paul: West, 1974); Morrison Torrey, Jackie Casey, and Karin Olson, "Teaching Law in a Feminist Manner: A Commentary from Experience," *Harvard Journal of Law and Feminism* 13 (1990): 87–136.

14. See Christine Boyle, "Teaching Law as If Women Really Mattered, or What about the Washrooms?," *Canadian Journal of Women and the Law* 2, no. 1 (1986): 108.

15. Catharine A. MacKinnon, "Feminism in Legal Education," *Legal Education Review* 1, no. 1 (1989): 1–7.

16. Katharine T. Bartlett, "Feminist Perspective on the Ideological Impact of Legal Education upon the Profession," *North Carolina Law Review* 72 (1994): 1259–70; Catherine A. MacKinnon, "Mainstreaming Feminism in Legal Education," *Journal of Legal Education* 53, no. 2 (June 2003): 200.

17. See, for example, Susan H. Williams, "Legal Education, Feminist Episte-mology, and the Socratic Method," *Stanford Law Review* 45, no. 6 (July 1993): 585–613.

18. Rhode, "Missing Questions," 1558.

19. See, for example, Garner, "Socratic Misogyny," 1630.

20. Carol Gilligan, *In a Different Voice: Psychological Theory and Women's Development* (Cambridge, MA: Harvard University Press, 1982), 1–2.

21. Bartlett, "Feminist Perspective," 1267.

22. Rhode, "Missing Questions," 1551.

23. Martha Minow, "Feminist Reason: Getting It and Losing It," *Journal of Legal Education* 38, nos. 1–2 (March–June 1998): 48.

24. See Carrie Menkel-Meadow, "Taking Law and _____ Really Seriously: Before, during and after 'The Law,'" *Vanderbilt Law Review* 60, no. 2 (2007): 563–68 (describing legal realism, its founders, its methods, and its enduring contributions); Mark Tushnet, "Critical Legal Studies: A Political History," *Yale Law Journal* 100, no. 5 (1990–91): 1515–44 (noting that this movement is generally connected to influences of the civil rights movement and the Warren Court); Tushnet, "Critical Legal Studies: An Introduction to Its Origins and Underpinnings," *Journal of Legal Education* 36, no. 4 (1986): 505–17.

25. Robert W. Gordon, "Unfreezing Legal Reality: Critical Approaches to Law," *Florida State University Law Review* 15, no. 2 (1987): 197.

26. Duncan Kennedy, *Legal Education and the Reproduction of Hierarchy* (New York: New York University Press, 2004), 15, 19, 31, 62, 77 (reproducing a work previously published in 1983, with more critical commentary, an intro-duction, and an afterword).

27. Kennedy, *Legal Education,* 160 (reflections by Peter Gabel).

28. E. Dana Neacsu, "CLS Stands for Critical Legal Studies, If Anyone Remembers," *Journal of Law and Policy* 8, no. 2 (2000): 418 (explaining that CLS urged legal educators to resist "and to avoid or at least postpone becoming innocent ideological instruments employed and exploited for the illegitimate reproduction of hierarchy" but noting that this "sense of social injustice" does not carry through to solutions).

29. Joan C. Williams, "Critical Legal Studies: The Death of Transcendence and the Rise of the New Langdells," *NYU Law Review* 62, no. 3 (June 1987): 430.

30. Robert W. Gordon, "Critical Legal Studies as a Teaching Method, against the Background of the Intellectual Politics of Modern Legal Education in the United States," *Legal Education Review* 1, no. 1 (1989): 68.

31. Gordon, "Critical Legal Studies."

32. See, for example, Jose A. Bracamonte, "Minority Critiques of the Critical Legal Studies Movement: Foreword," *Harvard Civil Rights–Civil Liberties Law Review* 22, no. 2 (Spring 1987): 421–510; Harlon L. Dalton, "The Clouded Prism," *Harvard Civil Rights–Civil Liberties Law Review* 22, no. 2 (Spring 1987): 435–47 (describing how legal scholars of color within CLS wanted to focus more on practice and community-based applications than on theory); Mari J. Matsuda, "Looking to the Bottom: Critical Legal Studies and Reparations," *Harvard Civil Rights–Civil Liberties Law Review* 22, no. 2 (Spring 1987): 323–400.

33. Kimberlé Crenshaw, "The First Decade: Critical Reflections, or 'A Foot in the Closing Door,'" in *Crossroads, Directions, and a New Critical Race Theory*, ed. Francisco Valdes, Jerome McCristal Culp, and Angela P. Harris (Philadelphia: Temple University Press, 2002), 30.

34. Kimberlé Crenshaw, "Twenty Years of Critical Race Theory: Looking Back to Move Forward," *Connecticut Law Review* 43, no. 5 (2011): 1289, 1290–95.

35. Kimberlé Crenshaw et al., eds., *Critical Race Theory: The Key Writings That Formed the Movement* (New York: New Press, 1995), xix.

36. Derrick A. Bell Jr., "Who's Afraid of Critical Race Theory?," *University of Illinois Law Review* 1995, no. 4 (1995): 898; see also Khiara Bridges, *Critical Race Theory: A Primer* (Goleta: Foundation, 2019).

37. Richard Delgado and Jean Stefanic, "Critical Race Theory: An Annotated Bibliography," *Virginia Law Review* 79, no. 2 (March 1993): 461.

38. Bridges, *Critical Race Theory*, 7, 10–11.

39. Crenshaw, "Twenty Years," 1262–63.

40. Daniel G. Solozano and Tara J. Yosso, "Critical Race and LatCrit Theory and Method: Counter-Storytelling," *International Journal of Qualitative Studies in Education* 14, no. 1 (2001): 473–74 (noting CRT's emergence from ethnic studies, women's studies, cultural nationalism, Marxist and neo-Marxist approaches, and internal colonial frameworks).

41. Crenshaw, "Twenty Years," 1272–73 (noting that the group was known as the Third World Coalition), 1273–74.

42. Crenshaw, "Twenty Years," 1281. Derrick Bell Jr.'s central text, *Race, Racism, and American Law,* along with other materials introduced in this course, became part of the CRT canon, which introduced interdisciplinary approaches and new analytic methods. Crenshaw, "Twenty Years," 1281–85.

43. See, for example, Francis L. Ansley, "Race and the Core Curriculum in Legal Education," *California Law Review* 79, no. 6 (1991): 1520 (discussing how race is central to US legal history and should be integrated into classroom teaching); Derrick A. Bell Jr., "Humanity in Legal Education," *Oregon Law Review* 59, nos. 2–3 (May 1980): 243–48 (arguing that law schools should not be just *teaching* but should also strengthen character and sensitize students to the world around them).

44. Solozano and Yosso, "Critical Race," 472, 473.

45. See, for example, Linda S. Greene, "Serving the Community: Aspiration and Abyss for the Law Professor of Color," *Saint Louis University Public Law Review* 10, no. 1 (1991): 297–303; Linda S. Greene, "Tokens, Role Models, and Pedagogical Politics: Lamentations of an African American Female Law Professor," *Berkeley Journal of Gender, Law and Justice* 6, no. 1 (1990–91): 81–92; Angela P. Harris, "On Doing the Right Thing: Education Work in the Academy," *Vermont Law Review* 15 (1990–91): 125–38.

46. Yolanda Flores Niemann, Gabriella Gutiérrez y Muhs, and Carmen G. González, eds., *Presumed Incompetent II: Race, Class, Power, and Resistance of Women in Academia* (Denver: University Press of Colorado, 2012) (an edited volume capturing the testimonies of forty authors identifying the challenges faced by academic women of color).

47. Crenshaw, "Twenty Years," 1311.

48. Solozano and Yosso, "Critical Race," 474 (noting CRT's expansion into LatCrit, FemCrit, AsianCrit, and WhiteCrit); Francisco Valdes and Steven W. Bender, *LatCrit: From Critical Legal Theory to Academic Activism* (New York: New York University Press, 2021), 1.

49. Elizabeth M. Iglesias, "Foreword: International law, Human Rights, and LatCrit Theory," *University of Miami Inter-American Law Review* 28, no. 2 (Winter 1996–97): 178. But see Athena D. Mutua, "Shifting Bottoms and Rotating Centers: Reflections on LatCrit III and the Black/White Paradigm," *University of Miami Law Review* 53, no. 4 (July 1999): 1177–218.

50. See Margaret E. Montoya, "Mascaras, Trenzas, y Greñas: Un/Masking the Self While Un/Braiding Latina Stories and Legal Discourse," *Harvard Journal of Law and Gender* 17 (1994): 1–37.

51. Francisco Valdes, "Legal Reform and Social Justice: An Introduction to LatCrit Theory, Praxis, and Community," *Griffith Law Review* 14, no. 2 (2005): 153.

52. Valdes and Bender, *LatCrit*, 1, x, 27–28.

53. Valdes and Bender, *LatCrit*, 30, 107, 3 (noting LatCrit's particularly close relationship to CRT).

54. Valdes and Bender, *LatCrit*, 35, 36–37, 13, 50–56 (describing the movement's robust discussions and convenings over decades and the breadth and depth of topics covered), 2.

55. Valdes and Bender, *LatCrit*, 27.

56. See Luz E. Herrara, "Challenging a Tradition of Exclusion: The History of an Unheard Story at Harvard Law School," *Harvard Latino Law Review* 5, no. 3 (Spring 2002): 54 (describing the founding of the Chicano Law Student Association), 80.

57. Valdes and Bender, *LatCrit*, 119. These data look at the enrollment of Latinx students in ABA-accredited law schools.

58. *ABA Annual Reports*, American Bar Association, 2020, www.abarequireddisclosures.org/Disclosure509.aspx.

59. The law schools that reported their data to the American Bar Association are not the same when comparing the 2012 and 2022 enrollment data: Arizona Summit Law School lost their accreditation in 2017; Charlotte School of Law closed in 2017; Florida Coastal School of Law ended classes in the spring of 2021 and initiated a teach-out plan; Thomas Jefferson Law School lost their ABA accreditation in 2019; University of La Verne converted from an ABA-accredited school to a California State Bar's Committee of Bar Examiners accreditation; UNT Dallas College of Law became fully ABA accredited in 2017; Valparaiso University closed in 2017; Whittier Law School closed, deciding in 2017 not to accept new 1L classes starting fall 2017; Hamline University and William Mitchell College of Law merged to Mitchell Hamline School of Law; Rutgers University merged its two campuses (Camden and Newark) in 2015; and Pennsylvania State—Dickinson and Pennsylvania State Law merged to Pennsylvania State University.

60. "Rosenblatt's Deans Database," Mississippi College School of Law, accessed July 13, 2022, https://lawdeans.com/results.php?s=14/.

61. Valdes and Bender, *LatCrit*, 79, 10, 14, 32–33, 80.

62. Donna Saadati-Soto, "The Experience of Latinx Students with the Harvard Law School First-Year Curriculum," Social Science Research Network, May 2020, 11–12, https://ssrn.com/abstract=3579132.

63. Aníbal Rosario-Lebrón, "If These Blackboards Could Talk: The Crit Classroom, a Battlefield," *Charlestown Law Review* 9 (2015): 305, 313, cited in Valdes and Bender, *LatCrit*, 80, 82.

64. Valdes and Bender, *LatCrit*, 59.

65. See Carl F. Stychin, *Law's Desire: Sexuality and the Limits of Justice* (London: Routledge, 1995).

66. Kevin S. Reuther, "Dorothy's Friend Goes to Law School," *National Journal of Sexual Orientation Law* 1, no. 2 (1995): 253, www.ibiblio.org /gaylaw/issue2/reuther.html; and Brad Sears, "Queer L," *National Journal of Sexual Orientation Law* 1, no. 2 (1995): 246, www.ibiblio.org/gaylaw/issue2 /sears.html, both cited in Kim Brooks and Debra Parkes, "Queering Legal Education: A Project of Theoretical Discovery," *Harvard Journal of Law and Gender* 27 (Spring 2004): 89, 90, 92.

67. Brooks and Parkes, "Queering Legal Education," 101–9, 90, 102 (describing legal education as "impoverished when it is based only upon the experiences of dominant groups"). The authors note that the experiences that are centered must be understood in their full diversity and that LGBTQ+ students and faculty must not be expected to perform this work for others.

68. See Ruthann Robson, "Educating the Next Generation of LGBTQ Attorneys," *Journal of Legal Education* 66, no. 3 (Spring 2017): 504–5 (describing use of a notecard system to create an inclusive classroom).

69. Robson, "Educating the Next Generation" ("Law cannot be divorced from the society in which it operates and that it helps to construct").

70. Robson, "Educating the Next Generation."

71. See Robert S. Chang, "Toward an Asian American Legal Scholarship: Critical Race Theory, Post-structuralism, and Narrative Space," *California Law Review* 81, no. 5 (October 1993): 1247–48 (noting that CRT does not "address fully the needs of Asian Americans" and suggesting that the discrimination and violence against them are "quantitatively and qualitatively different from that suffered by other disempowered groups"); John H. Török, "The Story of 'Towards Asian American Jurisprudence' and Its Implications for Latinas/os in American Law Schools," *Berkeley La Raza Law Journal* 13 (Fall 2002): 271 (describing advocacy efforts to diversify the faculty and strengthen the curriculum on Asian American Jurisprudence); Christina Payne-Tsoupros, "A Starting Point for Disability Justice in Legal Education," *Journal Committed to Social Change on Race and Ethnicity* 6, no. 1 (2020): 181–82 (proposing a set of initial questions governing disability justice to reveal "how far legal education is from embracing the structural transformation and re-centering of power necessary for disability justice" and a roadmap to begin the work).

72. Francisco Valdes, "Barely at the Margins: Race and Ethnicity in Legal Education; A Curricular Study with LatCritical Commentary," *Berkeley La Raza Law Journal* 13 (January 2002): 146.

3. STUDENTS REVEAL THAT WE SHOULD NOT FEAR CURRICULAR CHANGE

1. National Task Force on Lawyer Well-Being, *The Path to Lawyer Well-Being: Practical Recommendations for Positive Change,* American Bar Association, August 14, 2017, 35. www.americanbar.org/content/dam/aba/images/abanews /ThePathToLawyerWellBeingReportRevFINAL.pdf.

2. Janet Thompson Jackson, "Wellness and Law: Reforming Legal Education to Support Student Wellness," *Howard Law Journal* 65, no. 1 (2021): 45–102.

3. Kathryne M. Young, "Understanding the Social and Cognitive Process in Law School That Creates Unhealthy Lawyers," *Fordham Law Review* 89, no. 6 (2021): 2575–76.

4. See Nerissa Soh et al., "Law Student Mental Health Literacy and Distress: Finances, Accommodation and Travel Time," *Legal Education Review* 25, no 1 (January 2015): 31–32 (summarizing prevalent studies of university students).

5. Young, "Social and Cognitive Process," 2576.

6. Soh et al., "Law Student Mental Health," 36 (reporting on research using Brief Symptom Inventory scores).

7. Kennon M. Sheldon and Lawrence S. Krieger, "Does Legal Education Have Undermining Effects on Law Students? Evaluation Changes in Motivation, Values, and Well-Being," *Behavioral Sciences and the Law* 22, no. 2 (2004): 272.

8. Nancy J. Soonpaa, "Stress in Law Students: A Comparative Study of First-Year, Second-Year, and Third-Year Student," *Connecticut Law Review* 36 (2004): 377–78.

9. See Soh et al., "Law Student Mental Health"; Todd David Peterson and Elizabeth Waters Peterson, "Stemming the Tide of Law Student Depression: What Law Schools Need to Learn from the Science of Positive Psychology," *Yale Journal of Health Policy, Law, and Ethics* 9, no. 2 (2009): 357–434 (presenting a literature review of law student–distress studies); Molly Townes O'Brien, Stephen Tang, and Kath Hall, "No Time to Lose: Negative Impact on Law Student Wellbeing May Begin in Year One," *International Journal of the First Year in Higher Education* 2, no. 2 (June 2011): 56 (directing careful study to the "interaction between a rational thinking style and the culture of law school, especially during the first year" because it compels emotional detachment and concluding that "law schools are contributing to student distress and dysfunction").

10. Lawrence S. Krieger, "Institutional Denial about the Dark Side of Law School, and Fresh Empirical Guidance for Constructively Breaking the Silence," *Journal of Legal Education* 52, nos. 1–2 (2002): 119–20.

11. Krieger, "Institutional Denial," 119–20.

12. Krieger, "Institutional Denial," 122.

13. Jackson, "Wellness and Law."

14. Meera E. Deo, Jacquelyn Petzold, and Chad Christensen, *The COVID Crisis in Legal Education, Law School Survey of Student Engagement Annual Report,* LSSSE, 2021, https://lssse.indiana.edu/wp-content/uploads/2015/12 /COVID-Crisis-in-Legal-Education-Final-10.28.21.pdf, 5, 12, 15 (collecting responses from thirteen thousand law students across sixty-one law schools throughout the spring of 2021).

15. Deo, Petzold, and Christensen, *COVID Crisis*, 5, 9, 10, 12.

16. Deo, Petzold, and Christensen, *COVID Crisis*, 10, 11.

17. David Jaffe, Katherine M. Bender, and Jerome Organ, "'It Is Okay to Not Be Okay:' The 2021 Survey of Law Student Well-Being," *University of Louisville Law Review* 60 (Spring 2022): 456–59.

18. "Addiction Recovery Poses Special Challenges for Legal Professionals," Hazelden Betty Ford Foundation, March 16, 2017, https://www.hazeldenbetty ford.org/education/bcr/addiction-research/substance-abuse-legal-professionals-ru-317.

19. Jaffe, Bender, and Organ, "It Is Okay," 461.

20. Jerome M. Organ, David B. Jaffe, and Katherine M. Bender, "Suffering in Silence: The Survey of Law Student Well-Being and the Reluctance of Law Students to Seek Help for Substance Use and Mental Health Concerns," *Journal of Legal Education* 66, no. 1 (2016): 135.

21. Lawrence S. Krieger, "Inseparability of Professionalism and Personal Satisfaction: Perspectives on Values, Integrity and Happiness" *Clinical Law Review* 11 (Spring 2005): 434.

22. See Krieger, "Inseparability of Professionalism" (noting that the "most stressed law students may also be the most fulfilled").

23. Nisha C. Gottfredson et al., "Identifying Predictors of Law Student Life Satisfaction," *Journal of Legal Education* 58, no. 4 (December 2008): 520, 522.

24. Nancy Levit and Douglas O. Linder, "Happy Law Students, Happy Lawyers," *Syracuse Law Review* 58 (January 2008): 362.

25. Levit and Linder, "Happy Law Students," 362.

26. Tracie Marcella Addy, Derek Dube, Khadijah A. Mitchell, and Mallory SoRelle, *What Inclusive Instructors Do* (Sterling, VA: Stylus, 2021), 24.

27. Levit and Linder, "Happy Law Students."

28. Brigette LuAnn Willauer, "The Law School Honor Code and Collaborative Learning: Can They Coexist?," *UMKC Law Review* 73 (2004): 525–34.

29. O'Brien, Tang, and Hall, "No Time to Lose," 57.

30. Young, "Social and Cognitive Process," 2584.

31. Young, "Social and Cognitive Process," 2585–87.

32. Wendy Larcombe et al., "Does an Improved Experience of Law School Protect Students against Depression, Anxiety and Stress? An Empirical Study of Wellbeing and the Law School Experience of LLB and JD Students," *Sydney Law Review* 35, no. 2 (2013): 424–25.

33. Levit and Linder, "Happy Law Students."

34. Larcombe et al., "Improved Experience," 426.

35. Peterson and Peterson, "Stemming the Tide," 360 (describing some of their programming at AALS annual meetings), 361, 371–75 (concluding at the time of publication that most schools only referred students for help), 373–74.

36. *Creating a Movement to Improve the Legal Profession*, American Bar Association, August 14, 2017, www.americanbar.org/content/dam/aba/images/abanews/ThePathToLawyerWellBeingReportRevFINAL.pdf.

37. Young, "Social and Cognitive Process," 2585, 2595.

38. Jaffe, Bender, and Organ, "Is It Okay," 469, 472.

39. Jaffe, Bender, and Organ, "Is It Okay," 449.

4. THE LEGAL PROFESSION FACES SYMBIOTIC STRUGGLES

1. Stephanie Francis Ward, "Pulse of the Legal Profession," *American Bar Association Journal,* October 1, 2007, 33, www.abajournal.com/magazine/article/pulse_of_the_legal_profession.

2. Ward, "Legal Profession," 30.

3. *2022 Profile of the Legal Profession,* American Bar Association, 2022, 25, 26, 22, www.americanbar.org/content/dam/aba/administrative/news/2022/07/profile-report-2022.pdf.

4. *2022 Profile,* 25.

5. Laina Hammond, "The Pay Gap between Male and Female Law Partners Is Real: Litigation Finance Can Help Women Close It," Texas Lawyer, October 22, 2021, www.law.com/texaslawyer/2021/10/22/the-pay-gap-between-male-and-female-law-partners-is-real-litigation-finance-can-help-women-close-it/.

6. *Behind the Numbers: Feedback from Stakeholders,* 2022 NAWL Report, May 2023, www.nawl.org/p/cm/ld/fid=2019.

7. *Household Data: Annual Averages,* Bureau of Labor Statistics, accessed November 12, 2023, www.bls.gov/cps/cpsaat39.pdf.

8. Destiny Peery, *It's Time to Move beyond the Numbers,* National Association of Women Lawyers (NAWL) Survey on the Promotion and Retention of Women in Law Firms, April 18, 2022, https://issuu.com/nawl1899/docs/2021_nawl_survey_report.

9. Jeffrey A. Lowe, *2022 Partner Compensation Survey,* Major, Lindsey and Africa, 2022, https://209075.fs1.hubspotusercontent-na1.net/hubfs/209075/MLA%20%20Web%20Research%20Page%20PDFs/2022_Partner%20Compensation%20Survey_FINAL101822.pdf.

10. *2022 Profile.*

11. Peery, *It's Time to Move.*

12. Harry Keshet and Angela A. Meyer, *Compensation in Law Firms: The Impact of Gender, Race and Ethnicity,* Keshet Consulting, 2013, 6, www.yumpu.com/en/document/read/34378992/compensation, cited in Lauren Stiller Rikleen, *Closing the Gap: A Road Map for Achieving Gender Pay Equity in Law Firm Partner Compensation,* ABA Presidential Task Force on Gender Equity and the Commission on Women in the Profession, 2013, 12, www.americanbar.org/content/dam/aba/administrative/women/closing_the_gap.authcheckdam.pdf.

13. Rikleen, *Closing the Gap,* 13–14.

14. Joan C. Williams et al., *You Can't Change What You Can't See: Interrupting Racial and Gender Bias in the Legal Profession,* American Bar Association Commission on Women in the Profession and the Minority Corporate Counsel Association, 2018, 56, 6, https://mcca.com/wp-content/uploads/2018/09/You-Cant-Change-What-You-Cant-See-Executive-Summary.pdf.

15. Williams et al., *You Can't Change.*

16. *2022 Report on Diversity in U.S. Law Firms,* National Association of Law Placement, January 2023, www.nalp.org/uploads/Research/2022NALPReportonDiversity_Final.pdf.

17. *2022 Report on Diversity,* 14–15.

18. Rikleen, *Closing the Gap,* 14, 15. In 2014, 21.05 percent of partners in all law firms were women, 17.1 percent of equity partners were women, and 28.2

percent of nonequity partners were women. In 2022, 26.65 percent of partners were women, 22.6 percent of equity partners were women, and 32.7 percent of nonequity partners were women. In 2014, 44.94 percent of associates were women, and, in 2022, 49.42 percent of associates were women. Regarding counsel, 34.63 percent of counsel were women in 2014 and 38 percent of counsel were women in 2022. In 2014 women represented 55.74 percent of nontraditional track and staff attorneys, but in 2022 the percentage of women dropped to 54.85 percent.

19. Roberta D. Liebenberg and Stephanie A. Scharf, *Walking Out the Door: The Facts, Figures, and Future of Experienced Women Lawyers in Private Practice,* American Bar Association, 2019, 85, www.abajournal.com/files/WALKING_OUT_THE_DOOR_-_FINAL_AS_OF_NOV_14_2019_pm.pdf.

20. Kim Elsesser, "Female Lawyers Face Widespread Gender Bias, According to New Study," *Forbes,* October 1, 2018, www.forbes.com/sites/kimelsesser/2018/10/01/female-lawyers-face-widespread-gender-bias-according-to-new-study/?sh=5293a8144b55.

21. Matt Zapotosky, "Judge Who Quit over Harassment Allegations Reemerges, Dismaying Those Who Accused Him," *Washington Post,* July 24, 2018, www.washingtonpost.com/world/national-security/judge-who-quit-over-harassment-allegations-reemerges-dismaying-those-who-accused-him/2018/07/23/750a02f2-89db-11e8-a345-a1bf7847b375_story.html; Nina Totenberg, "Federal Panel of Judges Dismisses All 83 Ethics Complaints against Brett Kavanaugh," NPR, December 18, 2018, www.npr.org/2018/12/18/678004085/federal-panel-of-judges-dismiss-all-83-ethics-complaints-against-brett-kavanaugh; Dan Margolies, "Before He Quit, Federal Judge in Kansas City, Kansas, Faced Possible Impeachment for Misconduct," NPR Kansas, March 4, 2020, www.kcur.org/news/2020-03-04/before-he-quit-federal-judge-in-kansas-city-kansas-faced-possible-impeachment-for-misconduct. See also Renee Knake Jefferson, "Judicial Ethics in the #MeToo World," *Fordham Law Review* 89, no. 4 (2021): 1197–221.

22. John G. Roberts Jr., *2018 Year-End Report on the Federal Judiciary,* Supreme Court, December 31, 2018, 3–4, www.supremecourt.gov/publicinfo/year-end/2018year-endreport.pdf, cited in Pamela J. White, "Thirty Years Later: Recalling the Gender Bias Report and Asking What's Next in the Legal Profession," *Maryland Law Review* 80, no. 1 (2020): 32.

23. Derald Wing Sue et al., "Racial Microaggressions in Everyday Life: Implications for Clinical Practice," *American Psychologist* 62, no. 4 (May–June 2007): 271–86; *Merriam-Webster,* s.v. "mansplaining," accessed November 8, 2023, www.merriam-webster.com/dictionary/mansplain; Lindsay Dodgson, "Men Are Getting the Credit for Women's Work through Something Called 'Hepeating'—Here's What It Means," *Business Insider,* March 8, 2018, www.businessinsider.com/what-is-hepeating-2017-9; John Blake, "Stop 'Whitesplaining' Racism to Me," CNN, accessed February 17, 2019, www.cnn.com/2019/02/17/us/whitesplaining-racism-blake-analysis/index.html.

24. See, for example, Deborah L. Rhode, "Perspectives on Professional Women," *Stanford Law Review* 40, no. 5 (May 1988): 1188–91.

25. See Liebenberg and Scharf, *Walking Out the Door* (listing factors for reasons for leaving a firm and the percentages of women who believe the reason is either a very important or somewhat important reason for leaving).

26. Leopard Solutions, "Why Are Women Lawyers Leaving the Legal Indus-try?," *JD Supra,* March 9, 2022, www.jdsupra.com/legalnews/why-are-women-lawyers-leaving-the-legal-3000987/.

27. *2022 Profile,* 26.

28. Deborah L. Rhode and Lucy B. Ricca, "Diversity in the Legal Profession: Perspectives from Managing Partners and General Counsel," *Fordham Law Review* 83, no. 5 (2015): 2489, 2490.

29. Rikleen, *Closing the Gap,* 3, 21, 19.

30. Rikleen, *Closing the Gap,* 20.

31. *2022 Report on Diversity,* 15 (noting that Black and Latinx women reported higher levels of bias than White and Asian women), 9–10, 16, 17.

32. *2022 Report on Diversity,* 8.

33. Peery, *It's Time to Move,* 30, 31, 50–54.

34. Gabriele Plickert, *After the JD III: Third Results of a National Study of Legal Careers,* American Bar Foundation, 2014, 72–74, 194, www.americanbarfoundation.org/uploads/cms/documents/ajd3report_final_for_distribution.pdf.

35. *2022 Profile,* 52, 24–25.

36. See, for example, Williams et al., *You Can't Change.*

37. Aietie Akpan and Mia Lorick, "Lawyering While Black: Examining the Practice of Law through the Prism of the Black Experience," *Houston Lawyer* 58, no. 2 (October 2020): 26.

38. "Law School Enrollment by Race and Ethnicity (2019)," Enjuris, accessed June 20, 2021, www.enjuris.com/students/law-school-race-2019.html; *2019 Report on Diversity in U.S. Law Firms,* National Association for Law Placement, December 2019, 8, www.nalp.org/uploads/2019_DiversityReport.pdf.

39. *2019 Report on Diversity.*

40. Swethaa S. Ballakrishnen, "Law School as Straight Space," *Fordham Law Review* 91, no. 4 (2023): 1122.

41. *2022 Profile,* 39.

42. *State Nondiscrimination Laws,* Movement Advancement Project, March 6, 2023, www.lgbtmap.org/img/maps/citations-nondisc-employment.pdf. The states that do not have explicit sex-discrimination state laws are Alabama, Arkansas, Georgia, Indiana, Louisiana, Mississippi, Missouri, Montana, North Carolina, Oklahoma, South Carolina, South Dakota, Tennessee, West Virginia, and Wyoming. Arkansas and Tennessee take it a step further by passing state laws preventing the passage or enforcement of local nondiscrimination laws. The District of Columbia and thirty-three states have explicit laws or have extended existing sex-discrimination laws to include sexual orientation and gender identity: Alaska, Arizona, California, Colorado, Connecticut, Delaware, Florida, Hawaii, Idaho, Illinois, Iowa, Kansas, Kentucky, Maine, Maryland, Massachusetts, Michigan, Minnesota, Nebraska, Nevada, New Hampshire, New Mexico, New York, North Dakota, Ohio, Oregon, Pennsylvania, Rhode Island, Texas, Utah, Vermont, Virginia, and Washington. Wisconsin law only mentions sexual orientation, but federal law offers protections for gender identity.

43. Peter Blanck, Fitore Hyseni, and Fatma Altunkol Wise, "Diversity and Inclusion in the American Legal Profession: Discrimination Reported by Law-

yers with Disabilities and Lawyers Who Identify as LGBTQ+," *American Journal of Law and Medicine* 47, no. 1 (March 2021): 46.

44. Brad Sears, Christy Mallory, Andrew R. Flores, and Keith J. Conron, *LGBT People's Experiences of Workplace Discrimination and Harassment*, Williams Institute, September 2021, https://williamsinstitute.law.ucla.edu/wp-content/uploads/Workplace-Discrimination-Sep-2021.pdf.

45. Williams et al., *You Can't Change*, 14–16 (explaining that "Prove-It-Again" refers to how attorneys of color and women of color have to go above and beyond to get the same recognition and respect as colleagues), 16–18.

46. Janee T. Prince, "'Can I Touch Your Hair?' Exploring Double Binds and the Black Tax in Law School," *University of Pennsylvania Journal of Law and Social Change* 20, no. 1 (2017): 33.

47. See, for example, Dorothy W. Nelson, "Introduction to the Effects of Gender in the Federal Courts: The Final Report of the Ninth Circuit Gender Bias Task Force," *Southern California Law Review* 67 (1994): 731–38; Mary-Christine Sungaila, "Combating Bias Inside and Outside the Courtroom," *Perspectives* 5, no. 1 (Summer 1996): 12; North Dakota Commission on Gender Fairness in the Courts, "A Difference in Perceptions: The Final Report of the North Dakota Commission on Gender Fairness in the Courts," *North Dakota Law Review* 72, no. 4 (1996): 1113–42.

48. "Model Code of Professional Conduct Rule 8.4(g)," American Bar Association, 2020, www.americanbar.org/groups/professional_responsibility/publications/model_rules_of_professional_conduct/rule_8_4_misconduct/. See Kristen A. Kubes, Cara D. Davis, and Mary E. Schwind, *The Evolution of Model Rule 8.4(g): Working to Eliminate Bias, Discrimination, and Harassment in the Practice of Law*, American Bar Association, March 12, 2019, www.americanbar.org/groups/construction_industry/publications/under_construction/2019/spring/modelrule-8-4/.

49. See Latonia Haney Keith, "Cultural Competency in a Post-model 8.4(g) World," *Duke Journal of Gender Law and Policy* 25, no. 1 (2017): 5.

50. Kristy D'Angelo-Corker, "Don't Call Me Sweetheart! Why the ABA's New Rule Addressing Harassment and Discrimination Is So Important for Women Working in the Legal Profession Today," *Lewis and Clark Law Review* 23, no. 1 (May 2019): 267.

51. Patrick R. Krill, Ryan Johnson, and Linda Albert, "The Prevalence of Substance Use and Other Mental Health Concerns among American Attorneys," *Journal of Addiction Medicine* 10, no. 1 (February 2016): 49.

52. Matthew S. Thiese et al., "Depressive Symptoms and Suicidal Ideation among Lawyers and Other Law Professionals," *Journal of Occupational and Environmental Medicine* 63, no. 5 (2021): 381.

53. Rosa Flores and Rose Marie Arce, "Why are Kentucky Lawyers Killing Themselves?," CNN, January 20, 2014, www.cnn.com/2014/01/19/us/lawyer-suicides/index.html.

54. Michael S. Webb, "Dissenting from Death: Preventing Lawyer Suicide," American Bar Association, November 24, 2021, www.americanbar.org/groups/senior_lawyers/publications/voice_of_experience/2021/voice-of-experience-november-2021/dissenting-from-death-preventing-lawyer-suicide/.

55. Jeena Cho, "Attorney Suicide: What Every Lawyer Needs to Know," *ABA Journal,* January 1, 2019, www.abajournal.com/magazine/article/attorney_suicide_what_every_lawyer_needs_to_know?fbclid=IwAR0Ty-2FmxG6zHS-HYSFrQJUgQ4sZaBCyWmwJAt-P-SL1_FfeTIfr21aTpA; Jacquelyn Palmer and Linda Ouyang, "Analysis: Survey Finds Lawyer Burnout Rising, Well-Being Falling," *Bloomberg Law,* June 28, 2021, https://news.bloomberglaw.com/business-and-practice/analysis-survey-finds-lawyer-burnout-rising-well-being-falling; Jarrod F. Reich, "Capitalizing on Healthy Lawyers: The Business Case for Law Firms to Promote and Prioritize Lawyer Well-Being," *Villanova Law Review* 65, no. 2 (2020): 361–418; Anne Bradford, "Supervisor Relationships Are Key to Beating Attorney Burnout," Institute for Well-Being in Law, January 25, 2022, https://lawyerwellbeing.net/wp-content/uploads/2022/03/Brafford-burnout-article_newsletter-format-3-31-22.pdf.

56. Colin James, "Towards Trauma-Informed Legal Practice: A Review," *Psychiatric, Psychology and Law* 27, no. 2 (2020).

57. "Lawyers and Depression," David Nee Foundation, accessed November 14, 2023, www.mightycause.com/organization/Dave-Nee-Foundation.

58. Michael R. Oreskovich, "Prevalence of Alcohol Use Disorders among American Surgeons," *Archives of Surgery* 147, no. 2 (2012): 168–74, cited in *Substance Use Disorders among Legal Professionals,* Hazelden Betty Ford Foundation, March 2017, 2, www.hazeldenbettyford.org/education/bcr/addiction-research/substance-abuse-legal-professionals-ru-317.

59. *Substance Use Disorders,* 1.

60. Bethany L. Peters and Edward P. Stringham, "No Booze? You May Lose: Why Drinkers Earn More Money Than Nondrinkers," *Journal of Labor Research* 23, no. 3 (December 2006): 411–21, cited in *Substance Use Disorders,* 2.

61. Nancy McCarthy, "Statistics Tell Story of Stress, Addiction in Lives of Lawyers," *California Bar Journal,* November 2000, https://archive.calbar.ca.gov/archive/calbar/2cbj/00nov/index.htm, cited in *Substance Use Disorders,* 1.

62. Marjorie A. Silver, *Substance Abuse, Stress, Mental Health and the Legal Profession,* Touro Law Center, 2002, 7, www.nylat.org/documents/CourseinaBox.pdf.

63. Paula Davis, "Lawyer Strong®: The Legal Profession's Journey toward Well-Being," *Forbes,* May 18, 2023, www.forbes.com/sites/pauladavis/2023/05/18/lawyer-strong-the-legal-professions-journey-toward-well-being/?sh=17dbff7d2boa.

64. "Directory of Lawyer Assistance Programs," American Bar Association, accessed November 12, 2023, www.americanbar.org/groups/lawyer_assistance/resources/lap_programs_by_state/.

65. "Supporting Recovery in the Legal Community," The Other Bar, accessed November 13, 2023, https://otherbar.org/.

66. National Task Force on Lawyer Well-Being, *The Path to Lawyer Well-Being: Practical Recommendations for Positive Change,* American Bar Association, August 14, 2017, 1, 10–1, www.americanbar.org/content/dam/aba/images/abanews/ThePathToLawyerWellBeingReportRevFINAL.pdf.

67. "Well-Being Pledge Campaign," American Bar Association, accessed March 28, 2022, www.americanbar.org/groups/lawyer_assistance/well-being-in-the-legal-profession/.

68. *Creating a Movement.*

69. Jerome M. Organ, David B. Jaffe, and Katherine M. Bender, "Suffering in Silence: The Survey of Law Student Well-Being and the Reluctance of Law Students to Seek Help for Substance Use and Mental Health Concerns," *Journal of Legal Education* 66, no. 1 (2016): 145.

70. Marilyn Cavicchia, "A New Look at Character and Fitness: Bar Leaders, Lawyers, Others Urge Elimination of Mental Health Questions," *Bar Leader* 44, no. 3 (January–February 2020), www.americanbar.org/groups/bar-leadership/publications/bar_leader/2019_20/january-february/a-new-look-at-character-and-fitness-bar-leaders-lawyers-others-urge-elimination-of-mental-health-questions/.

71. Commission on Disability Rights, *Mental Health Character and Fitness Questions for Bar Admission,* American Bar Association, July 6, 2023, www.americanbar.org/groups/diversity/disabilityrights/resources/character-and-fitness-mh/.

72. Cavicchia, "New Look."

73. See Heidi K. Brown, *The Flourishing Lawyer: A Multi-dimensional Approach to Performance and Well-Being* (Chicago: ABA, 2022).

5. THE IMPERATIVE OF INCLUSIVE SOCRATIC CLASSROOMS

1. See Malcolm Gladwell, *The Tipping Point: How Little Things Can Make a Big Difference* (New York: Back Bay Books, 2006).

2. W. C. Kim and Renee Mauborgne, "Tipping Point Leadership," *Harvard Business Review* 50, no. 4 (2003) (explaining that the biggest challenge in achieving change is convincing people that there is a problem and a need for change), 52.

3. Damon Centola et al., "Experimental Evidence for Tipping Points in Social Convention," *American Association for the Advancement of Science* 360, no. 6393 (2018): 1116.

4. See Kim and Mauborgne, "Tipping Point Leadership," 52.

5. Doug Lederman, "How Teaching Changed in the (Forced) Shift to Remote Learning," Inside Higher Ed, April 22, 2020, www.insidehighered.com/digital-learning/article/2020/04/22/how-professors-changed-their-teaching-springs-shift-remote (reporting that survey respondents communicated a "level of anxiety and scrambling" in the pivot to online but that "despite that anxiety, institutions and instructors made significant changes on the fly in their teaching practices and expectations to try to pull off [the transition]").

6. See, for example, "Socratic Zooming: Faculty Weigh In on Teaching Remotely," Columbia Law School, April 27, 2020, www.law.columbia.edu/news/archive/socratic-zooming-faculty-weigh-teaching-remotely (noting that the analysis seems more probing and exploratory and that students are relaxed enough to let an exchange linger); and Kim Wright, How the Socratic Method Translates Online, *Harvard Gazette,* March 24, 2020, https://news.harvard.edu/gazette/story/2020/03/harvard-law-school-professor-was-prepared-for-zoom-debut (stating that teaching online was "surprisingly more personable and less performative than standing at a podium at the front of a large lecture hall").

7. Lederman, "How Teaching Changed."

8. "Socratic Zooming."

9. See, for example, Reuters, "U.S. Saw Summer of Black Lives Matter Protests Demanding Change," *U.S. News and World Report,* December 7, 2020, www.usnews.com/news/top-news/articles/2020-12-07/us-saw-summer-of-black-lives-matter-protests-demanding-change (describing these protests as the biggest protests in a generation).

10. For policing practices, see *The Other Epidemic: Fatal Police Shootings in the Time of COVID-19,* American Civil Liberties Union, 2020, 3, www.aclu.org/report/other-epidemic-fatal-police-shootings-time-covid-19 ("Our country has to reckon with the scope and impact of centuries of systemic police violence and racism"); Robert Klemko and John Sullivan, "The Push to Remake Policing Takes Decades, Only to Begin Again," *Washington Post,* June 10, 2021, www.washingtonpost.com/investigations/interactive/2021/police-reform-failure. For hyperincarceration, see Zina Makar, "Unnecessary Incarceration," *Oregon Law Review* 98, no. 2 (2020): 649. For monuments and naming practices, see Lyra D. Monteiro, "Power Structures: White Columns, White Marble, White Supremacy," *Medium,* October 27, 2020, https://intersectionist.medium.com/american-power-structures-white-columns-white-marble-white-supremacy-d43aa091b5f9.

11. See, for example, Justin Worland, "America's Long Overdue Awakening to Systemic Racism," *Time,* June 11, 2020, https://time.com/5851855/systemic-racism-america.

12. See, for example, Alaa Elassar, "The University of Louisville's Law School Is Offering a Class on Systemic Racism Titled 'Breonna Taylor's Louisville,'" CNN, September 23, 2020, www.cnn.com/2020/09/23/us/university-of-louisville-breonna-taylor-class-trnd/index.html.

13. "SALT Virtual Series: Social Justice in Action, Incorporating Anti-racism Frameworks into Core Law School Classes," Society of American Law Teachers, July 10, 2020, www.saltlaw.org/salt-virtual-series-social-justice-in-action (hosting the programs Incorporating Anti-racism Frameworks into Core Law School Classes, Promoting Equity and Inclusion in Online Teaching, Racialized Trauma and Fatigue among Academic Activists, and Anti-racist Hiring Practices).

14. "Racial Bias, Disparities and Oppression in the 1L Curriculum: A Critical Approach to the Canonical First Year Law School Subjects" (symposium, Boston University School of Law, Boston, February 28–29, 2020), www.bu.edu/law/files/2019/12/BU-Symposium-schedule-2320201-1.pdf.

15. See, for example, "Fordham Law's Anti-racism Action Plan," Fordham University, accessed November 12, 2023, www.fordham.edu/info/30269/addressing_racism_in_the_legal_system_and_our_community (expressing a commitment to "addressing racial injustice while responding to the needs of directly impacted individuals" and describing webinars, discussions, student groups, clinical work, mentoring, and career development).

16. Meera E. Deo, Jacquelyn Petzold, and Chad Christensen, *The COVID Crisis in Legal Education: Law School Survey of Student Engagement Annual Report,* 2021, 16, https://lssse.indiana.edu/wp-content/uploads/2015/12/COVID-Crisis-in-Legal-Education-Final-10.28.21.pdf.

17. Tracie Marcella Addy et al., *What Inclusive Instructors Do* (Sterling, VA: Stylus, 2021), 4.

18. Peter Felter and Leo M. Lambert, *Relationship-Rich Education: How Human Connections Drive Success in College* (Baltimore: Johns Hopkins University Press, 2020), 19.

19. See Genevieve Blake Tung, "Working towards Equitable Outcomes in Law School: The Role of the ABA Standards," in *Integrating Doctrine and Diversity: Inclusion and Equity in the Law School Classroom*, ed. Nicole P. Dyszlewski et al. (Durham: Carolina Academic Press, 2021), 15–22 (explaining that diversity in the curricula is largely left to individual law professors and that this existing model is inadequate).

20. Dyszlewski et al., *Integrating Doctrine and Diversity*, xi, 5.

21. Felter and Lambert, *Relationship-Rich Education*, ix.

22. Teri A. McMurtry-Chubb, *Strategies and Techniques for Integrating Diversity, Equity, and Inclusion into the Core Law Curriculum: A Comprehensive Guide to DEI Pedagogy, Course Planning, and Classroom Practice* (Philadelphia: Wolters Kluwer, 2021), 80.

23. McMurtry-Chubb, *Strategies and Techniques*, 80.

24. See Bennett Capers, "The Law School as a White Space," *Minnesota Law Review* 106 (2021): 34; Danielle M. Conway, Bekah Saidman-Krauss, and Rebecca Schreiber, "Building an Antiracist Law School: Inclusivity in Admissions and Retention of Diverse Students; Leadership Determines DEI Success," *Rutgers Race and the Law Review* 23, no. 1 (2021): 1–38; Doron Samuel-Siegel, "Reckoning with Structural Racism in Legal Education: Methods toward a Pedagogy of Antiracism," *Cardozo Journal of Equal Rights and Social Justice* 29, no. 1 (December 2022): 1–68.

25. L. Danielle Tully, "The Cultural (Re)Turn: The Case for Teaching Culturally Responsive Lawyering," *Stanford Journal of Civil Rights and Civil Liberties* 16, no. 2 (June 2020): 224.

26. *Functions and Structure of a Medical School: Standards for Accreditation of Medical Education Programs Leading to the MD Degree,* Liaison Committee on Medical Education, March 2016, https://lcme.org/publications/, cited in Tully, "Cultural (Re)Turn," 225.

27. *Educational Policy and Accreditation Standards for Baccalaureate and Master's Social Work Programs,* Council on Social Work Education 1, 7, 14, 2015, www.cswe.org/getmedia/23a35a39-78c7-453f-b805-b67f1dca2ee5/2015-epas-and-glossary.pdf, cited in Tully, "Cultural (Re)Turn," 225.

28. Deborah Jones Merritt and Logan Cornett, *Building a Better Bar: The Twelve Building Blocks of Minimum Competence,* Institute for the Advancement of the American Legal System, October 2020, 30, https://iaals.du.edu/sites/default/files/documents/publications/building_a_better_bar.pdf.

29. See Addy et al., *What Inclusive Instructors Do,* 156 (capturing the experiences of hundreds of instructors identifying what inclusive teaching is and how to incorporate it into their courses).

30. McMurtry-Chubb, *Strategies and Techniques,* xvii, 21, 28 ("Without White faculty members' purposeful investment in and willingness to move forward with DEI efforts, these efforts will most assuredly fail").

31. Kathryne M. Young, "Understanding the Social and Cognitive Process in Law School That Creates Unhealthy Lawyers," *Fordham Law Review* 89, no. 6 (2021): 2594 ("The root cause of law student unwellness is not cranky old professors who refuse to 'change with the times'; rather, it is a fidelity to long-standing structures even when those structures do not serve all students").

32. Lani Guinier, Michelle Fine, and Jane Balin, "Becoming Gentlemen: Women's Experiences at One Ivy League Law School," *University of Pennsylvania Law Review* 143, no. 1 (November 1994): 45.

33. McMurtry-Chubb, *Strategies and Techniques,* 30.

34. *Section of Legal Education and Admissions to the Bar: Report to the House of Delegates, Resolution 300,* American Bar Association Section of Legal Education and Admissions to the Bar, February 14, 2022, www.americanbar.org /content/dam/aba/administrative/news/2022/02/midyear-hod-resolutions/300.pdf.

35. "Student Learning Outcomes," New York Law School, accessed July 31, 2021, www.nyls.edu/academics/programs-of-study/student-competencies-and-learning-outcomes ("Understands the fundamentals of basic lawyering skills such as interviewing, fact development and analysis, client counseling, negotiation, advocacy, document drafting, cross-cultural competency, organization and management of legal work, and the use of technology to aid practice").

36. I extend a warm and hearty note of thanks and acknowledgement to my colleague Dean Lisa Taylor for pointing out this disconnect and thoughtfully flagging the concern that I had not previously seen.

37. *Section of Legal Education,* Interpretation 303-6.

38. I credit my talented colleague Lisa Taylor, the assistant dean for diversity, inclusion, and affinity relations at the American University Washington College of Law, for first identifying this incongruity with the measurable learning-outcomes approaches.

39. *Section of Legal Education,* Interpretation 303-7.

40. *Section of Legal Education,* Standard 303-7.

41. *Section of Legal Education,* Interpretation 303-5.

42. Young, "Social and Cognitive Process," 2585.

6. PIVOTING AWAY FROM PROBLEMATIC SOCRATIC PERFORMANCES

1. See William M. Sullivan et al., *Educating Lawyers: Preparation for the Profession of Law,* Carnegie Foundation for the Advancement of Teaching, 2007, 50–59, http://archive.carnegiefoundation.org/publications/pdfs/elibrary /elibrary_pdf_632.pdf.

2. Jeannie Suk Gersen, "The Socratic Method in the Age of Trauma," *Harvard Law Review* 130, no. 9 (October 2017): 2346.

3. John Jay Osborn, *The Paper Chase* (Boston: Houghton Mifflin, 1971); "Awards Databases," Oscars, accessed October 15, 2023, www.oscars.org /oscars/awards-databases-0.

4. James Bridges, dir., *The Paper Chase* (Los Angeles: 20th Century Fox, 1978).

5. J. Bridges, *Paper Chase.*

6. Jamie R. Abrams, "Legal Education's Curricular Tipping Point," *Hofstra Law Review,* 49 (November 2021): 898; Beth Hirschfelder Wilensky, "Dethroning Langdell," *Minnesota Law Review* 107, no. 6 (2023): 2701.

7. Steven I. Friedland, "How We Teach: A Survey of Teaching Techniques in American Law School," *Seattle University Law Review* 20 (1996): 31.

8. Martha Chamallas, "The Shadow of Professor Kingsfield: Contemporary Dilemmas Facing Women Law Professors," *William and Mary Journal of Race, Gender, and Social Justice* 11, no. 2 (2005): 199.

9. See Yolanda Flores Niemann, Gabriella Gutiérrez y Muhs, and Carmen G. González, eds. *Presumed Incompetent II: Race, Class, Power, and Resistance of Women in Academia* (Denver: University Press of Colorado, 2020), 106.

10. See, for example, Darby Dickerson, "President's Message: Abolish the Academic Caste System," Association of American Law Schools, accessed June 17, 2021, www.aals.org/about/publications/newsletters/aals-news-fall-2020 /presidents-message-abolish-the-academic-caste-system; and Rachel López, "Unentitled: The Power of Designation in the Legal Academy," *Rutgers University Law Review* 73, no. 3 (Spring 2021): 923–32 (describing how labels and titles become proxies for "abusive, and even invidious, treatment, all under the veil of objective neutrality").

11. See, for example, Duncan Kennedy, *Legal Education and the Reproduction of Hierarchy* (New York: New York University Press, 2004), 21 (explaining how professors who do not use these approaches are perceived to lack "rigor").

12. Donna Saadati-Soto, "The Experience of Latinx Students with the Harvard Law School First-Year Curriculum," Social Science Research Network, May 2020, 12, https://ssrn.com/abstract=3579132.

13. Lani Guinier, Michelle Fine, and Jane Balin, "Becoming Gentlemen: Women's Experiences at One Ivy League Law School," *University of Pennsylvania Law Review* 143, no. 1 (November 1994), 21–32, 42 (describing their first year of law school as a "radical, painful, or repressive experience").

14. Carrie Menkel-Meadow, "Feminist Legal Theory, Critical Legal Studies, and Legal Education, or 'The Fem-Crits Go to Law School,'" *Journal of Legal Education* 38, nos. 1–2 (March–June 1988): 80; see also Kimberlé Crenshaw, "Foreword: Toward a Race-Conscious Pedagogy in Legal Education," *Southern California Review of Law and Women's Studies* 4 (1994): 49.

7. IDENTIFYING THE SHARED VALUES THAT SHAPE SOCRATIC CLASSROOMS

1. See, for example, Lisa Radtke Bliss and Donald C. Peters, "Delivering Effective Education in In-House Clinics," in *Building on Best Practices: Transforming Legal Education in a Changing World,* ed. Deborah Maranville et al. (Durham: Carolina Academic Press, 2015), 188–215 (describing the pedagogical values that shape in-house clinics).

2. Beth Hirschfelder Wilensky describes the importance of authentic teaching and deploys an "Authentic Pedagogy Test." See "Dethroning Langdell," *Minnesota Law Review* 107, no. 6 (2023): 2716.

3. See Jamie R. Abrams, "Reframing the Socratic Method," *Journal of Legal Education* 64, no. 4 (2015): 565–68.

4. Tracie Marcella Addy, Derek Dube, Khadijah A. Mitchell, and Mallory SoRelle, *What Inclusive Instructors Do* (Sterling, VA: Stylus, 2021), 24.

5. See Michael Hunter Schwartz, Gerald F. Hess, and Sophie M. Sparrow, *What the Best Law Teachers Do* (Cambridge, MA: Harvard University Press, 2013), 76–150.

6. See, for example, Eun Hee Han, "What to Learn from Pandemic Teaching? Our Student's Names," *Journal of Legal Education* 69, no. 3 (Spring 2020): 819 (cautioning that this explanation might be a manifestation of exposure bias, whereby professors are less adept at distinguishing students from races other than their own, which can result in exclusionary classroom cultures, impose burdens on students, and rise to the level of a microaggression).

7. Addy et al., *What Inclusive Instructors Do,* 24.

8. "Law School Survey of Student Engagement," LSSSE, accessed November 21, 2023, https://lssse.indiana.edu ("As part of the Indiana University Center for Postsecondary Research, LSSSE has been a provider of research products and services centered on the study of the law student experience since 2004"). This site allows law schools to register for the survey and explains how this research and data can support law schools.

9. Meera E. Deo, Jacquelyn Petzold, and Chad Christensen, *The COVID Crisis in Legal Education: Law School Survey of Student Engagement Annual Report,* LSSSE, 2021, 5, https://lssse.indiana.edu/wp-content/uploads/2015/12/COVID-Crisis-in-Legal-Education-Final-10.28.21.pdf.

10. Peter Felter and Leo M. Lambert, *Relationship-Rich Education: How Human Connections Drive Success in College* (Baltimore: Johns Hopkins University, 2020), 10.

11. Felter and Lambert, *Relationship-Rich Education,* 52–53 ("The overall ecosystem of higher education does not reward good teaching in the same way it rewards (and requires) measurable 'outputs'—peer-reviewed articles, books, professional papers, and grants").

12. See "Explanation of Changes," American Bar Association Section of Legal Education and Admission to the Bar, 2014, www.americanbar.org/content/dam/aba/administrative/legal_education_and_admissions_to_the_bar/council_reports_and_resolutions/201408_explanation_changes.pdf.

13. Paulo Freire, *Pedagogy of the Oppressed* (New York City: Penguin, 2017), 34, 45; Sherri Lee Keene and Susan A. McMahon, "The Contextual Case Method: Moving beyond Opinions to Spark Students' Legal Imaginations," *Virginia Law Review Online* 108 (February 2022): 80.

14. Heather L. Reynolds and Katherine Dowell Kearns, "A Planning Tool for Incorporating Backward Design, Active Learning, and Authentic Assessment in the College Classroom," *College Teaching* 65, no. 1 (2016): 17–21; Nitza Davidovitch, "Learning-Centered Teaching and Backward Course Design: From Transferring Knowledge to Teaching Skills," *Journal of International Education Research* 9, no. 4 (2013): 332–34.

15. Davidovitch, "Learning-Centered Teaching," 333–34.

16. See Teri A. McMurtry-Chubb, *Strategies and Techniques for Integrating Diversity, Equity, and Inclusion into the Core Law Curriculum: A Comprehensive Guide to DEI Pedagogy, Course Planning, and Classroom Practice* (Philadelphia: Wolters Kluwer, 2021).

17. Reynolds and Kearns, "Planning Tool," 17–18.

18. Davidovitch, "Learning-Centered Teaching," 333–34.

19. Davidovitch, "Learning-Centered Teaching," 333–34.

20. Schwartz, Hess, and Sparrow, *Best Law Teachers,* 177–80.

21. Marjorie M. Shultz and Sheldon Zedeck, *Final Report: Identification, Development, and Validation of Predictors for Successful Lawyering,* SSRN, 2008, 25, https://papers.ssrn.com/sol3/papers.cfm?abstract_id=1353554, cited in Deborah Jones Merritt and Logan Cornett, *Building a Better Bar: The Twelve Building Blocks of Minimum Competence,* Institute for the Advancement of the American Legal System, October 2020, 12, https://iaals.du.edu/sites/default/files/documents/publications/building_a_better_bar.pdf.

22. Alli Gerkman and Logan Cornett, "Foundations for Practice: The Whole Lawyer and the Character Quotient," Institute for the Advancement of the American Legal System, July 26, 2016, https://iaals.du.edu/publications/foundations-practice-whole-lawyer-and-character-quotient, cited in Merritt and Cornett, *Building a Better Bar,* 15–16.

23. Paula Schaefer, "Integrating Professionalism into Doctrinally-Focused Courses," in Maranville et al., *Building on Best Practices,* 275–78.

24. See Freire, *Pedagogy of the Oppressed,* 53–54.

25. Jamie R. Abrams, *Tort Law Simulations,* Bridge to Practice Series (Saint Paul: West Academic, 2020); Jessica Dixon Weaver and Jamie R. Abrams, *Family Law Simulations,* Bridge to Practice Series (Saint Paul: West Academic, 2021).

26. See, for example, Julie Heflin, "UofL Law, Dental Faculty Receive International Award for Novel Teaching Method," *UofL News,* August 20, 2021, www.uoflnews.com/post/uofltoday/uofl-law-dental-faculty-receive-international-award-for-novel-teaching-method/.

27. "Multistate Performance Test," National Conference of Bar Examiners, accessed November 13, 2023, www.ncbex.org/exams/mpt/.

28. *Final Report of the Testing Task Force,* National Conference of Bar Examiners, April 2021, https://nextgenbarexam.ncbex.org/reports/final-report-of-the-ttf/.

29. Judith A. Gundersen, "Leaving Langdell Behind: Reimagining Legal Education for a New Era," *Minnesota Law Review* 105 (2023): 2414, 2411 (describing, from the author's role in the National Conference of Bar Examiners, how legal education and bar licensure are both integral parts of the profession).

30. Merritt and Cornett, *Building a Better Bar,* 7–12 (summarizing research that memorizing legal concepts from appellate federal cases had little value to the practice of law, with one study concluding that nine out of ten hiring partners wanted new lawyers to have strong oral and written communication skills, whereas less than a third wanted new lawyers to have existing knowledge of substantive or procedural law).

31. Merritt and Cornett, *Building a Better Bar,* 30.

32. Wilensky, "Dethroning Langdell," 2701–2.

33. Karen Sloan, "Law School Applications Plummet as Law Schools Raise Their Sights," Reuters, August 22, 2022, www.reuters.com/legal/legalindustry/law-professor-applications-plummet-law-schools-raise-their-sights-2022-08-22/.

34. Abrams, *Tort Law Simulations*.

35. See, for example, Michael Hunter Schwartz, "Improving Legal Education by Improving Casebooks: Fourteen Things Casebooks Can Do to Produce Better and More Learning," *Elon Law Review* 3, no. 1 (2011): 27–63 (documenting critiques of existing casebooks and proposing further reforms, including a greater focus on skills development). See also Stephen M. Johnson, "The Course Source: The Casebook Evolved," *Capital University Law Review* 44, no. 3 (2016): 593 (describing the history of casebook development, arguing that "major shifts in pedagogy require major shifts in pedagogical tools," and advocating for the "course source" instead of the "casebook," in which a compiled suite of open-source materials support student learning).

36. Aníbal Rosario Lebrón, "If These Blackboards Could Talk: The Crit Classroom, a Battlefield," *Charleston Law Review* 9 (2015): 320.

37. Wilensky, "Dethroning Langdell," 2722.

38. "Model Rules of Professional Conduct," American Bar Association, accessed November 6, 2023, www.americanbar.org/groups/professional_responsibility/publications/model_rules_of_professional_conduct/model_rules_of_professional_conduct_table_of_contents/ (emphasis added).

39. See Serena Patel, "Cultural Competency Training: Preparing Law Students for Practice in Our Multicultural World," *UCLA Law Review Discourse* 62, no. 7 (2014): 151 (emphasizing how cultural competency connects to building trusting relationship with clients and how important it is to build these skills for all students, not just in clinics).

40. Deborah Jones Merritt, "Client-Centered Legal Education and Licensing," *Minnesota Law Review* 107 (2023): 101–47.

41. Merritt, "Client-Centered Legal Education."

42. *Section of Legal Education and Admissions to the Bar: Report to the House of Delegates, Resolution 300,* American Bar Association Section of Legal Education and Admissions to the Bar, February 14, 2022, www.americanbar.org/content/dam/aba/administrative/news/2022/02/midyear-hod-resolutions/300.pdf.

43. Wilensky, "Dethroning Langdell," 2701.

44. Wilensky, "Dethroning Langdell," 2701.

45. "Sixth Circuit Court of Appeals Visits Louisville," University of Louisville, accessed November 6, 2023, https://louisville.edu/law/banners/sixth-circuit-court-of-appeals-visits-louisville-law/view.

46. Felter and Lambert, *Relationship-Rich Education*, 10–11 (stating that "institutions must develop structures and practices that value students, recognize and reward the efforts faculty and staff devote to building relationships with students, value and practice excellent teaching, encourage all on campus to see themselves as part of a web of important interactions students will experience, and think critically about how metrics are used to assess student experiences as well as the work of faculty, staff, and administrators").

47. "Torts and Contract Law Meet at Axe-Throwing Event, University of Louisville Brandeis School of Law," University of Louisville, accessed November 6, 2023, https://louisville.edu/law/news/torts-and-contract-law-meet-at-axe-throwing-event.

48. L. Danielle Tully, "The Case for Teaching Culturally Responsive Lawyering," *Stanford Journal of Civil Rights and Civil Liberties* 16, no. 2 (June 2020): 219 (stating, "From influencing how lawyers read, interpret and apply legal rules to communicating this information to clients, community members, public representatives, and the legal community, law students should understand that culture impacts how law is made and how the profession is practiced").

49. *Standards and Rules of Procedure for Approval of Law Schools,* American Bar Association, 2023, www.americanbar.org/content/dam/aba/administrative /legal_education_and_admissions_to_the_bar/standards/2023-2024/2023-2024-aba-standards-rules-for-approval.pdf.

50. Chris Chambers Goodman and Sarah E. Redfield, "A Teacher Who Looks Like Me," *Journal of Civil Rights and Economic Development* 27 (2013): 160–63.

51. Linda L. Berger, Kathryn M. Stanchi, and Bridget J. Crawford, "Learning from Feminist Judgments: Lessons in Language and Advocacy," *Texas Law Review* 98 (2019): 41–42.

8. MEASURING EFFECTIVE, INCLUSIVE, AND EQUITABLE SOCRATIC CLASSROOMS

1. Kellye Y. Teste, "Advancing an Evidence-Based Approach to Improving Legal Education," *Journal of Legal Education* 69, no. 2 (2020): 563.

2. L. Danielle Tully, "What Law Schools Should Leave Behind," *Utah Law Review* 22, no. 4 (2022): 857.

3. "Law School Enrollment by Race and Ethnicity (2019)," Enjuris, accessed June 20, 2021, www.enjuris.com/students/law-school-race-2019.html.

4. Barbara E. Walvoord, *Assessment Clear and Simple: A Practical Guide for Institutions, Departments, and General Education* (San Francisco: Jossey-Bass, 2010), 2.

5. Debra Moss Vollweiler, "Don't Panic! The Hitchhiker's Guide to Learning Outcomes: Eight Ways to Make Them More Than (Mostly) Harmless," *Dayton Law Review* 44 (July 2018): 17–52.

6. Vollweiler, "Don't Panic!"

7. Rachel Gurvich et al., "Reimagining Langdell's Legacy: Puncturing the Equilibrium in Law School Pedagogy," *North Carolina Law Review Addendum* 101 (2023): 159 (asking, "As we strive for inclusive legal education, we should ask ourselves: If our grading methods don't necessarily assess and communicate competency, shouldn't we reimagine them?").

8. Herb D. Vest, "Felling the Giant: Breaking the ABA's Stranglehold on Legal Education in America," *Journal of Legal Education* 50, no. 4 (2000): 502.

9. James E. Moliterno, "And Now a Crisis in Legal Education," *Seton Hall Law Review* 44, no. 4 (2014): 1097–98.

10. *Final Report of the Testing Task Force,* National Conference of Bar Examiners, April 2021, https://nextgenbarexam.ncbex.org/reports/final-report-of-the-ttf/.

11. See Stephanie Francis Ward, "New ABA Data Parses Out Bar Exam Pass Rates by Race and Ethnicity," *ABA Journal,* June 22, 2021, www.abajournal.com/news/article/new-aba-data-parses-out-bar-exam-pass-rates-by-ethnicity.

12. See Linda Suskie, *Assessing Student Learning* 86–97 (San Francisco: Jossey-Bass, 2009); Barbara Glesner Fines, "An Institutional Culture of Assessment for Student Learning," in *Building on Best Practices: Transforming Legal Education in a Changing World,* ed. Maranville et al. (Durham: Carolina Academic Press, 2015), 94–101.

13. Andrea Susnir Funk, *The Art of Assessment: Making Outcomes Assessment Accessible, Sustainable, and Meaningful* (Durham: Carolina Academic Press, 2017), 8–11.

14. Jamie R. Abrams, "A Synergistic Pedagogical Approach to First-Year Teaching," *Duquesne Law Review* 48, no. 2 (2010): 438.

15. Tully, "Law Schools Should Leave Behind," 870.

16. Tully, "Law Schools Should Leave Behind," 870.

17. Tully, "Law Schools Should Leave Behind," 870.

18. See Gurvich et al., "Reimagining Langdell's Legacy," 152.

19. Kristina W.M. Mitchell and Jonathan Martin, *Gender Bias in Student Evaluations* (Cambridge: Cambridge University Press, 2018), 648 (stating, "We contend that women are evaluated differently in at least two ways: intelligence/competence and personality").

20. McMurtry-Chubb, *Strategies and Techniques,* 33.

21. McMurtry-Chubb, *Strategies and Techniques,* 71–72, 73.

22. Peter Seldin, "Self-Assessment of College Teaching," *Improving College and University Teaching* 30, no. 2 (1982): 71.

23. *Managing Director's Guidance Memo,* American Bar Association, June 2015, 1, www.americanbar.org/content/dam/aba/administrative/legal_education_and_admissions_to_the_bar/governancedocuments/2015_learning_outcomes_guidance.pdf (noting that schools could also add additional learning outcomes).

24. See *Standards and Rules of Procedure for Approval of Law Schools,* American Bar Association, 2023, www.americanbar.org/content/dam/aba/administrative/legal_education_and_admissions_to_the_bar/standards/2023-2024/2023-2024-aba-standards-rules-for-approval.pdf.

25. See, for example, Sarah Valentine, "Flourish or Founder: The New Regulatory Regime in Legal Education," *Journal of Law and Education* 44, no. 4 (Fall 2015): 474–75 (explaining how law schools historically distanced themselves from reforms occurring in other sectors of undergraduate and higher education: "Law schools now find themselves isolated: untethered from the profession, unmoored from higher education, and beset by unrelenting calls to reform").

26. Peter A. Joy, "The Uneasy History of Experiential Education in U.S. Law Schools," *Dickinson Law Review* 122, nos. 2–4 (2018): 554–55; Trudy W. Banta and Catherine A. Palomba, *Assessment Essentials* (San Francisco: Jossey-Bass, 2015), 3–9.

27. See A. Benjamin Spencer, "The Law School Critique in Historical Perspective," *Washington and Lee Law Review* 69, no. 4 (Fall 2012): 1949–2063 (chronicling the historical shifts in legal education from apprenticeships to the Langdell method to the ABA's centralized regulation); Judith Welch Wagner, "Creating an Effective Law School Mission," in *Building on Best Practices: Transforming Legal Education in a Changing World,* ed. Maranville et al. (Durham: Carolina Academic Press, 2015), 6–11.

28. See E. Eugene Clark, "Legal Education and Professional Development: An Educational Continuum; Report of the Task Force on Law Schools and the Profession: Narrowing the Gap," *Legal Education Review* 4, no. 1 (1993).

29. Anthony Niedwiecki, "Prepared for Practice? Developing a Comprehensive Assessment Plan for a Law School Professional Skills Program," *University of San Francisco Law Review* 245, no. 2 (2016): 255–57.

30. Valentine, "Flourish or Founder," 484–89.

31. See Mary A. Lynch, "Contemporary Issues in Outcomes-Based Education: An Examination of Ten Concerns about Using Outcomes in Legal Education," *William Mitchell Law Review* 38, no. 3 (2012): 976–1016 (responding to common critiques).

32. Valentine, "Flourish or Founder," 484–89.

33. See *Standards and Rules,* 26–27.

34. See Genevieve Blake Tung, "Working towards Equitable Outcomes in Law School: The Role of the ABA Standards," in *Integrating Doctrine and Diversity: Inclusion and Equity in the Law School Classroom,* ed. Nicole P. Dyszlewski et al. (Durham: Carolina Academic Press, 2021), 15–22 (explaining that diversity in the curricula is largely left to individual law professors and that this existing model is inadequate).

35. L. Danielle Tully, "The Cultural (Re)Turn: The Case for Teaching Culturally Responsive Lawyering," *Stanford Journal of Civil Rights and Civil Liberties* 16, no. 2 (June 2020): 220–33 (critiquing the impact of revisions to Standards 301 and 302); Gurvich et al., "Reimagining Langdell's Legacy," 152.

Bibliography

2019 Report on Diversity in U.S. Law Firms. National Association for Law Placement. December 2019. www.nalp.org/uploads/2019_DiversityReport .pdf.

2020 Diversity and Exclusion: 2020 Annual Survey Results. Law School Survey of Student Engagement. September 29, 2020. https://lssse.indiana.edu/wp-content/uploads/2020/09/Diversity-and-Exclusion-Final-9.29.20.pdf.

2021–2022 Standards and Rules of Procedure for Approval of Law Schools. American Bar Association Section of Legal Education and Admissions to the Bar. August 23, 2021. www.americanbar.org/groups/legal_education/resources /standards/.

2022 Profile of the Legal Profession. American Bar Association. July 2022. www. americanbar.org/content/dam/aba/administrative/news/2022/07/profile-report-2022.pdf.

2022 Report on Diversity in U.S. Law Firms. National Association of Law Placement. January 2023. www.nalp.org/uploads/Research/2022NALPRep ortonDiversity_Final.pdf.

ABA Annual Reports. American Bar Association. 2020. www.abarequired disclosures.org/Disclosure509.aspx.

ABA Approved Law Schools. American Bar Association. 2022. www.americanbar .org/content/dam/aba/administrative/legal_education_and_admissions_to_the_ bar/Questionnaires/2022/2022-aba-standard-509-data-overview-final.pdf.

Abrams, Jamie R. "Feminism's Transformation of Legal Education and Unfinished Agenda." In *Oxford Handbook of Feminism and Law in the U.S.,* edited by Deborah L. Brake, Martha Chamallas, and Verna L. Williams, 494–516. Oxford: Oxford University Press, 2023.

———. "Legal Education's Curricular Tipping Point." *Hofstra Law Review* 49 (November 2021): 897–943.

———. "Reframing the Socratic Method." *Journal of Legal Education* 64, no. 4 (2015): 562–85.

———. "A Synergistic Pedagogical Approach to First-Year Teaching." *Duquesne Law Review* 48, no. 2 (2010): 423–53.

———. *Tort Law Simulations*. Bridge to Practice Series. Saint Paul: West Academic, 2020.

Abrams, Jamie R., and Daniela Kraiem. "Banding Together: Reflections on the Role of the Women's Bar Association of the District of Columbia and the Washington College of Law in Promoting Women's Rights." *Modern American* 4, no. 2 (Fall 2008): 42–56.

"Addiction Recovery Poses Special Challenges for Legal Professionals." Hazelden Betty Ford Foundation. March 16, 2017. www.hazeldenbettyford.org/education/bcr/addiction-research/substance-abuse-legal-professionals-ru-317.

Addy, Tracie Marcella, Derek Dube, Khadijah A. Mitchell, and Mallory SoRelle. *What Inclusive Instructors Do*. Sterling, VA: Stylus, 2021.

Akpan, Aietie, and Mia Lorick. "Lawyering While Black: Examining the Practice of Law through the Prism of the Black Experience." *Houston Lawyer* 58, no. 2 (October 2020).

American Association of Law Schools. "Highlights from the American Law School Dean Study." *ABA Journal*, 2021. www.abajournal.com/files/Deans_Study_Short_Report.pdf.

American Bar Association Required Disclosures on Faculty Resources. American Bar Association. 2022. www.abarequireddisclosures.org/Disclosure509.aspx.

Ansley, Francis L. "Race and the Core Curriculum in Legal Education." *California Law Review* 79, no. 6 (1991): 1511–97.

Archer, Deborah, Caitlin Barry, G. S. Hans, Derrick Howard, Alexis Karteron, Shobha Mahadev, and Jeff Selbin. "The Diversity Imperative Revisited: Racial and Gender Inclusion in Clinical Law Faculty." *Clinical Law Review* 26, no. 1 (August 2019): 127–46.

"Are 1L Grades Really That Important in Law School?" J.D. Advising. Accessed October 15, 2023. https://jdadvising.com/are-1l-grades-really-that-important-in-law-school/.

"Awards Databases." Oscars. Accessed October 15, 2023. www.oscars.org/oscars/awards-databases-0.

Babcock, Barbara Allen, Ann E. Freedman, Eleanor H. Norton, and Susan Ross. *Sex Discrimination and the Law: Causes and Remedies*. Boston: Little, Brown, 1975.

Bagby, Laura, "ABA Profile of the Legal Profession: Diversity and Well-Being." 2Civility. August 13, 2020. www.2civility.org/aba-profile-of-the-legal-profession-diversity-and-well-being/.

Ballakrishnen, Swethaa S. "Law School as Straight Space." *Fordham Law Review* 91, no. 4 (2023): 1113–38.

Banks, Taunya Lovell. "Gender Bias in the Classroom." *Journal of Legal Education* 38, no. 1 (March 1988): 137–46.

Banta, Trudy W., and Catherine A. Palomba. *Assessment Essentials*. San Francisco: Jossey-Bass, 2015.

Barnhizer, David R. "The Purposes and Methods of American Legal Education." *Journal of the Legal Profession* 36, no. 1 (March 2011).

Bartlett, Katharine T. "Feminist Perspective on the Ideological Impact of Legal Education upon the Profession." *North Carolina Law Review* 72 (1994): 1259–70.

Bashi, Sari, and Maryana Iskander. "Why Legal Education Is Failing Women." *Yale Journal of Law and Feminism* 18, no. 2 (2006): 389–449.

Behind the Numbers: Feedback from Stakeholders. 2022 NAWL Report. May 2023. www.nawl.org/p/cm/ld/fid=2019.

Bell, Derrick A., Jr. "Humanity in Legal Education." *Oregon Law Review* 59, nos. 2–3 (May 1980): 243–48.

———. "Who's Afraid of Critical Race Theory?" *University of Illinois Law Review* 1995, no. 4 (1995): 893–971.

Berenguer, Elizabeth, Lucy Jewel, and Teri A. McMurtry-Chubb. "Gut Renovations: Using Critical and Comparative Rhetoric to Remodel How the Law Addresses Privilege and Power." *Harvard Latinx Law Review* 23, no. 2 (2020): 205–32.

Berger, Linda L., Kathryn M. Stanchi, and Bridget J. Crawford. "Learning from Feminist Judgments: Lessons in Language and Advocacy." *Texas Law Review* 98 (2019): 40–70.

Blake, John. "Stop 'Whitesplaining' Racism to Me." CNN. February 17, 2019. www.cnn.com/2019/02/17/us/whitesplaining-racism-blake-analysis/index.html.

Blanck, Peter, Fitore Hyseni, and Fatma Altunkol Wise. "Diversity and Inclusion in the American Legal Profession: Discrimination Reported by Lawyers with Disabilities and Lawyers Who Identify as LGBTQ+." *American Journal of Law and Medicine* 47, no. 1 (March 2021): 9–61.

Bliss, Lisa Radtke, and Donald C. Peters. "Delivering Effective Education in In-House Clinics." In Maranville et al., *Building on Best Practices,* 188–215.

Bloch, Kate E. "A Rape Law Pedagogy." *Yale Journal of Law and Feminism* 7, no. 2 (1995): 307–40.

Bodamer, Elizabeth. "Do I Belong Here? Examining Perceived Experiences of Bias, Stereotype Concerns, and Sense of Belonging in U.S. Law Schools." *Journal of Legal Education* 69, no. 2 (2020): 455–90.

Boyle, Christine. "Teaching Law as If Women Really Mattered, or What about the Washrooms?" *Canadian Journal of Women and the Law* 2, no. 1 (1986): 96–112.

Bracamonte, Jose A. "Minority Critiques of the Critical Legal Studies Movement: Foreword." *Harvard Civil Rights–Civil Liberties Law Review* 22, no. 2 (Spring 1987): 421–510.

Bradford, Anne. "Supervisor Relationships Are Key to Beating Attorney Burnout." Institute for Well-Being in Law. January 25, 2022. https://lawyerwellbeing.net/wp-content/uploads/2022/03/Brafford-burnout-article_newsletter-format-3-31-22.pdf.

Bridges, James, dir. *The Paper Chase.* Los Angeles: 20th Century Fox, 1978.

Bridges, Khiara. *Critical Race Theory: A Primer.* Goleta: Foundation, 2019.

Brooks, Kim, and Debra Parkes. "Queering Legal Education: A Project of Theoretical Discovery." *Harvard Journal of Law and Gender* 27 (Spring 2004): 89–136.

Brown, Heidi K. *The Flourishing Lawyer: A Multi-dimensional Approach to Performance and Well-Being.* Chicago: ABA, 2022.

———. *The Introverted Lawyer: A Seven-Step Journey Toward Authentically Empowered Advocacy.* Chicago: ABA, 2017.

———. *Untangling Fear in Lawyering: A Four-Step Journey toward Powerful Advocacy.* Chicago: ABA, 2019.

Capers, Bennett. "The Law School as a White Space." *Minnesota Law Review* 106 (2021): 7–57.

Cavicchia, Marilyn. "A New Look at Character and Fitness: Bar Leaders, Lawyers, Others Urge Elimination of Mental Health Questions." *Bar Leader* 44, no. 3 (January–February 2020). www.americanbar.org/groups/bar-leadership/publications/bar_leader/2019_20/january-february/a-new-look-at-character-and-fitness-bar-leaders-lawyers-others-urge-elimination-of-mental-health-questions/.

Centola, Damon, Joshua Becker, Devon Brackbill, and Andrea Baronchelli. "Experimental Evidence for Tipping Points in Social Convention." *American Association for the Advancement of Science* 360, no. 6393 (2018): 1116–19.

Chamallas, Martha. "The Shadow of Professor Kingsfield: Contemporary Dilemmas Facing Women Law Professors." *William and Mary Journal of Race, Gender, and Social Justice* 11, no. 2 (2005): 195–208.

Chang, Julia H. "Spectacular Bodies." In Niemann, Gutiérrez y Muhs, and González, *Presumed Incompetent II,* 259–68.

Chang, Robert S. "Toward an Asian American Legal Scholarship: Critical Race Theory, Post-structuralism, and Narrative Space." *California Law Review* 81, no. 5 (October 1993): 1241–1323.

Chatman, Carliss N., and Najarian R. Peters. "The Soft-Shoe and Shuffle of Law School Hiring Committee Practices." *UCLA Law Review* 69, *Discourse* 2 (2021): 2–17.

Chew, Alexa Z., and Rachel Gurvich. "Saying the Quiet Parts Out Loud: Teaching Law Students How Law School Works." *Nebraska Law Review* 904 (2022): 887–904.

Cho, Jeena. "Attorney Suicide: What Every Lawyer Needs to Know." *ABA Journal,* January 1, 2019. www.abajournal.com/magazine/article/attorney_suicide_what_every_lawyer_needs_to_know?fbclid=IwARoTy-2FmxG6zHS-HYSFrQJUgQ4sZaBCyWmwJAt-P-SL1_FfeTIfr21aTpA.

Chused, Richard H. "The Hiring and Retention of Minorities and Women on American Law School Faculties." *University of Pennsylvania Law Review* 137 (1988): 537–69.

Clark, E. Eugene. "Legal Education and Professional Development: An Educational Continuum; Report of the Task Force on Law Schools and the Profession: Narrowing the Gap." *Legal Education Review* 4, no. 1 (1993).

Clark, Mary L. "The Founding of the Washington College of Law: The First Law School Established by Women for Women." *American University Law Review* 47 (1998): 613–76.

Commission on Disability Rights. *Mental Health Character and Fitness Questions for Bar Admission*. American Bar Association. July 6, 2023. www .americanbar.org/groups/diversity/disabilityrights/resources/character-and-fitness-mh/.

Conway, Danielle M., Bekah Saidman-Krauss, and Rebecca Schreiber. "Building an Antiracist Law School: Inclusivity in Admissions and Retention of Diverse Students; Leadership Determines DEI Success." *Rutgers Race and the Law Review* 23, no. 1 (2021): 1–38.

The Cost of Women's Success. Law School Survey of Student Engagement. 2019. https://lssse.indiana.edu/wp-content/uploads/2015/12/LSSSE-Annual-Survey-Gender-Final.pdf.

Cox, Prentiss. "1L Curricula in the United States: 2023 Data and Historical Comparison." Research paper, University of Minnesota Law School. 2023. https://ssrn.com/abstract=4450371.

Creating a Movement to Improve Well-Being in the Legal Profession. American Bar Association. August 14, 2017. www.americanbar.org/content/dam/aba /images/abanews/ThePathToLawyerWellBeingReportRevFINAL.pdf.

Crenshaw, Kimberlé. "The First Decade: Critical Reflections, or 'A Foot in the Closing Door.'" In *Crossroads, Directions, and a New Critical Race Theory*, edited by Francisco Valdes, Jerome McCristal Culp, and Angela P. Harris, 9–31. Philadelphia: Temple University Press, 2002.

———. "Foreword: Toward a Race-Conscious Pedagogy in Legal Education." *Southern California Review of Law and Women's Studies* 4 (1994): 33–52.

———. "Twenty Years of Critical Race Theory: Looking Back to Move Forward." *Connecticut Law Review* 43, no. 5 (2011): 1253–353.

Crenshaw, Kimberlé, Neil Gotanda, Gary Peller, and Kendall Thomas, eds. *Critical Race Theory: The Key Writings That Formed the Movement*. New York: New Press, 1995.

Dalton, Harlon L. "The Clouded Prism." *Harvard Civil Rights–Civil Liberties Law Review* 22, no. 2 (Spring 1987): 435–47.

D'Angelo-Corker, Kristy. "Don't Call Me Sweetheart! Why the ABA's New Rule Addressing Harassment and Discrimination Is So Important for Women Working in the Legal Profession Today." *Lewis and Clark Law Review* 23, no. 1 (May 2019): 267–309.

Davidovitch, Nitza. "Learning-Centered Teaching and Backward Course Design: From Transferring Knowledge to Teaching Skills." *Journal of International Education Research* 9, no. 4 (2013): 329–38.

Davidson, Kenneth, Ruth B. Ginsburg, and Herma Hill Kay. *Text, Cases, and Materials on Sex-Based Discrimination*. Saint Paul: West, 1974.

Davis, Paula. "Lawyer Strong®: The Legal Profession's Journey toward Well-Being." *Forbes*, May 18, 2023. www.forbes.com/sites/pauladavis/2023/05/18 /lawyer-strong-the-legal-professions-journey-toward-well-being/?sh= 17dbff7d2b0a.

"Deans by Ethnicity and Gender: Listed Alphabetically." Mississippi College School of Law. Accessed November 12, 2023. https://lawdeans.com/results .php?s=15.

Delgado, Richard, and Jean Stefanic. "Can Lawyers Find Happiness?" *Syracuse Law Review* 58 (2008): 241–59.

———. "Critical Race Theory: An Annotated Bibliography." *Virginia Law Review* 79, no. 2 (March 1993): 461–515.

Deo, Meera E. "Investigating Pandemic Effects on Legal Academia." *Fordham Law Review* 89, no. 6 (2021): 2467–95.

———. "Trajectory of a Law Professor." *Michigan Journal of Race and Law* 20, no. 2 (2015): 441–57.

———. *Unequal Profession: Race and Gender in Legal Academia.* Redwood City: Stanford University Press, 2019.

Deo, Meera E., Jacquelyn Petzold, and Chad Christensen. *The COVID Crisis in Legal Education: Law School Survey of Student Engagement Annual Report.* LSSSE. 2021. https://lssse.indiana.edu/wp-content/uploads/2015/12/COVID-Crisis-in-Legal-Education-Final-10.28.21.pdf.

Dickerson, Darby. "President's Message: Abolish the Academic Caste System." Association of American Law Schools. Accessed July 17, 2021. www.aals.org/about/publications/newsletters/aals-news-fall-2020/presidents-message-abolish-the-academic-caste-system.

"Directory of Lawyer Assistance Programs." American Bar Association. Accessed November 12, 2023. www.americanbar.org/groups/lawyer_assistance/resources/lap_programs_by_state/.

Dodgson, Lindsay. "Men Are Getting the Credit for Women's Work through Something Called 'Hepeating'—Here's What It Means." *Business Insider,* March 8, 2018. www.businessinsider.com/what-is-hepeating-2017-9.

Drachman, Virginia G. *Sisters in Law: Women Lawyers in Modern American History.* Cambridge, MA: Harvard University Press, 2001.

Dyszlewski, Nicole P., Raquel J. Gabriel, Suzanne Harrington-Steppen, Anna Russell, and Genevieve B. Tung, eds. *Integrating Doctrine and Diversity: Inclusion and Equity in the Law School Classroom.* Durham: Carolina Academic Press, 2021.

Educational Policy and Accreditation Standards for Baccalaureate and Master's Social Work Programs. Council on Social Work Education. 2015. www.cswe.org/getmedia/23a35a39-78c7-453f-b805-b67f1dca2ee5/2015-epas-and-glossary.pdf.

Elassar, Alaa. "The University of Louisville's Law School Is Offering a Class on Systemic Racism Titled 'Breonna Taylor's Louisville.'" CNN. Sept. 23, 2020. www.cnn.com/2020/09/23/us/university-of-louisville-breonna-taylor-class-trnd/index.html.

Elsesser, Kim. "Female Lawyers Face Widespread Gender Bias, According to New Study." *Forbes,* October 1, 2018. www.forbes.com/sites/kimelsesser/2018/10/01/female-lawyers-face-widespread-gender-bias-according-to-new-study/?sh=5293a8144b55.

"Explanation of Changes." American Bar Association Section of Legal Education and Admission to the Bar. 2014. www.americanbar.org/content/dam/aba/administrative/legal_education_and_admissions_to_the_bar/council_reports_and_resolutions/201408_explanation_changes.pdf.

Felter, Peter, and Leo M. Lambert. *Relationship-Rich Education: How Human Connections Drive Success in College.* Baltimore: Johns Hopkins University, 2020.

Final Report of the Testing Task Force. National Conference of Bar Examiners. April 2021. https://nextgenbarexam.ncbex.org/reports/final-report-of-the -ttf/.

Fines, Barbara Glesner. "An Institutional Culture of Assessment for Student Learning." In Maranville et al., *Building on Best Practices,* 94–101.

Finger, Davida. "CLEA Statement on Anti-racist Legal Education." Best Practices for Legal Education. April 22, 2021. https://bestpracticeslegaled.com /2021/04/22/clea-statement-on-anti-racist-legal-education.

Flores, Rosa, and Rose Marie Arce. "Why Are Kentucky Lawyers Killing Themselves?" CNN. January 20, 2014. www.cnn.com/2014/01/19/us/lawyer-suicides/index.html.

Ford, Christopher M. "The Socratic Method in the 21st Century." Master's thesis, United States Military Academy, 2008. www.westpoint.edu/sites /default/files/inline-images/centers_research/center_for_teching_excellence /PDFs/mtp_project_papers/Ford_08.pdf.

"Fordham Law's Anti-racism Action Plan." Fordham University. Accessed November 12, 2023. www.fordham.edu/info/30269/addressing_racism_in_ the_legal_system_and_our_community.

Fordyce-Ruff, Tenielle. "Research across the Curriculum: Using Cognitive Science to Answer the Call for Better Legal Research Instruction." *Dickinson Law Review* 125, no. 1 (2020): 1–46.

Freire, Paulo. *Pedagogy of the Oppressed.* New York: Penguin, 2017.

Friedland, Steven I. "How We Teach: A Survey of Teaching Techniques in American Law School." *Seattle University Law Review* 20 (1996): 1–44.

Functions and Structure of a Medical School: Standards for Accreditation of Medical Education Programs Leading to the MD Degree. Liaison Committee on Medical Education. March 2016. https://lcme.org/publications/.

Funk, Andrea Susnir. *The Art of Assessment: Making Outcomes Assessment Accessible, Sustainable, and Meaningful.* Durham: Carolina Academic Press, 2017.

Garner, David. "Socratic Misogyny: Analyzing Feminist Criticism of Socratic Teaching in Legal Education." *BYU Law Review* 2000, no. 4 (2000): 1587–650.

Gerkman, Alli, and Logan Cornett. "Foundations for Practice: The Whole Lawyer and the Character Quotient." Institute for the Advancement of the American Legal System. July 26, 2016. https://iaals.du.edu/publications /foundations-practice-whole-lawyer-and-character-quotient.

Gersen, Jeannie Suk. "The Socratic Method in the Age of Trauma." *Harvard Law Review* 130, no. 9 (October 2017): 2320–47.

Gilligan, Carol. *In a Different Voice: Psychological Theory and Women's Development.* Cambridge, MA: Harvard University Press, 1982.

Gladwell, Malcolm. *The Tipping Point: How Little Things Can Make a Big Difference.* New York: Back Bay Books, 2006.

González, Carmen G. *Women of Color in Legal Education Challenging the Presumption of Incompetence.* Federal Lawyer. July 2014. https://upcolorado.com/excerpts/PresumedIncompetent_FederalLawyer.pdf.

González, Carmen G., and Angela P. Harris. "Presumed Incompetent: Continuing the Conversation." *Berkeley Journal of Gender, Law and Justice* 29, no. 2 (Summer 2014): 183–94.

Goodman, Chris Chambers, and Sarah E. Redfield. "A Teacher Who Looks Like Me." *Journal of Civil Rights and Economic Development* 27 (2013): 105–66.

Gordon, Robert W. "Critical Legal Studies as a Teaching Method, against the Background of the Intellectual Politics of Modern Legal Education in the United States." *Legal Education Review* 1, no. 1 (1989): 59–84.

———. "Unfreezing Legal Reality: Critical Approaches to Law." *Florida State University Law Review* 15, no. 2 (1987): 195–220.

Gottfredson, Nisha C., A.T. Panter, Charles E. Daye, Walter T. Allen, Linda F. Wightman, and Meera E. Deo. "Identifying Predictors of Law Student Life Satisfaction." *Journal of Legal Education* 58, no. 4 (December 2008): 520–30.

Greene, Linda S. "Serving the Community: Aspiration and Abyss for the Law Professor of Color." *Saint Louis University Public Law Review* 10, no. 1 (1991): 297–303.

———. "Tokens, Role Models, and Pedagogical Politics: Lamentations of an African American Female Law Professor." *Berkeley Journal of Gender, Law and Justice* 6, no. 1 (1990–91): 81–92.

Guinier, Lani. "Of Gentlemen and Role Models." *Berkeley Women's Law Journal* 6, no. 1 (1991): 93–106.

Guinier, Lani, Michelle Fine, and Jane Balin. "Becoming Gentlemen: Women's Experiences at One Ivy League Law School." *University of Pennsylvania Law Review* 143, no. 1 (November 1994): 1–110.

Gundersen, Judith A. "Leaving Langdell Behind: Reimagining Legal Education for a New Era." *Minnesota Law Review* 105 (2023): 2407–29.

Gurvich, Rachel, L. Danielle Tully, Laura A. Webb, Alexa Z. Chew, Jane E. Cross, and Joy Kanwar. "Reimagining Langdell's Legacy: Puncturing the Equilibrium in Law School Pedagogy." *North Carolina Law Review Addendum* 101 (2023): 118–61.

Guthrie, Chris, and Emily Lamm. "The Aid Gap." *Journal of Legal Education* 69, no. 1 (Fall 2019): 123–37.

Halpern, Stephen C. "On the Politics and Pathology of Legal Education." *Journal of Legal Education* 32, no. 3 (September 1982): 383–94.

Hammond, Laina. "The Pay Gap between Male and Female Law Partners Is Real: Litigation Finance Can Help Women Close It." Texas Lawyer. October 22, 2021. www.law.com/texaslawyer/2021/10/22/the-pay-gap-between-male-and-female-law-partners-is-real-litigation-finance-can-help-women-close-it/.

Han, Eun Hee. "What to Learn from Pandemic Teaching? Our Student's Names." *Journal of Legal Education* 69, no. 3 (Spring 2020): 806–13.

Hanson, Melanie. "Average Law School Debt, Education." Education Data Initiative. June 15, 2023. https://educationdata.org/average-law-school-debt.

Harris, Angela P. "On Doing the Right Thing: Education Work in the Academy." *Vermont Law Review* 15 (1990–91): 125–38.

Hathaway, Grace. *Fate Rides a Tortoise: A Biography of Ellen Spencer Mussey.* Philadelphia: Winston, 1937.

Hayes, Elisabeth. "Insights from Women's Experiences for Teaching and Learning." *Effective Teaching Styles: New Directions for Continuing Legal Education* 1989, no. 43 (Fall 1989): 55–66.

Heflin, Julie. "UofL Law, Dental Faculty Receive International Award for Novel Teaching Method." *UofL News,* August 20, 2021. www.uoflnews.com/post /uofltoday/uofl-law-dental-faculty-receive-international-award-for-novel-teaching-method/.

Herrara, Luz E. "Challenging a Tradition of Exclusion: The History of an Unheard Story at Harvard Law School." *Harvard Latino Law Review* 5, no. 3 (Spring 2002): 51–140.

Hochschild, Arlie R. *Second Shift: Working Parents and the Revolution at Home.* New York: Viking Penguin, 1989.

Household Data: Annual Averages. Bureau of Labor Statistics. Accessed November 12, 2023. www.bls.gov/cps/cpsaat39.pdf.

Iglesias, Elizabeth M. "Foreword: International Law, Human Rights, and LatCrit Theory." *University of Miami Inter-American Law Review* 28, no. 2 (Winter 1996–97): 177–213.

Ihrig, Scott. "Sexual Orientation in Law School: Experiences of Gay, Lesbian, and Bisexual Law Students." *Minnesota Journal of Law and Inequity* 14, no. 2 (1996): 555–91.

Jackson, Janet Thompson. "Wellness and Law: Reforming Legal Education to Support Student Wellness." *Howard Law Journal* 65, no. 1 (2021): 45–102.

Jaffe, David, Katherine M. Bender, and Jerome Organ. "'It Is Okay to Not Be Okay': The 2021 Survey of Law Student Well-Being." *University of Louisville Law Review* 60 (Spring 2022): 441–96.

James, Colin. "Towards Trauma-Informed Legal Practice: A Review." *Psychiatric, Psychology and Law* 27, no. 2 (2020).

Jefferson, Renee Knake. "Judicial Ethics in the #MeToo World." *Fordham Law Review* 89, no. 4 (2021): 1197–221.

Jewel, Lucille A. "Oil and Water: How Legal Education's Doctrine and Skills Divide Reproduces Toxic Hierarchies." *Columbia Journal of Gender and Law* 31, no. 1 (2015): 111–34.

———. "Silencing Discipline in Legal Education." *University of Toledo Law Review* 49, no. 3 (Spring 2018): 657–83.

Johnson, Stephen M. "The Course Source: The Casebook Evolved." *Capital University Law Review* 44, no. 3 (2016): 591–664.

Joy, Peter A. "The Uneasy History of Experiential Education in U.S. Law Schools." *Dickinson Law Review* 122, nos. 2–4 (2018): 551–83.

Keene, Sherri Lee, and Susan A. McMahon. "The Contextual Case Method: Moving beyond Opinions to Spark Students' Legal Imaginations." *Virginia Law Review Online* 108 (February 2022): 72–90.

Keith, Latonia Haney. "Cultural Competency in a Post-model 8.4(g) World." *Duke Journal of Gender Law and Policy* 25, no. 1 (2017): 1–41.

Kennedy, Duncan. *Legal Education and the Reproduction of Hierarchy*. 1983. Reprint, New York: New York University Press, 2004.

Keshet, Harry, and Angela A. Meyer. *Compensation in Law Firms: The Impact of Gender, Race and Ethnicity*. Keshet Consulting. 2013. www.yumpu.com /en/document/read/34378992/compensation.

Kim, W. C., and Renee Mauborgne. "Tipping Point Leadership." *Harvard Business Review* 50, no. 4 (2003).

Kimball, Bruce A. "The Langdell Problem: Historicizing the Century of Historiography, 1906–2000s." *Law and History Review* 22, no. 2 (Summer 2004): 57–140.

Klemko, Robert, and John Sullivan. "The Push to Remake Policing Takes Decades, Only to Begin Again." *Washington Post*, June 10, 2021. www .washingtonpost.com/investigations/interactive/2021/police-reform-failure.

Kotkin, Minna J. "Clinical Legal Education and the Replication of Hierarchy." *Clinical Law Review* 26, no. 1 (Fall 2019): 287–306.

Krannich, Jess M., James R. Holbrook, and Julie J. McAdams. "Beyond 'Thinking Like a Lawyer' and the Traditional Legal Paradigm: Toward a Comprehensive View of Legal Education." *Denver University Law Review* 86, no. 2 (2009): 381–404.

Krieger, Lawrence S. "Inseparability of Professionalism and Personal Satisfaction: Perspectives on Values, Integrity and Happiness." *Clinical Law Review* 11 (Spring 2005): 425–45.

———. "Institutional Denial about the Dark Side of Law School, and Fresh Empirical Guidance for Constructively Breaking the Silence." *Journal of Legal Education* 52, nos. 1–2 (2002): 112–29.

Krill, Patrick R., Ryan Johnson, and Linda Albert. "The Prevalence of Substance Use and Other Mental Health Concerns among American Attorneys." *Journal of Addiction Medicine* 10, no. 1 (February 2016): 46–52.

Krook, Joshua. "The Real Socratic Method: At the Heart of Legal Education Lies a Fundamental Misunderstanding of Why Socrates Asked So Many Questions." *Griffith Journal of Law and Human Dignity* 5, no. 1 (2017): 32–44.

———. "The Real Socratic Method: Law Schools Fail to Understand Why Socrates Asked So Many Questions." *New Intrigue*, September 24, 2017. https://newintrigue.com/2017/09/24/the-real-socratic-method-law-schools-fail-to-understand-why-socrates-asked-so-many-questions/#_ftn22.

Kubes, Kristen A., Cara D. Davis, and Mary E. Schwind. *The Evolution of Model Rule 8.4(g): Working to Eliminate Bias, Discrimination, and Harassment in the Practice of Law*. American Bar Association. March 12, 2019. www.americanbar.org/groups/construction_industry/publications/under_ construction/2019/spring/modelrule-8-4/.

Kuehn, Robert R. "Shifting Law School Faculty Demographics." Best Practices for Legal Education. January 5, 2022. https://bestpracticeslegaled.com/2022 /01/05/clinical-legal-education-by-the-numbers/.

Kuehn, Robert R., Margaret Reuter, and David A. Santacroce. *2019–20 Survey of Applied Legal Education*. Center for the Study of Applied Legal Education. 2020. www.csale.org/#results.

"Lani Guinier." Harvard Law School. Accessed March 25, 2022. www.hls
.harvard.edu/faculty/directory/10344/Guinier.

Larcombe, Wendy, Letty Tumbaga, Ian Malkin, Penelope Nicholson, and Ora-
nia Tokatlidis. "Does an Improved Experience of Law School Protect
Students against Depression, Anxiety and Stress? An Empirical Study of
Wellbeing and the Law School Experience of LLB and JD Students." *Sydney
Law Review* 35, no. 2 (2013): 407–32.

"Law School Enrollment by Race and Ethnicity (2019)." Enjuris. Accessed June
20, 2021. www.enjuris.com/students/law-school-race-2019.html.

"Law School Enrollment by Race and Ethnicity (2022)." Enjuris. Accessed July
12, 2023. www.enjuris.com/students/law-school-race-2022/.

"Law School Rankings by Female Enrollment (2019)." Enjuris. Accessed
November 13, 2023. www.enjuris.com/students/law-school-female-enrollment-
2019.html.

"Law School Survey of Student Engagement." LSSSE. Accessed November 21,
2023. https://lssse.indiana.edu.

"Lawyers and Depression." David Nee Foundation. Accessed November 14,
2023. www.mightycause.com/organization/Dave-Nee-Foundation.

Lebrón, Aníbal Rosario. "If These Blackboards Could Talk: The Crit Classroom, a Battlefield." *Charleston Law Review* 9 (2015): 305–33.

Lederman, Doug. "How Teaching Changed in the (Forced) Shift to Remote
Learning." Inside Higher Ed. April 22, 2020. www.insidehighered.com/digital-
learning/article/2020/04/22/how-professors-changed-their-teaching-springs-
shift-remote.

Leopard Solutions. "Why Are Women Lawyers Leaving the Legal Industry?"
JD Supra, March 9, 2022. www.jdsupra.com/legalnews/why-are-women-
lawyers-leaving-the-legal-3000987/.

Levit, Nancy, and Douglas O. Linder. "Happy Law Students, Happy Lawyers."
Syracuse Law Review 58 (January 2008): 351–73.

Li, Miranda, Phillip Yao, and Goodwin Lui. "Who's Going to Law School?"
UC Davis Law Review 54, no. 2 (December 2020): 613–62.

Liebenberg, Roberta D., and Stephanie A. Scharf. *Walking Out the Door: The
Facts, Figures, and Future of Experienced Women Lawyers in Private
Practice.* American Bar Association. 2019. www.abajournal.com/files
/WALKING_OUT_THE_DOOR_-_FINAL_AS_OF_NOV_14_2019_pm
.pdf.

Liemer, Sue. "The Hierarchy of Law School Faculty Meetings: Who Votes?"
UMKC Law Review 73, no. 2 (2004): 351–418.

"List of Law Schools Withdrawing from *U.S. News and World Report* Rankings
Participation." Spivey Consulting. November 19, 2022. www.spiveyconsulting
.com/blog-post/list-of-law-schools-withdrawing-from-us-news-rankings/.

López, Rachel. "Unentitled: The Power of Designation in the Legal Academy."
Rutgers University Law Review 73, no. 3 (Spring 2021): 923–32.

Lowe, Jeffrey A. *2022 Partner Compensation Survey.* Major, Lindsey and
Africa. 2022. https://209075.fs1.hubspotusercontent-na1.net/hubfs/209075
/MLA%20%20Web%20Research%20Page%20PDFs/2022_Partner%20
Compensation%20Survey_FINAL101822.pdf.

Lynch, Mary A. "Contemporary Issues in Outcomes-Based Education: An Examination of Ten Concerns about Using Outcomes in Legal Education." *William and Mitchell Law Review* 38, no. 3 (2012): 976–1016.

MacKinnon, Catharine A. "Feminism in Legal Education." *Legal Education Review* 1, no. 1 (1989): 1–7.

———. "Mainstreaming Feminism in Legal Education." *Journal of Legal Education* 53, no. 2 (June 2003): 199–212.

Makar, Zina. "Unnecessary Incarceration." *Oregon Law Review* 98, no. 2 (2020): 607–70.

Managing Director's Guidance Memo. American Bar Association. June 2015. www.americanbar.org/content/dam/aba/administrative/legal_education_and_admissions_to_the_bar/governancedocuments/2015_learning_outcomes_guidance.pdf.

Maranville, Deborah, Lisa Radtke Bliss, Carolyn Wilkes Kaas, and Antoinette Sedillo Lopez, eds. *Building on Best Practices: Transforming Legal Education in a Changing World.* Durham: Carolina Academic Press, 2015.

Margolies, Dan. "Before He Quit, Federal Judge in Kansas City, Kansas, Faced Possible Impeachment for Misconduct." NPR Kansas, March 4, 2020. www.kcur.org/news/2020-03-04/before-he-quit-federal-judge-in-kansas-city-kansas-faced-possible-impeachment-for-misconduct.

Martin, Susan Ehrlich, and Nancy C. Jurik. *Doing Justice, Doing Gender: Women in Legal and Criminal Justice Occupations* (Thousand Oaks: Sage, 2006).

Matsuda, Mari J. "Looking to the Bottom: Critical Legal Studies and Reparations." *Harvard Civil Rights–Civil Liberties Law Review* 22, no. 2 (Spring 1987): 323–400.

———. "When the First Quail Calls: Multiple Consciousness as Jurisprudential Method." *Women's Rights Law Reporter* 11, no. 1 (1993): 7–10.

McCarthy, Nancy. "Statistics Tell Story of Stress, Addiction in Lives of Lawyers." *California Bar Journal,* November 2000. https://archive.calbar.ca.gov/archive/calbar/2cbj/00nov/index.htm.

McGinley, Ann C. "Reproducing Gender on Law School Faculties" *BYU Law Review* 99, no. 1 (2009): 99–156.

McMahon, Susan A. "What We Teach When We Teach Legal Analysis." *Minnesota Law Review* 107 (2023): 2511–60.

McMurtry-Chubb, Teri A. *Strategies and Techniques for Integrating Diversity, Equity, and Inclusion into the Core Law Curriculum: A Comprehensive Guide to DEI Pedagogy, Course Planning, and Classroom Practice.* Philadelphia: Wolters Kluwer, 2021.

Menkel-Meadow, Carrie. "Feminist Legal Theory, Critical Legal Studies, and Legal Education, or 'The Fem-Crits Go to Law School.'" *Journal of Legal Education* 38, nos. 1–2 (March–June 1988): 61–85.

———. "Taking Law and _____ Really Seriously: Before, during and after 'The Law.'" *Vanderbilt Law Review* 60, no. 2 (2007): 555–95.

Menkel-Meadow, Carrie, Martha Minow, and David Vernon. "From the Editors." *Journal of Legal Education* 38 (March–June 1988): 1–2.

Merritt, Deborah Jones. "Client-Centered Legal Education and Licensing." *Minnesota Law Review* 107 (2023): 101–47.

Merritt, Deborah Jones, and Logan Cornett. *Building a Better Bar: The Twelve Building Blocks of Minimum Competence.* Institute for the Advancement of the American Legal System. October 2020. https://iaals.du.edu/sites/default /files/documents/publications/building_a_better_bar.pdf.

Merritt, Deborah Jones, and Kyle McEntee. "Gender Equity in Law School Enrollment: An Elusive Goal." *Journal of Legal Education* 69, no. 1 (Fall 2019): 102–15.

Mertz, Elizabeth. *The Language of Law School: Learning to Think Like a Lawyer.* Oxford: Oxford University Press, 2007.

———. "Teaching Lawyers the Language of Law: Legal and Anthropological Translations." *John Marshall Law Review* 34, no. 4 (September 2000): 91–117.

Minow, Martha. "Feminist Reason: Getting It and Losing It." *Journal of Legal Education* 38, nos. 1–2 (March–June 1998): 47–60.

Mitchell, Kristina W. M., and Jonathan Martin. *Gender Bias in Student Evaluations.* Cambridge: Cambridge University Press, 2018.

"Model Code of Professional Conduct Rule 8.4(g)." American Bar Association. 2020. www.americanbar.org/groups/professional_responsibility/publications /model_rules_of_professional_conduct/rule_8_4_misconduct/.

"Model Rules of Professional Conduct." American Bar Association. Accessed November 6, 2023. www.americanbar.org/groups/professional_responsibility /publications/model_rules_of_professional_conduct/model_rules_of_ professional_conduct_table_of_contents/.

Moliterno, James E. "And Now a Crisis in Legal Education." *Seton Hall Law Review* 44, no. 4 (2014): 1069–129.

Monopoli, Paula. "Gender and the Crisis in Legal Education: Remaking the Academy in Our Image." *Michigan State Law Review* 5 (2012): 1745–75.

Monteiro, Lyra D. "Power Structures: White Columns, White Marble, White Supremacy." *Medium,* October 27, 2020. https://intersectionist.medium .com/american-power-structures-white-columns-white-marble-white-supremacy-d43aa091b5f9.

Montoya, Margaret E. "Mascaras, Trenzas, y Greñas: Un/Masking the Self While Un/Braiding Latina Stories and Legal Discourse." *Harvard Journal of Law and Gender* 17 (1994): 1–37.

———. "Silence and Silencing: Their Centripetal and Centrifugal Forces in Legal Communication, Pedagogy and Discourse." *Michigan Journal of Race and Law* 5, no. 3 (Summer 2000): 263–327.

Morse, Robert, Kenneth Hines, Eric Brook, and Sam Wellington. "Methodology: 2023–2024 Best Law Schools Rankings." U.S. News. May 10, 2023. www.usnews.com/education/best-graduate-schools/articles/law-schools-methodology.

"Multistate Performance Test." National Conference of Bar Examiners. Accessed November 13, 2023. www.ncbex.org/exams/mpt/.

Mutua, Athena D. "Shifting Bottoms and Rotating Centers: Reflections on LatCrit III and the Black/White Paradigm." *University of Miami Law Review* 53, no. 4 (July 1999): 1177–218.

NALP Foundation for Law Career Research and Education and the Center for Women in Law. *Women of Color: A Study of Law School Experiences (2020)*. 2020. www.nalpfoundation.org/product-page/women-of-color-a-study-of-law-school-experiences.

National Task Force on Lawyer Well-Being. *The Path to Lawyer Well-Being: Practical Recommendations for Positive Change*. American Bar Association. August 14, 2017. www.americanbar.org/content/dam/aba/images/abanews/ThePathToLawyerWellBeingReportRevFINAL.pdf.

Neacsu, E. Dana. "CLS Stands for Critical Legal Studies, If Anyone Remembers." *Journal of Law and Policy* 8, no. 2 (2000): 415–53.

Nelson, Dorothy W. "Introduction to the Effects of Gender in the Federal Courts: The Final Report of the Ninth Circuit Gender Bias Task Force." *Southern California Law Review* 67 (1994): 731–38.

Niedwiecki, Anthony. "Prepared for Practice? Developing a Comprehensive Assessment Plan for a Law School Professional Skills Program." *University of San Francisco Law Review* 245, no. 2 (2016): 245–89.

Niemann, Yolanda Flores, Gabriella Gutiérrez y Muhs, and Carmen G. González, eds. *Presumed Incompetent II: Race, Class, Power, and Resistance of Women in Academia*. Denver: University Press of Colorado, 2020.

North Dakota Commission on Gender Fairness in the Courts. "A Difference in Perceptions: The Final Report of the North Dakota Commission on Gender Fairness in the Courts." *North Dakota Law Review* 72, no. 4 (1996): 1113–42.

Norwood, Candice. "More Black Women Are Leading U.S. Law Schools and Changing the Conversation on Race and Gender." *19th News*, February 8, 2022. https://19thnews.org/2022/02/black-women-law-school-deans/.

O'Brien, Molly Townes, Stephen Tang, and Kath Hall. "No Time to Lose: Negative Impact on Law Student Wellbeing May Begin in Year One." *International Journal of the First Year in Higher Education* 2, no. 2 (June 2011): 49–60.

Olson, Elizabeth. "Women Make Up Majority of U.S. Law Students for First Time." *New York Times,* December 16, 2016. www.nytimes.com/2016/12/16/business/dealbook/women-majority-of-us-law-students-first-time.html.

Oreskovich, Michael R. "Prevalence of Alcohol Use Disorders among American Surgeons." *Archives of Surgery* 147, no. 2 (2012): 168–74.

Organ, Jerome M., David B. Jaffe, and Katherine M. Bender. "Suffering in Silence: The Survey of Law Student Well-Being and the Reluctance of Law Students to Seek Help for Substance Use and Mental Health Concerns." *Journal of Legal Education* 66, no. 1 (2016): 116–56.

Osborn, John Jay. *The Paper Chase*. Boston: Houghton Mifflin, 1971.

The Other Epidemic: Fatal Police Shootings in the Time of COVID-19. American Civil Liberties Union. 2020. www.aclu.org/report/other-epidemic-fatal-police-shootings-time-covid-19.

"Our Founding Mothers." American University Washington College of Law. Accessed July 17, 2023. www.wcl.american.edu/impact/history/.

Padilla, Laura M. "Presumptions of Incompetence, Gender, Sidelining, and Women Law Deans." In Niemann, Gutiérrez y Muhs, and González, *Presumed Incompetent II,* 117–28.

Palmer, Jacquelyn, and Linda Ouyang. "Analysis: Survey Finds Lawyer Burnout Rising, Well-Being Falling." *Bloomberg Law,* June 28, 2021. https://news.bloomberglaw.com/business-and-practice/analysis-survey-finds-lawyer-burnout-rising-well-being-falling.

Patel, Serena. "Cultural Competency Training: Preparing Law Students for Practice in Our Multicultural World." *UCLA Law Review Discourse* 62, no. 7 (2014): 140–56.

Payne-Tsoupros, Christina. "A Starting Point for Disability Justice in Legal Education." *Journal Committed to Social Change on Race and Ethnicity* 6, no. 1 (2020): 165–89.

Peery, Destiny. *It's Time to Move beyond the Numbers.* National Association of Women Lawyers (NAWL) Survey on the Promotion and Retention of Women in Law Firms. April 18, 2022. https://issuu.com/nawl1899/docs/2021_nawl_survey_report.

Peters, Bethany L., and Edward P. Stringham. "No Booze? You May Lose: Why Drinkers Earn More Money Than Nondrinkers." *Journal of Labor Research* 23, no. 3 (December 2006): 411–21.

Peterson, Todd David, and Elizabeth Waters Peterson. "Stemming the Tide of Law Student Depression: What Law Schools Need to Learn from the Science of Positive Psychology." *Yale Journal of Health Policy, Law, and Ethics* 9, no. 2 (2009): 357–434.

Pistone, Michele R., and John J. Hoeffner. "No Path but One: Law School Survival in an Age of Disruptive Technology." *Wayne Law Review* 59, no. 2 (Fall 2013): 193–268.

Plickert, Gabriele. *After the JD III: Third Results of a National Study of Legal Careers.* American Bar Foundation. 2014. www.americanbarfoundation.org/uploads/cms/documents/ajd3report_final_for_distribution.pdf.

Prince, Janee T. "'Can I Touch Your Hair?' Exploring Double Binds and the Black Tax in Law School." *University of Pennsylvania Journal of Law and Social Change* 20, no. 1 (2017): 29–49.

Purvis, Dara. "Legal Education as Hegemonic Masculinity." *Villanova Law Review* 65, no. 5 (January 2021): 1145–54.

"Racial Bias, Disparities and Oppression in the 1L Curriculum: A Critical Approach to the Canonical First Year Law School Subjects." Symposium, Boston University School of Law, Boston, February 28–29, 2020. www.bu.edu/law/files/2019/12/BU-Symposium-schedule-2320201-1.pdf.

Reich, Jarrod F. "Capitalizing on Healthy Lawyers: The Business Case for Law Firms to Promote and Prioritize Lawyer Well-Being." *Villanova Law Review* 65, no. 2 (2020): 361–418.

Reuters. "U.S. Saw Summer of Black Lives Matter Protests Demanding Change." *U.S. News and World Report,* December 7, 2020. www.usnews.com/news/top-news/articles/2020-12-07/us-saw-summer-of-black-lives-matter-protests-demanding-change.

Reuther, Kevin S. "Dorothy's Friend Goes to Law School." *National Journal of Sexual Orientation Law* 1, no. 2 (1995). www.ibiblio.org/gaylaw/issue2/reuther.html.

Reynolds, Heather L., and Katherine Dowell Kearns. "A Planning Tool for Incorporating Backward Design, Active Learning, and Authentic Assessment in the College Classroom." *College Teaching* 65, no. 1 (2016): 17–27.

Rhode, Deborah L. "Missing Questions: Feminist Perspectives on Legal Education." *Stanford Law Review* 45, no. 6 (1993): 1547–66.

———. "Perspectives on Professional Women." *Stanford Law Review* 40, no. 5 (May 1988): 1163–1207.

Rhode, Deborah L., and Lucy B. Ricca. "Diversity in the Legal Profession: Perspectives from Managing Partners and General Counsel." *Fordham Law Review* 83, no. 5 (2015): 2483–507.

Rikleen, Lauren Stiller. *Closing the Gap: A Road Map for Achieving Gender Pay Equity in Law Firm Partner Compensation.* ABA Presidential Task Force on Gender Equity and the Commission on Women in the Profession. 2013. www.americanbar.org/content/dam/aba/administrative/women/closing_the_gap.authcheckdam.pdf.

Ristroph, Alice. "The Curriculum of the Carceral State." *Columbia Law Review* 120, no. 6 (2020): 1631–1708.

Robbins, Ruth A., Kristen M. Tischione, and Melissa H. Weresh. "Persistent Structural Barriers to Gender Equity in the Legal Academy and the Efforts of Two Legal Writing Organizations to Break Them Down." *Villanova Law Review* 65, no. 5 (2021): 1155–85.

Roberts, John G., Jr. *2018 Year-End Report on the Federal Judiciary.* Supreme Court. December 31, 2018. www.supremecourt.gov/publicinfo/year-end/2018year-endreport.pdf.

Robson, Ruthann. "Educating the Next Generation of LGBTQ Attorneys." *Journal of Legal Education* 66, no. 3 (Spring 2017): 502–9.

———. *Sappho Goes to Law School: Fragments in Lesbian Legal Theory.* New York: Columbia University Press, 1998.

"Rosenblatt's Deans Database." Mississippi College School of Law. Accessed July 13, 2022. https://lawdeans.com/results.php?s=14/.

Rubin, Edward. "What's Wrong with Langdell's Method, and What to Do About It." *Vanderbilt Law Review* 60, no. 2 (2007): 609–65.

Rubino, Kathryn. "Black at Harvard Law School Is the Instagram Account You Need to Read Right Now." Above the Law. June 24, 2020. https://abovethelaw.com/2020/06/black-at-harvard-law-school-is-the-instagram-account-you-need-to-read-right-now.

Ryan, Christopher J., Jr., and Meghan Dawe. "Mind the Gap: Gender Pay Disparities in the Legal Academy." *Georgetown Journal of Legal Ethics* 34, no. 3 (2021): 567–611.

Saadati-Soto, Donna. "The Experience of Latinx Students with the Harvard Law School First-Year Curriculum." Social Science Research Network. May 2020. https://ssrn.com/abstract=3579132.

"SALT Virtual Series: Social Justice in Action, Incorporating Anti-racism Frameworks into Core Law School Classes." Society of American Law Teachers. July 10, 2020. www.saltlaw.org/salt-virtual-series-social-justice-in-action.

Samuel-Siegel, Doron. "Reckoning with Structural Racism in Legal Education: Methods toward a Pedagogy of Antiracism." *Cardozo Journal of Equal Rights and Social Justice* 29, no. 1 (December 2022): 1–68.

Schaefer, Paula. "Integrating Professionalism into Doctrinally-Focused Courses." In Maranville et al., *Building on Best Practices,* 271–89.

Schwartz, Michael Hunter. "Improving Legal Education by Improving Casebooks: Fourteen Things Casebooks Can Do to Produce Better and More Learning." *Elon Law Review* 3, no. 1 (2011): 27–63.

Schwartz, Michael Hunter, Gerald F. Hess, and Sophie M. Sparrow. *What the Best Law Teachers Do.* Cambridge, MA: Harvard University Press, 2013.

Sears, Brad. "Queer L." *National Journal of Sexual Orientation Law* 1, no. 2 (1995). www.ibiblio.org/gaylaw/issue2/sears.html.

Sears, Brad, Christy Mallory, Andrew R. Flores, and Keith J. Conron. *LGBT People's Experiences of Workplace Discrimination and Harassment.* Williams Institute. September 2021. https://williamsinstitute.law.ucla.edu /wp-content/uploads/Workplace-Discrimination-Sep-2021.pdf.

Section of Legal Education and Admissions to the Bar: Report to the House of Delegates, Resolution 300. American Bar Association Section of Legal Education and Admissions to the Bar. February 14, 2022. www.americanbar .org/content/dam/aba/administrative/news/2022/02/midyear-hod-resolutions /300.pdf.

Seldin, Peter. "Self-Assessment of College Teaching." *Improving College and University Teaching* 30, no. 2 (1982): 70–74.

Shadel, Molly Bishop, Sophie Trawalter, and J.H. Verkerke. "Gender Differences in Law School Classroom Participation: The Key Role of Social Context." *Virginia Law Review Online* 108 (February 2022): 55–71.

Shaw, Gary. "A Heretical View of Teaching: A Contrarian Look at Teaching, the Carnegie Report, and Best Practices." *Touro Law Review* 28, no. 4 (November 2012): 1239–303.

Sheldon, Kennon M., and Lawrence S. Krieger. "Does Legal Education Have Undermining Effects on Law Students? Evaluation Changes in Motivation, Values, and Well-Being." *Behavioral Sciences and the Law* 22, no. 2 (2004): 261–86.

Shultz, Marjorie M., and Sheldon Zedeck. *Final Report: Identification, Development, and Validation of Predictors for Successful Lawyering.* SSRN. 2008. https://papers.ssrn.com/sol3/papers.cfm?abstract_id=1353554.

Silver, Marjorie A. *Substance Abuse, Stress, Mental Health and the Legal Profession.* Touro Law Center, 2002. www.nylat.org/documents/CourseinaBox .pdf.

"Sixth Circuit Court of Appeals Visits Louisville." University of Louisville. Accessed November 6, 2023. https://louisville.edu/law/banners/sixth-circuit-court-of-appeals-visits-louisville-law/view.

Sloan, Karen. "ABA Votes to Keep Law School Standardized Test Requirement." Reuters. February 6, 2023. www.reuters.com/legal/legalindustry /aba-votes-keep-law-school-standardized-test-requirement-2023-02-06/.

———. "Law School Applications Plummet as Law Schools Raise Their Sights." Reuters. August 22, 2022. www.reuters.com/legal/legalindustry/law-professor-applications-plummet-law-schools-raise-their-sights-2022-08-22/.

"Socratic Zooming: Faculty Weigh In on Teaching Remotely." Columbia Law School. April 27, 2020. www.law.columbia.edu/news/archive/socratic-zooming-faculty-weigh-teaching-remotely.

Soh, Nerissa, Fiona Burns, Rita Shackel, and Bruce Robinson. "Law Student Mental Health Literacy and Distress: Finances, Accommodation and Travel Time." *Legal Education Review* 25, no 1 (January 2015): 29–63.

Solozano, Daniel G., and Tara J. Yosso. "Critical Race and LatCrit Theory and Method: Counter-Storytelling." *International Journal of Qualitative Studies in Education* 14, no. 1 (2001): 471–95.

Soonpaa, Nancy J. "Stress in Law Students: A Comparative Study of First-Year, Second-Year, and Third-Year Students." *Connecticut Law Review* 36 (2004): 353–83.

Spade, Dean. "For Those Considering Law School." *Unbound* 6 (2010): 111–19.

Spencer, A. Benjamin. "The Law School Critique in Historical Perspective." *Washington and Lee Law Review* 69, no. 4 (Fall 2012): 1949–2063.

Stanchi, Kathryn M. "Who Next, the Janitors? A Socio-feminist Critique of the Status Hierarchy of Law Professors." *UMKC Law Review* 73, no. 2 (2004): 469–97.

Standards and Rules of Procedure for Approval of Law Schools. American Bar Association. 2023. www.americanbar.org/content/dam/aba/administrative/legal_education_and_admissions_to_the_bar/standards/2023-2024/2023-2024-aba-standards-rules-for-approval.pdf.

State Nondiscrimination Laws. Movement Advancement Project. March 6, 2023. www.lgbtmap.org/img/maps/citations-nondisc-employment.pdf.

Statistics. American Bar Association. February 10, 2023. www.americanbar.org/content/dam/aba/administrative/legal_education_and_admissions_to_the_bar/statistics/2023/2022-jd-non-jd-enrollment.xlsx.

Strader, Kelly, Brietta R. Clark, Robin Ingli, Elizabeth Kransberger, Lawrence Levine, and William Perez. "An Assessment of the Law School Climate for GLBT Students." *Journal of Legal Education* 58, no. 2 (2008): 212–44.

Stropus, Ruta K. "Mend It, Bend It, and Extend It: The Fate of Traditional Law School Methodology in the 21st Century." *Loyola University Chicago Law Journal* 27, no. 3 (1996): 449–89.

"Student Learning Outcomes." New York Law School. Accessed July 31, 2021. www.nyls.edu/academics/programs-of-study/student-competencies-and-learning-outcomes.

Stychin, Carl F. *Law's Desire: Sexuality and the Limits of Justice.* London: Routledge, 1995.

Substance Use Disorders among Legal Professionals. Hazelden Betty Ford Foundation. March 2017. www.hazeldenbettyford.org/education/bcr/addiction-research/substance-abuse-legal-professionals-ru-317.

Sue, Derald Wing, Christina M. Capodilupo, Gina C. Torino, Jennifer M. Bucceri, Aisha M.B. Holder, Kevin L. Nadal, and Marta Esquilin. "Racial

Microaggressions in Everyday Life: Implications for Clinical Practice." *American Psychologist* 62, no. 4 (May–June 2007): 271–86.

Sullivan, William M., Anne Colby, Judith Welch Wegner, Lloyd Bond, and Lee S. Shulman. *Educating Lawyers: Preparation for the Profession of Law.* Carnegie Foundation for the Advancement of Teaching. 2007. http://archive .carnegiefoundation.org/publications/pdfs/elibrary/elibrary_pdf_632.pdf.

Sungaila, Mary-Christine. "Combating Bias Inside and Outside the Courtroom." *Perspectives* 5, no. 1 (Summer 1996).

"Supporting Recovery in the Legal Community." The Other Bar. Accessed November 13, 2023. https://otherbar.org/.

Suskie, Linda. *Assessing Student Learning.* San Francisco: Jossey-Bass, 2009.

Teste, Kellye Y. "Advancing an Evidence-Based Approach to Improving Legal Education." *Journal of Legal Education* 69, no. 2 (2020): 561–67.

Thiese, Matthew S., Joseph A. Allen, Martha Knudson, Kim Free, and Paige Petersen. "Depressive Symptoms and Suicidal Ideation among Lawyers and Other Law Professionals." *Journal of Occupational and Environmental Medicine* 63, no. 5 (2021): 381–86.

Török, John H. "The Story of 'Towards Asian American Jurisprudence' and Its Implications for Latinas/os in American Law Schools." *Berkeley La Raza Law Journal* 13 (Fall 2002): 271.

Torrey, Morrison, Jackie Casey, and Karin Olson. "Teaching Law in a Feminist Manner: A Commentary from Experience." *Harvard Journal of Law and Feminism* 13 (1990): 87–136.

"Torts and Contract Law Meet at Axe-Throwing Event, University of Louisville Brandeis School of Law." University of Louisville. Accessed November 6, 2023. https://louisville.edu/law/news/torts-and-contract-law-meet-at-axe-throwing-event.

Totenberg, Nina. "Federal Panel of Judges Dismisses All 83 Ethics Complaints against Brett Kavanaugh." NPR. December 18, 2018. www.npr.org/2018 /12/18/678004085/federal-panel-of-judges-dismiss-all-83-ethics-complaints-against-brett-kavanaugh.

Toussaint, Etienne C. "The Purpose of Legal Education." *California Law Review* 111 (February 2023): 1–70.

Tully, L. Danielle. "The Cultural (Re)Turn: The Case for Teaching Culturally Responsive Lawyering." *Stanford Journal of Civil Rights and Civil Liberties* 16, no. 2 (June 2020): 201–58.

———. "What Law Schools Should Leave Behind." *Utah Law Review* 22, no. 4 (2022): 837–70.

Tung, Genevieve Blake. "Working towards Equitable Outcomes in Law School: The Role of the ABA Standards." In Dyszlewski et al., *Integrating Doctrine and Diversity,* 15–22.

Tushnet, Mark. "Critical Legal Studies: An Introduction to Its Origins and Underpinnings." *Journal of Legal Education* 36, no. 4 (1986): 505–17.

———. "Critical Legal Studies: A Political History." *Yale Law Journal* 100, no. 5 (1990–91): 1515–44.

Valdes, Francisco. "Barely at the Margins: Race and Ethnicity in Legal Education; A Curricular Study with LatCritical Commentary." *Berkeley La Raza Law Journal* 13 (January 2002): 119–269.

———. "Legal Reform and Social Justice: An Introduction to LatCrit Theory, Praxis, and Community." *Griffith Law Review* 14, no. 2 (2005): 148–73.

Valdes, Francisco, and Bender, Steven W. *LatCrit: From Critical Legal Theory to Academic Activism.* New York: New York University Press, 2021.

Valentine, Sarah. "Flourish or Founder: The New Regulatory Regime in Legal Education." *Journal of Law and Education* 44, no. 4 (Fall 2015): 473–578.

"Various Statistics on ABA-Approved Law Schools." American Bar Association. Accessed June 20, 2021. www.americanbar.org/groups/legal_education/resources/statistics.

Vest, Herb D. "Felling the Giant: Breaking the ABA's Stranglehold on Legal Education in America." *Journal of Legal Education* 50, no. 4 (2000): 494–503.

Vollweiler, Debra Moss. "Don't Panic! The Hitchhiker's Guide to Learning Outcomes: Eight Ways to Make Them More Than (Mostly) Harmless." *Dayton Law Review* 44 (July 2018): 17–52.

Wagner, Judith Welch. "Creating an Effective Law School Mission." In Maranville et al., *Building on Best Practices,* 3–11.

Walvoord, Barbara E. *Assessment Clear and Simple: A Practical Guide for Institutions, Departments, and General Education.* San Francisco: Jossey-Bass, 2010.

Ward, Stephanie Francis. "Diversity Increases with Law School Deans, According to New AALS Study." *ABA Journal,* April 4, 2022. www.abajournal.com/web/article/diversity-increases-with-law-school-deans-according-to-aals-study.

———. "New ABA Data Parses Out Bar Exam Pass Rates by Race and Ethnicity." *ABA Journal,* June 22, 2021. www.abajournal.com/news/article/new-aba-data-parses-out-bar-exam-pass-rates-by-ethnicity.

———. "Pulse of the Legal Profession." *American Bar Association Journal,* October 1, 2007. www.abajournal.com/magazine/article/pulse_of_the_legal_profession.

Weaver, Jessica Dixon, and Jamie R. Abrams. *Family Law Simulations.* Bridge to Practice Series. Saint Paul: West Academic, 2021.

Webb, Michael S. "Dissenting from Death: Preventing Lawyer Suicide." American Bar Association. November 24, 2021. www.americanbar.org/groups/senior_lawyers/publications/voice_of_experience/2021/voice-of-experience-november-2021/dissenting-from-death-preventing-lawyer-suicide/.

"Well-Being Pledge Campaign." American Bar Association. Accessed March 28, 2022. www.americanbar.org/groups/lawyer_assistance/well-being-in-the-legal-profession/.

White, Pamela J. "Thirty Years Later: Recalling the Gender Bias Report and Asking What's Next in the Legal Profession." *Maryland Law Review* 80, no. 1 (2020): 13–35.

Wildman, Stephanie. "The Question of Silence: Techniques to Ensure Full Class Participation." *Journal of Legal Education* 38, no. 1 (March 1988): 147–54.

Wilensky, Beth Hirschfelder. "Dethroning Langdell." *Minnesota Law Review* 107, no. 6 (2023): 2701–28.

Willauer, Brigette LuAnn. "The Law School Honor Code and Collaborative Learning: Can They Coexist?" *UMKC Law Review* 73 (2004): 574–91.

Williams, Joan C. "Critical Legal Studies: The Death of Transcendence and the Rise of the New Langdells." *NYU Law Review* 62, no. 3 (June 1987): 429–96.

Williams, Joan C., Marina Multhaup, Su Li, and Rachel Korn. *You Can't Change What You Can't See: Interrupting Racial and Gender Bias in the Legal Profession*. American Bar Association Commission on Women in the Profession and the Minority Corporate Counsel Association. 2018. https://mcca.com/wp-content/uploads/2018/09/You-Cant-Change-What-You-Cant-See-Executive-Summary.pdf.

Williams, Patricia. *The Alchemy of Race and Rights: The Diary of a Law Professor*. Cambridge, MA: Harvard University Press, 1991.

Williams, Susan H. "Legal Education, Feminist Epistemology, and the Socratic Method." *Stanford Law Review* 45, no. 6 (July 1993): 585–613.

Worland, Justin. "America's Long Overdue Awakening to Systemic Racism." *Time,* June 11, 2020. https://time.com/5851855/systemic-racism-america.

Wright, Kim. "How the Socratic Method Translates Online." *Harvard Gazette,* March 24, 2020. https://news.harvard.edu/gazette/story/2020/03/harvard-law-school-professor-was-prepared-for-zoom-debut.

Young, Kathryne M. "Understanding the Social and Cognitive Process in Law School That Creates Unhealthy Lawyers." *Fordham Law Review* 89, no. 6 (2021): 2575–95.

Zapotosky, Matt. "Judge Who Quit over Harassment Allegations Reemerges, Dismaying Those Who Accused Him." *Washington Post,* July 24, 2018. www.washingtonpost.com/world/national-security/judge-who-quit-over-harassment-allegations-reemerges-dismaying-those-who-accused-him/2018/07/23/750a02f2-89db-11e8-a345-a1bf7847b375_story.html.

Zimmerman, Emily. "Do Grades Matter?" *Seattle University Law Review* 35, no. 2 (2012): 305–76.

Index

Founded in 1893,
UNIVERSITY OF CALIFORNIA PRESS
publishes bold, progressive books and journals
on topics in the arts, humanities, social sciences,
and natural sciences—with a focus on social
justice issues—that inspire thought and action
among readers worldwide.

The UC PRESS FOUNDATION
raises funds to uphold the press's vital role
as an independent, nonprofit publisher, and
receives philanthropic support from a wide
range of individuals and institutions—and from
committed readers like you. To learn more, visit
ucpress.edu/supportus.